Published by Ockley Books Ltd

First published September, 2016

All text copyright of the author.

The moral right of all the author to be identified as the author of this work
has been asserted. All chapters written by Stuart Fuller and edited by John Dobson.
All rights reserved. No part of this book may be reproduced
in any form without prior permission in writing from the author
and publisher Ockley Books.

ISBN 978-1910906040

Front Cover, layout & design by Michael Kinlan

Printed & bound in Scotland by:

Bell & Bain, Glasgow, www.bell-bain.com

the
football
tourist
THE SECOND HALF

Stuart Fuller

OCKLEY BOOKS
.com

Contents

———

Introduction

I'm a rubbish liar. After I had finishing writing The Football Tourist back in January 2013, I made some vague promise to those around me that my days of flying off at every opportunity to watch football across the globe were over. My family looked forward to me being around more. I was swapping the Belgrade derby for Thorpe Park, the Sud Tribune in Dortmund for B&Q. My days of being on the road were finished.

Yeah, because that lasted all of four weeks before I was back on the terrace, beer in one hand, sausage in the other, in Münster with Kenny Legg, Stoffers and Danny Last.

Of course Danny Last, always Danny Last.

I couldn't give this up just like the Current Mrs Fuller couldn't give up shopping for candles. It was in my blood. My publisher, Dave Hartrick, tried to convince me not to write another book. "That's the last thing everyone wants Stu" he told me whilst on hands free, driving his new Aston Martin DB7 in the South of France which he bought around six months after my book came out. Eventually both The Current Mrs Fuller and Hartrick gave in. Passport returned, the planning phase began.

So here we go again, my friends, back on the road. The cast is much the same, most of the destinations are new. Thanks for that have to go to my employers for deciding to expand into new regions and making me travel there. So whilst The Football Tourist was focused on Europe, my new adventures spanned four continents over a period of close to two years.

Sequels are often a bit of a let-down. The original raises you up and your expectations are high, but then the same trusted formula doesn't work, the jokes are the same and there's little new content. But once in a while they do deliver, packing a mighty punch that has the audience calling for a more. For every Godfather 2 there is a Back to the Future 2, a Porky's 2 to Oceans 12, or On the Buses to Debbie Does Dallas. I'd like to think I've produced the former rather than the latter in this publication, and that's not easy working with a cast containing the likes of Last, Adam Lloyd and new to this world, Ed Seaford down in Australia.

The premise is the same. I fly to somewhere, have a beer, eat some food, watch people acting like they are kids (sometimes that just may include me, it also might just be me on my own in truth) and then watch some football, and then after I get over my hangover, I write about it, changing some of the names to protect the guilty and ridicule those who stood on the side lines. More often than not the game is the low point of the trip, the bit where expectations fall short. Whilst I may sometimes bemoan my predicament, living out of a suitcase full of Mars Bars, I know that I am lucky to get to see and do the things I do.

My objectives for writing this book are still the same – sharing some of the wonderful places to watch football around the world, with an added portion of enjoyment. Experiencing the pleasure and the pain, the triumphs and tragedies. There are guidebooks in every bookshop about cities and regions around the world. Every bar, restaurant and attraction has a review these days on websites such as TripAdvisor, taking the danger, the risk, the step into the unknown of traveling abroad away from the virgin traveller. And that is my mission (not to meet virgin travellers I hasten to add). To find places where these guides don't reach. To share the experience of landing in a foreign land and seeing what football really means through the local eyes.

Whilst my travels take me to see some of the biggest games in the world, I am equally happy to watch a game or two in the most basic surroundings. Nothing sums up my footballing watching life than the month of May 2013. During those 31 days I saw six games, slightly below my average attending month. But it was the sheer variety of the matches and venues that defines my passion for watching the beautiful game.

In the classic episode of Only Fools and Horses screened in December 1982 called A Touch of Glass, Del explains to Rodney that he is a man for all seasons; "I'm one of them that's accepted anywhere, whether it's drinking lager with the market boys down at Nine Elms, or sipping Pimms fruit cup at Hendon regatta!"

That's how I would describe my football watching in that month. Three visits to Wembley, a trip to the capital of cool, Stockholm, to experience one of the last games in one of Europe's best-preserved stadiums and a match that couldn't be more grass roots if it tried. In the middle of the month I saw Manchester City humiliated in the FA Cup final by Wigan Athletic thanks to the free drink, free food and free hostesses provided by Budweiser. Two weeks later a global insurance company gave me the hottest ticket in town to watch the Champions League final in exchange for some arty photos of the German fans taking over London. In between I paid the princely sum of

£3 to watch FC Metrogas lose the Kent Invicta League title on the last day of the season in front of 17 fans and four dogs. It's hard for me to choose the best experience to tell you the truth.

Travel has made the world a more accessible place. There has never been a better time to experience some of the Wonders of the Footballing World. And whisper it quietly, there are also other sports that ignite the passions just as much and are worth a visit. In the next two-hundred or so pages I will share the emotions and passions of watching different variants of football; Australian Rules, Rugby and, of course, the American version.

Any author will tell you that the hours spent researching, the missing of family events and the endless note taking in the middle of the most inappropriate situations are difficult, but the reward is when you, dear reader, pick up this book and buy it. 99% of authors do not write for the money, they write to feed their passion. Nothing gives us a bigger buzz than someone contacting you to say "I enjoyed that."

I tried to think of something different to write as an introduction. We've all read books with lots of waffle and hot air, promising the world and delivering nothing – a bit like Chessington World of Adventures. So I asked my children to write something. And here it is, the words of my two daughters on what it is like to be the child of a Football Tourist.

ISABELLA FULLER – AGED 13 YEARS OLD

Don't get me wrong - I love it when my Dad is at home but then I always am being told off for having a messy room. It's not mess, it is organised mess. After a while you get used to waking up to snoring in the night from next door, despite him saying he doesn't snore, but it's strange not to wake up to it too when he is off on his travels. I always look forward to my Dad's homecoming, not just because he always brings presents, but he always seems to stay at hotels where One Direction have stayed or are about to. I always asked to go with him on his trips but the answer is always "No!", giving me excuses like "You don't understand football", "You don't drink beer" or that "You will tell Mummy that I wasn't just asking that lady for directions". I wonder what he gets up to when he is away. My silence is bought for a present and for now that will do me nicely.

LAUREN FULLER – AGED 16 YEARS OLD

My sister and I can both agree on one thing, which for siblings is pretty rare. Our Dad is a workaholic. Now this trait on its own is fine, in fact it's probably quite a good thing to describe some as. However, when teamed with other his traits it can become less positive. You see, our Dad is also a footballaholic. Football's OK - I used to go all the time with Dad, but only to escape having to tidy my room or do the chores. But let's be honest. Football today is all about a bunch of overpaid *word probably removed as it's a bit rude* who could fake their way to moon and back and have no grip on the real world.

Now being a footballaholic is fine as well. But his addiction doesn't stop there. School has taught me that certain chemical elements can bond together and create a much stronger element (see, I do pay attention in Chemistry!). My Dad is also a travelaholic. Combining these two elements produces something akin to carbon monoxide - you can't see it, smell it, taste it, hear it or touch it until it's too late and you're dead. Obviously it's not that extreme, but it's a very dangerous mixture. Add in a "cheeky pint" and you have Dad's ideal day out and our nightmare.

Our Dad is amazing however if he writes like he keeps his word on buying me a puppy then this book will be terrible and full of lies, but if he writes like he travels then this book will probably be amazing. Let's be honest, he's not great at being at home all the time, but his writing always makes people smile so it's probably half-decent. Alas, as I'm only a child and apparently the book has rude words in I cannot comment any further.

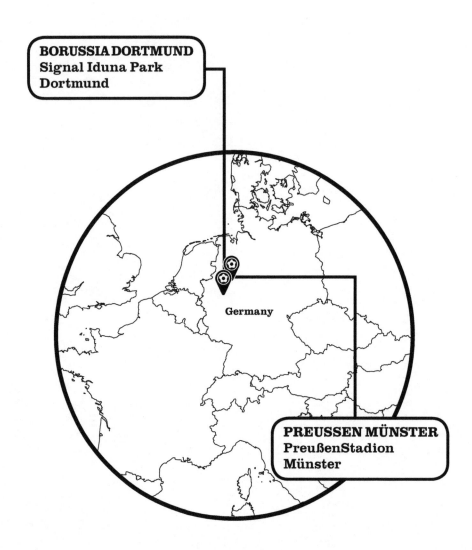

BORUSSIA DORTMUND
Signal Iduna Park
Dortmund

Germany

PREUSSEN MÜNSTER
PreußenStadion
Münster

As any schoolboy knows, baby elephants
and suspended monorails do not mix.

1. Herman the German Münster

I bloody love Germany. That's hardly a surprising statement. My publisher suggested I started this book with a "strong, positive statement. A battle cry that would be echoed throughout the whole book." But what does he really know about European football? To him a trip to see Ossett Town is continental. I love you Hartch, but you have to let me be my own man on this one. I know my audience and they want the reassurance that their frequent excursions to the land of our Teutonic brothers is a perfectly acceptable way of spending a weekend.

So I will say it again. I bloody love Germany. After all, I am of that age where good value football, good value beer and accessibility to good-value hardcor — . . . ah, OK, sorry Mum . . . good-value nocturnal entertainment is more important than DJ Jazzy J and a foam-filled dance floor of scantily clad girls off their ti— . . . sorry again Mum . . . nightclubs, are more important to me. And Germany ticks all of those boxes thrice-times over and also does have those foam-filled dance floors full of scantily clad semi-naked girls . . . apparently. Despite spending the last eight years exploring every corner of the Bundesliga there are still little pockets I have always wanted to visit and never had an opportunity to do so, mainly because of the lack of reasonably priced travel options. Exotic locations such as Cottbus and Rostock, clubs like Carls Zeiss Jena and Dynamo Dresden that are forever etched on my memories of David Coleman and *Sportsnight* and of course Wuppertal. Possibly the best-named place in the whole of Europe, behind Middelfart in Denmark. Oh, and of course Wank, on the German/Dutch border. It just sounds like the best place in the world. Woo-per-tal. If you want to be all posh and continental, add an extra "e" at the end as you say it. Nobody will mind. It's not like saying Wrotham when you should pronounce it as Rootam, or my favourite from my courting days with The Current Mrs Fuller (for a number of reasons that will not be revealed on these pages): Beaver Castle, which is of course written Belvoir.

What do you mean, where? Come on! Wuppertal, sitting on the River Wupper slap-bang in the middle of the Bergisches Land to the east of Düsseldorf. Home to the Von der Heydt Museum, the Arboretum Burgholz, which even Wikipedia enthused over as an EXTENSIVE arboretum, and of course the eighteenth-century Engels house. But put all that excitement to one side when I tell you it is the spiritual home of the Schwebebahn, or as we may say in England, the Monorail. Not just your run-of-the-mill monorail either. This is the oldest electric elevated railway in the world, having opened in 1901. And catch this. It's only bloody suspended (not in a closed way but in a hanging down, swinging way).

Those clever Germans eh? Well no, let me stop you there before you get too excited and crack open a Hofmeister. This was actually invented by the British. God Save the Queen and all that. A man called Henry Robinson Palmer (of course, Henry Robinson Palmer) first suggested the idea of a suspended rail network, pulled along by horses, back in 1824 to the elders of Wuppertal. Alas, his original route had one flaw that saw him dismissed as a country bumpkin. His proposed network didn't go as far as reaching the Stadion am Zoo to the west of the city centre. What was the point of that, said the town council, with amazing forethought as football was still nearly 50 years away from becoming a regulated game in Germany. But Palmer was out and so was his horse-drawn plan.

There was a small issue of horses getting too frisky and running off, pulling dozens of passengers behind them as well, but that was not the real issue, as we know today.

Instead, in 1901 the current line was opened to global acclaim, linking Oberbarmen in the east to Vohwinkel in the west and having a stop at the stadium of Wuppertaler SV Borussia, making it the first football ground in the world to have its own monorail station. Around 25 million passengers today travel on the line, which travels about 10 metres above the River Wupper in swinging comfort. Back in 1950 so popular was the railway as a way to get from the centre of the city to the Zoo that a passenger decided to bring his baby elephant on board. As any schoolboy knows, baby elephants and suspended monorails do not mix and poor Tufti got a bit concerned at the swaying motion on the route, pressed the emergency door release button and promptly fell into the river below. She was fine but hasn't been back on any railways since. To stop such recurrences the authorities quickly passed a by-law that even today prohibits anyone bringing four-legged mammals onto the carriages.

I could kid you by saying that riding on the monorail was the only reason that I, along with Danny Last, Spencer Webb, Big Deaksy and Andy Hudson, had arrived in Germany some hours before but I would be sticking two fingers up at your intellect. Of course we were here to see Kenny Legg in his Düsseldorf outpost. He gets lonely does our Kenny, and had asked for some company, so we all arrived on the same weekend. Alas, this meant there was no room at the Legg Inn so we decamped to the local 5-star hotel at the end of his road. It just happened that there was a couple of decent games on, which we vaguely discussed on the way over as time-fillers while we rode the monorail.

The headline act for the weekend would be a trip to the Westfalenstadion to watch the mighty Borussia Dortmund. In the space of a couple of years they had become one of the most popular teams to watch in Europe, and the question "How do I get tickets for the SüdTribüne?" was the most popular poser on our Facebook page those days. Tickets in general to watch BVB are hard to get. Not impossible, just hard, but with careful planning, the right words whispered in the right ears, and an endless supply of The Ball is Round badges, we had procured six bright yellow, beautiful tickets for the biggest and best football party in Europe. That was Saturday night's entertainment taken care of after our exciting day of riding the monorail in Wuppertal.

But the weather had been proving to be as much of a pain in the arse in these parts as in England. Rain, snow, ice – you name it and it was falling in Nordrhein-Westfalen. However, in the knowledge that six Englishmen would be arriving, Wuppertaler SV would surely be up all night with hairdryers to get the pitch playable for the game versus VfB Hüls, right?

On Thursday, 48 hours before kick-off, the game was postponed. Thursday. Really? Heck, the weather must be really bad out in Germany for our "Big Match" to have already been postponed.

Who wasn't looking forward to the joys of Wuppertaler SV, and of course the trip on the monorail?

Five very sad Englishmen met at Gatwick Airport for our short hop across to Düsseldorf via Cologne.

It was like waiting decades for the new *Star Wars* film only to see it and just remember the character Jar Jar Binks (not to be confused with J J Okocha). We still had Dortmund, with the biggest terrace in the world and a guaranteed 80,500 sell-out, but this weekend was all about riding that suspended single rail automated railway to the ground, wasn't it? Oh, and maybe a beer or two.

The scene certainly wasn't encouraging as we touched down early doors on Friday at Cologne-Bonn, or CGN for those who live their lives in transport codes (for the record, the trip from NEH to LGW had been textbook around the M25 and down the M23). Snow lay everywhere and the mercury was struggling to break the zero barrier. Bugger – football certainly didn't look like being the winner on this weekend.

We'd arranged a little private tour around the Bayer Arena, home of Bayer Leverkusen, where just 14 hours previously the home side had lost to Benfica in the Europa League, and just 26 hours later they would be taking on Greuther Fürth. We needed something to entertain us, otherwise, come knocking-off time back in Düsseldorf, Kenny would find five gibbering idiots with bellies full of Alt beer. Our tour guide, Nick, got very excited as he took us around the stadium, saying it was the first time he'd done it with five English boys. We put the comment down to his English grammar, although the wink he kept giving Spencer did make us a bit uneasy when he asked if we wanted to go into the showers. He couldn't understand our excitement at being let into the away end where all the "Ultras" stand. "Such bad boys," he said. We asked who the worst away fans were. "Those naughty men from Frankfurt. They fired flares into the home fans." Something to look forward to at Dortmund then! Nick was a legend, allowing us to stop every few metres to take a picture of something, and he was soon joining in with our English banter.

As a fond farewell, Nick presented us all with a certificate that confirmed we had completed the tour and wished us Auf Wiedersehen. Danny was tempted to invite him out with us for the rest of the day but we got that feeling his idea of a good time in Düssers might be a bit different to ours. We still had no idea what games would be on over the weekend as we headed back to meet Kenny, who had his usual hard Friday's graft that saw him finish at 4pm.

"Don't worry lads, I have a plan B, C, D and Z for tomorrow," he told us over the phone as we were on the train. "Meet me in the Legg Arms at 5.04pm." It could be the best of times, or the worst of times, to nick a phrase from Charles Dickens.

We'd been in Kenny's local for a few Alt beers before he arrived with the fruits of a hard day at work. It seemed he;d printed off every railway timetable in Germany and he proceeded to talk us through potential plans for the morning. We went to the public vote and option C, Prueßen Münster v Hallescher in Bundesliga 3, was the clear winner. This would be preceded by a tour of a number of the city's more bohemian drinking establishments.

At 10am on Saturday we did what every good German would do. We bought a six-pack of beer, some Fisherman's Friends (I still think they've missed a trick by not using the marketing slogan "Sucking on a Fisherman's Friend is more rewarding than you may think"), and a bag of German Frazzles, and jumped on the train to Münster, the cultural capital of Westphalia. Despite being less than 40 miles from the Dutch border, the city is as German as they come. Well, apart from the thousands of British servicemen and their families who are still stationed here and swell the attendances at Prueßen and other local clubs including Osnabrück and Bielefeld.

The area in front of the main station was already busy with football fans tucking into the 75-cents beers, although most seemed to be decked out in the yellow and black of Borussia Dortmund rather than the green and black of the local team. These were hardcore fans and the presence of the riot police watching their every sip put us off, so we decided to head to the ground.

One bus ride later and we pulled up at the Preußen Stadion. They cater for all needs in these parts, with a supermarket selling cheap bottles of beer, a casino and an Erotik superstore across the road from the ground if the football didn't float your boat or the home team were getting stuffed and you wanted to sneak out. "Know your customer base" is one thing I have learnt from various business books I have read, and here is the perfect example.

Once again German football wins the Top Trumps for cheapest standing ticket at €10 for a place on the terrace here. You have to drop down into the eighth tier of England (Isthmian North or South for instance) to find a comparable price. Oh, and the ticket of course then allowed free train travel in the region after the game, meaning we would be travelling to Dortmund courtesy of Preußen Münster. Now that was worth a beer to celebrate, as if we needed a reason.

The stadium looked fantastic. Old school, if you will allow me to use such a phrase. Yes, there was an athletics track but the stands oozed nostalgia, and despite the fact it was the coldest day ever, you couldn't help feeling that this was what football was supposed to be like. We had a choice of where to stand but before we could start jumping around like loons with the Ultras, Andy Hudson had a word of caution for us. Apparently relations had been strained for some time between the Ultras factions at Münster, so much so that three groups now existed, and really didn't like each other. Our tickets were for Sektor M, where you could find one group, unsurprisingly called "Sektor M". This group included a drummer who was no more than eight and a few young girls patiently taping banners up. To our left the more threatening-looking group were readying themselves. And then in the middle were the undecided ones, not sure if they should go left or right.

A wrong decision here could prove dangerous and mark our cards in terms of ever being accepted by the Preußen faithful. So we took the easy option and stood on the far side of the terrace, close to the bar, food and toilets, where we could get a good view if anything kicked off on the terrace.

Want some more German third-tier footballing trivia? Of course you do! Preußen, or Die Adler (the Eagles) as they are still known, were one of the founding members of the Bundesliga in 1963. In fact their opening game in August 1963 against Hamburg was the ONLY sell-out on that historic day.

They can also lay claim to being the only side included in the original 16-team league that has never played back at this level, after relegation in the first season. Only two teams from that inaugural championship now play in the third tier of German football – the Eagles and fellow relegated side 1. FC Saarbrücken.

The club were also the first in Germany to shun the idea of football as an amateur game, and as early as 1948 started paying their players, much to the disgust of many of their peers. These paid players meant the club could compete at the top levels in the German Oberliga, eventually leading to their invitation to play in that first Bundesliga season.

The club continued to fall through the divisions after their first and only Bundesliga season, and ironically ended up back as an amateur side in the Eighties. Their one major honour came during this period when in 1994 they won the German Amateur Championships, beating Kickers Offenbach.

It took a change in club management at the highest level to start their climb back up the tables, with an investment in the youth policy and set-up of the club. In 2011 the policy paid off as they made it out of the regional leagues and back into the third tier of German football, where they now held their own and played in front of an average attendance of over 9,000. Again, compare that to England and you will see very few third-tier teams get close to such a gate every two weeks. Unfortunately, and this is where the comparison with England is true, there are more than a few fallen giants in Tier 3 in Germany, meaning promotion is incredibly difficult. Karlsruher SC had fallen through the divisions in a similar way to Wolves, Aachen were playing in a brand new stadium but had suffered off-the-field problems akin to Coventry City, and Hansa Rostock came from a port where the fans had a bit of a reputation (Portsmouth anyone?).

The teams took to the field with a flourish of activity from the Ultras, with the 500 or so away fans at the far end suddenly pulling their hoods up and deciding to try to leave *en masse*. Andy Hudson was once again on hand to give us the lowdown on their protest, which was aimed at the lack of investment in the team. The police were having none of it. "If we have to stay and watch this rubbish, then so do you" was the message relayed back to the Hallescher fans. So they did what any other self-respecting fan would do on such a chilly day. They whipped their tops off and starting dancing around like loons. Welcome to German football.

PREUSSEN MÜNSTER 2, HALLESCHER 0
Saturday 16th February 2013 – PreußenStadion

Despite the brave attempts by the away fans to inspire the former East Germans, it was an easy run-out for the promotion-chasing home side. A goal in each half from the Turk Mehmet Kara, his first since returning to Germany from his home country, saw the Eagles consolidate third place in the league, and close the gap on the leaders Karlsruher and Osnabrück to just three points.

It was gloves all around, apart from Big Deaksy who wanted to whip his top off in support of the away fans as the game kicked off, and our beers developed a frosty head. The opening exchanges were accompanied by the beat of 7,000 fans stamping their feet trying to keep warm as the mercury plummeted. Despite some early incursions into the home side's penalty area, Hallescher didn't look too convinced that they could win the game and, like their fans, clearly wanted to be somewhere else.

With most of the home crowd lost in debate about the quality of the Currywürst, Deaksy spotted an offence in the Hallescher penalty area, told the assistant referee and he flagged for the penalty.

Eagle-eyed like an Action Man is Big Deaksy. Kara stepped up and sent the keeper the wrong way.

Cue a further attempt by the away fans to leave. Perhaps if they'd tried to leave in twos or threes every 30 seconds rather than all at once they could have got away with it.

With so many games off in the area due to the freezing conditions, the bumper crowd of over 7,000 who braved the cold were rewarded with a decent game of football and in the process deprived the various establishments across the road of thousands of euros. After the break the away side briefly threatened to equalise but any ambition they had to put up a fight was soon extinguished as Kara scored a well-taken second goal. Last season's Regionaliga Nord champions, Hallescher, simply had no answer. It was left to their fans to liven up the afternoon for us all with a brief scuffle with the police. Nobody wants to see that, unless the game you are watching has petered out and it's bloody freezing; then it is the best thing ever.

Having a date with 80,496 others in Dortmund we made a swift exit with a few minutes to go, stocking up with our 75-cent beers from the supermarket, slipping 10 euros on black and visiting the . . . well, let's just leave that there, for the hour-long journey to Dortmund, the current European capital of football.

Despite having the biggest average home league attendance in the world, Borussia Dortmund surprisingly only generate around £25 million from match-day income each season out of a total of £189 million of total revenue, according to the most recent Football Money League report published annually by Deloitte. Although they lead the way in terms of passionate home support, their approach on ticket pricing puts them firmly behind "smaller" clubs such as Arsenal and Chelsea where money is no object for the majority of their fans.

The German footballing philosophy of football for the masses is all well and good in getting ticks in the boxes for affordability, but in terms of the one true global measure of how big a club is, it is a contentious issue. Match-day revenues make up nearly a third of the income sources for Manchester United, and around 40 per cent for Arsenal. If Borussia Dortmund wanted to be mentioned in the same breath as Real Madrid, Barcelona and, dare I say it in these parts, Bayern Munich, an increase in ticket prices would need to be put in place. But that's not how clubs roll here in Germany. For, as those who have experienced a Bundesliga game or two will know, the fans actually mean more to a club than simply being a walking wallet filled with cash. Just because you can put your logo on everything in a club shop doesn't mean you should.

You get the feeling that even if Dortmund increased ticket prices by 20–30 per cent the fans would still flock to the Signal Iduna Park week in, week out. Even such a Greek debt-busting inflation hike would still make ticket prices cheaper than they are for all but a few Premier League sides. The demand for tickets from visitors and Dortmund virgins far outstrips supply. I've yet to meet a serious Football Tourist who doesn't have a visit to the SüdTribüne on their tick list. However, thanks to the contacts of Danny Last, we had four tickets for the game in the bag as our train from Münster eased into the Signal Iduna Park station and a wall of yellow and black hit us firmly in the face.

On paper this was a banker home win, with some of the shortest odds I had seen for a while, suggesting the visitors Eintracht Frankfurt had as much chance of coming away with three points as the Lewes Veterans side, marshalled by yours truly, would have had. Similar odds had been on offer for the visit of Hamburg the previous weekend, but in a coupon-busting result, the 'Rothosen' had run out 4-1 winners, leading a few journalists to question whether Germany's "super team" had run out of steam. Even with joint Bundesliga top scorer Robert Lewandowski serving a suspension, surely Dortmund would have enough quality to see off the visitors -lightning wouldn't strike twice in a week, would it?

I made my "debut" here back in 2001 when the stadium had a capacity of JUST 65,000. It was a chilly night of UEFA Cup football against Slovan

Liberec from the Czech Republic. These were dark days for the club on and off the pitch as after the glory years of the late 1990s investments had failed to return the predicted returns. I paid just €10 for my seat among the 36,500 crowd on the gate, spending treble that on an assortment of German football fare that included a few sausages, a beer or two and of course a pair of Dortmund socks. It would be unheard of today to see a crowd that low in the stadium, irrespective of the competition.

Today it was a different story. This is the team that everyone is trying to emulate. While it looks like this season they may have play second fiddle to Bayern Munich, the team built by Jürgen Klopp is still the envy of most. Even when one of the stars is sold, another steps up their game, meaning the team has never yet suffered. Although, at the time we watched them, they hadn't written off their chances of catching Bayern, both the domestic and the European cups offered them an additional prize. A place in the knock-out stages of the Champions League against Shakhtar Donetsk was just a few days away: the reward of qualifying from a group featuring two of the richest clubs in the world in Manchester City and Real Madrid.

The huge demand for tickets to see them obviously leads to the question of why they wouldn't expand the stadium even more. But when is too much enough? That's a question you are left asking yourself when you finally manage to exit the Signal Iduna Park after 20 minutes of squeezing down stairwells. Compared to my last visit to Borussia in 2002, this was a wholly different ball game.

There were 80,500 fans shoe-horned into an immense cauldron of noise. Thousands locked out. What's next? Ninety thousand? A hundred thousand? Build it and they will come was the message in *Field of Dreams* but what will the experience be like?

Rolling up 10 minutes prior to kick-off, expecting to get in the stadium, is not a good idea in Dortmund. Allow at least 45 minutes and be prepared to use those elbows. Once inside, if you are in the cheap seats, strap on the oxygen pack and start the long climb upwards. Any expansion would have to be upwards, meaning you would be closer to Mars than the pitch. You can now understand why they play in such bright yellow – it's the only way you can make out the players from the upper reaches of the stadium.

Big Deaksy and I took our places in the north-west corner as the wall of noise was whipped into a crescendo. "You'll Never Walk Alone" was belted out for the second time in the day and the teams emerged from the tunnel, each member holding a heart-shaped balloon to mark Valentine's Day. It's touches like those that restore your faith in football. The countdown clock reached zero. Showtime!

BORUSSIA DORTMUND 3, EINTRACHT FRANKFURT 0
Saturday 16th February 2013 – Signal Iduna Park

In truth this game was dead and buried before the Frankfurt fans had found their voice. After missing two golden opportunities to take the lead within the first five minutes Borussia finally opened the scoring in the seventh minute when Marco Reus finished off a move that Klopp's team had become known for. Fast, flowing football from one end of the pitch to the other in what seemed like a move perfected on FIFA13. Frankfurt were simply chasing shadows. One became two just four minutes later when Reus again finished well after the Eintracht defence had been carved open by Julian Schieber. This had the potential to be highly embarrassing for the away side.

However, the fans around us didn't seem to be overly enthused about the master class being given on the pitch in front of them. Some years ago I'd been a guest in the 'International Lounge' at Old Trafford. It was actually the game when Manchester United keeper Massimo Taibi let THAT goal in against Southampton. Halfway through the first half of that game I noticed two "fans" sitting near me. One was reading a book, the other knitting. Nobody was quit that disengaged here, but there was nevertheless an almost uninterested feel among many of the fans. Despite the wall of noise at the far end of the SüdTribüne, the main noise at our end came from those naughty Frankfurt fans way down in the lower tier, who were yelling bad things about Klopp, Dortmund and where they could stick their yellow and black gnomes.

It might have been so different if only Eintracht could have been bothered. After no more than 30 minutes Dortmund lost Schieber thanks to two harsh yellow cards in just four minutes, but even then Frankfurt didn't step up a gear. Perhaps they had read the Pleat philosophy about playing against 10 men, although they would then have also noted that 2-0 is the most dangerous scoreline in football to be defending. What does that mean? Only the great skipping man in slip-on loafers knows the actual rules of Pleatism. Borussia Dortmund continued to purr, slick and quick in their passing, although without Schieber they seemed to over-complicate things and more often than not ended up giving the ball directly to a Frankfurt player in the wrong place (or right place) for their perfect passing game.

Talking of unnecessary complication, Deaksy and I headed down to get a beer as the half wound down. We figured that with nearly 80,000 Germans having gone almost 45 minutes without a beer they may be getting thirsty, so we needed to put our towels down first.

Borussia Dortmund use one of those card systems similar to that used in Amsterdam and many other new stadiums. The logic is that it reduces the queues for food and drink because no one has to handle cash. For one-time visitors like Deaksy and me, they are basically a pain in the arse. But a craving for a beer meant we had no option but to queue for one.

"Can I have a €20 card please?"

"Sure. Here you go," says a young lady. "It's got €18 on now."

"But I gave you €20?"

"You have to pay a deposit for the card. But you can top it up when you come back to visit the ground."

"I've been once in 10 years."

"Oh. You can give it to your friend then."

"He's been twice in 10 years."

"Oh. Perhaps you can make a friend in the stadium and give it to them."

Pointless conversation number 1. So we took our card and joined another queue to buy two beers. "That will be €10.40 please."

"But they are only €3.70 each!"

"You have to pay a deposit on your limited-edition cup of €1.50 each."

"Can I have it in a non-limited-edition cup for just €3.70?"

"No."

Pointless conversation number 2. We were fighting a losing battle on this one. With half-time coming to an end we worked out we had enough cash left after Deaksy's large sausage for one more beer, which we would share. So we returned to said girl at the beer counter.

"One beer please," I said, offering her my limited-edition cup.

"You do not have enough money on your card."

"I have €5 left -the beer is €3.70."

"No, it's €5.20."

"But I have my cup here."

"You can't re-use them. You have to buy a new one."

"But you just pour the beer from bottles into them?"

"I'm sorry, that's the rules. It's unhygienic to pour them into a used cup. It may have germs in it."

Pointless conversation number 3. So we had to go down two flights of steps to get our €1.50 put back on our card by handing in our used cups, then go back upside to get another beer at €5.20.

Of course by which point half-time is over and we have a card that we will never use again with €2.70 on.

So the second period and we are looking forward to the Eintracht manager having given his side a rocket and them racing out of the box. Errr no. Despite the passionate support from the away fans their performance was toothless, almost as if they were suffering from stage fright. Meanwhile Dortmund continued to make a mockery of Eintracht having an extra man and drove forward. It was inevitable that they would get their third, and Reus completed a hat-trick thanks to some unselfish work by Mario Götze. Boom.

"That shot, sponsored by Timex, was measured at 78kmph." Thanks for that. Everything is sponsored at Dortmund.

Despite a second yellow for Frankfurt's Japanese midfielder Takashi Inui evening up the sides, there were no more goals in a disappointing second period. Somehow, despite the goal, the sending off and five substitutions, only one added minute was due to be played at the end of the game. With 90 minutes up the referee went to issue a yellow card, slipped on his arse and, as 80,000 fans laughed in unison, blew the final whistle, picked up the ball and walked off in a huff.

We all piled out into the Westfalon night, satisfied that the yellow and black juggernaut was back on the road again. Bayern may be out of sight in the league, but who would bet against Dortmund as an outside punt for the Champions League. Oh, and there is also the small matter of the DFB-Pokal game at the Allianz Arena in a couple of weeks. Surely it would all go Bayern's way.

Outside the stadium we found Danny, who had managed to pay for his evening by collecting the "limited edition" beer cups and taking them back to claim the deposit. Kenny's latest lady friend, affectionately known as "Dorty Slippers" (she once bought him a pair of Dortmund slippers – it really is that simple), joined us to say hello. It was, as Kenny had warned her, like meeting the in-laws for the first time. She soon won us over – her dad has his own Borussia-themed bar in his basement. Surely that was enough to have Kenny dropping down on one knee? Well, at least while he was sober. Another successful trip negotiated without injury, arrest or catching of a contagious disease. That's a winner in anyone's book. Bloody love Germany, me.

REAL MADRID
Bernabéu Stadium
Madrid

Spain

He sent me a tweet at 3.35am simply saying "Help".

2. Gareth Baled on Us
Tiers, Tapas and Tantrums in the Spanish Capital

It's 7am and out of the window the yellow beaches of the Atlantic coast of France kiss the blue sea. The Bay of Biscay is still asleep, as every sane person should be at this hour on a Sunday. I think it is fair to say that the evidence of my insanity is irrefutable. I don't need much of an excuse to travel when the opportunity arises so today is no real exception. I mean, how often do you get a chance to see the world's most expensive player on his home debut? Well, apart from the boy Shearer wearing his £15,000,000 price tag around his neck for Newcastle United against Wimbledon back in 1996.

It's been a few years since I was last in the Spanish capital, Madrid. February 2009 to be precise, when I passed through on the way to and from Seville, where England were due to lose to Spain. It was a trip remembered for excruciating toothache, caused by an infected root canal. Despite the pain, there was an opportunity to tour the Bernabéu, in my opinion one of the finest stadiums in the world. The last time I had seen a game there was again when I was on England duty in November 2003 for one of those mid-season pointless friendlies. You remember the one? Ashley Cole and Shaun Wright-Phillips were racially abused, the England fans were attacked by the Spanish police and Asier Del Horno scored the only goal. The normally mild-mannered Henry Winter pulled no punches the following day in his *Daily Telegraph* column: "England lost a football match last night but Spain shamefully lost something far more important; Spain lost their right to be considered a civilised footballing nation. The Bernabéu's relentless racial barracking of Shaun Wright-Phillips and Ashley Cole disfigured a match that was supposed to be about bringing people together, about celebrating Spain's 500th fixture. A friendly? No chance."

This was when Spain were considered "big tournament bottlers" and few would have believed the dominance of the global game they would soon embark on. The trip to Madrid was one of those regrettable England fans day trips where we paid a king's ransom to see lots of the city's outskirts from a coach with a police escort, six hours of empty stadium seats, and finally a crap game of football. Great times indeed.

But my first visit to the stadium had been back in January 2000. Budget airlines were just starting to grow, and exotic places such as Berlin, Copenhagen and Madrid were now in the price range for your average European Football Weekender. Me and The Current Mrs Fuller booked up to go on a month of footballing fun as soon as the flights were released in the glorious summer of 1999. Instead of buying each other Christmas (and in my case, birthday) presents, we planned to hit the cultural highways of Europe with four consecutive weekends of art galleries, fine wine, damn good food and the odd football match or two. Milan, Madrid, Munich and Rome.

Alas, a small matter of the conception of our first child sort of put paid to the fine-wine element, but come January time, a five-month pregnant Bridget wasn't going to let 230 steps up to the top tier of the San Siro beat her as we sampled our first ever European away game together. A week later and I managed to secure some tickets behind the goal in the Bernabéu in the lower tier. Yes, it was in the Ultras section, and yes there is medical evidence to suggest that passive smoking is bad for an unborn baby, but flares? There hasn't been any research done to date that identifies birth defects with being an Ultra.

In those days the Bernabéu was still missing a top tier on the east stand, but it was still an impressive edifice, a far cry from the 1982 World Cup version which, while it had a capacity of 91,000, was a bit of a dump.

This was to be a day of adventure at both ends of the footballing spectrum. Just like any big city in the world, Madrid is the home of football teams right up and down the Spanish footballing pyramid. Everyone has obviously heard of Real and Atletico, probably a few less realise that Getafe and Rayo Vallecano, both plying their trade in La Liga, are from the south and south-eastern suburbs respectively. Spain also allows clubs to enter reserve teams (and even third teams) into the league structure, so on a typical weekend you could also find Real Madrid II or III playing out at the impressive training complex, Cuidad Real Madrid, near the airport.

The day before I arrived in the city, Real II (also known as Castilla) had hosted Real Zaragoza in the Segunda Division in front of over 3,000 at the shiny complex that had cost over €250 million to develop. Not that the club were short of money, even with the acquisition of Messrs Zidane, Figo, Roberto Carlos, Beckham and Jonathan Woodgate. Indeed not. They simply sold their old training ground to the city council for €480 million and moved into the barren wastelands near Barajas, although disappointingly the Real Madrid Theme Park, promised at the time by President Florentino Pevez, has still failed to materialise.

But it's not all about Real and Atletico in the city. There are the other clubs, representing the smaller neighbourhoods, where tourists have little reason to visit. The start of my weekend adventure in Madrid would be in one such suburb called Carabanchel, just three stops on the metro from the Estadio Vincente Calderon, home of Atletico Madrid. But first I had to find Danny Last.

On landing at Barajas I turned on my phone and saw his text explaining where I needed to head to.

"Tell cab driver to head to Calle (pronounced Ka-yee) Siena. If he can't find it then make the universal sign for a bull and he will know where to go." Ten minutes later we pulled up outside the Bull Ring and there was Danny, sunglasses on, looking a little "delicate".

Danny had been out into the wee-small hours "somewhere in Vallacances". He was on his holidays with his good wife Ana up in her village in the middle of rural Spain where wireless still means an AM radio, the net refers to what they use to catch olives and the nearest football ground is a two-hour bus ride away. As he had been a good boy all week, walking dogs, making chorizo and doing quality assurance on the locally produced wine, he was allowed a weekend back in the "smoke" to watch some football. On Saturday it was Rayo Vallecano versus Barcelona and he decided to have a swift half post-match. As we all know, one drink can soon turn to fifteen and before you know it is 3.35am and you have no idea where you are. He knew I would be worried after I didn't get three rings to say he's arrived home safely. Finally he sent me a tweet at 3.35am simply saying "Help". Of course I knew he didn't really need any help. If he did he would text me, or WhatsApp me. Tweeting is reserved for banter. Never one to miss an opportunity to experience the authentic side of the beautiful game he had tagged along with some of the Rayo fans and ended up in their Ultras Bar.

Google "Carabanchel" and the most notable result will be about the prison that used to be here. The notorious jail was used extensively during the reign of General Franco to house his enemies, whether they were military or political. Thankfully, today the only remains of the building are those in cyberspace, and as we emerged from the metro on a sunny morning we were met with a typically Spanish scene. A small market was set up outside the metro station, some old chaps played cards for matches and taxi drivers snoozed in their cars. Our destination was the Campo de la Mino, one of the oldest stadiums in Madrid, for a Sunday morning game in the Tercera Division, Group 7 . . . or the fourth tier of Spanish football to you and me.

We were fashionably late for kick-off. It's the done thing in these parts, so much so that the club delayed the kick-off for 10 minutes to ensure there were at least some fans in the ground. The sun was beating down and it was officially hotter than Greece. Despite our delay, the good news was we were still in time to take part in the half-time raffle to win a whole leg of Iberian cured pork. Perfect for a day when the mercury was topping 30 degrees. The Campo de la Mino didn't look like one of the oldest stadiums in Madrid. In fact it looked the most modern little stadium in the whole of Spain, complete with a 3G pitch and a nice stand surrounded on two sides by residential apartments. The stand was almost full with an eclectic mix of fans. Young girls showing off their tans, old chaps munching down on their big bags of sunflower seeds, teenagers squaring up to each other. The club seemed to be pretty happy playing at this level, having spent only two seasons at a higher level, between 1995 and 1998, and based on this game you can see why. This was their fourth draw in five games this season, and despite all of their efforts, they only really created one chance, a late penalty they converted to level the visitors' strike, which could have been the best goal ever but Danny and I were in negotiations at the gate over the terms and conditions for the half-time meat raffle.

The highpoint, apart from the raffle, was half-time. As you should do in any event in Spain, we simply went with the flow. There was no club house in the Mino, so everyone piled across the road to the bar, where for €3.60 we had two cold beers and our first tapas of the day – an egg and cheese number, fried in breadcrumbs, which I think was called something like Cojonudo. Whatever it was, it was the best thing we had ever eaten.

We got back into the ground just in time to see a few of the younger fans trying to turn on the water cannons around the edge of the pitch before being chased off by the groundsman armed with a mop.

The second half was a lively affair, full of passion but little in the way of creativity. The visitors, CD Los Yébenes San Bruno from Toledo, had taken a very early lead. This was the first season they had played at this level since being formed back in 1970. They certainly had a unique kit, combining yellow and red striped shirts (à la Lens or Lecce) with blue sleeves and shorts. The home side huffed and puffed trying to get the equaliser that their possession deserved. Finally, with a few minutes left, they got a penalty. The decision seemed quite harsh but the home striker made no mistake from the spot, sparking one of those amusing scuffles in the net when the keeper holds on to the ball while the attacking side want to restart quickly. Full time brought a round of pleasant applause and our departure for more tapas before the main event.

The day was young and we had a good few hours to fill before the game at the Estadio Santiago Bernabàu. Danny was keen to introduce me to a little street called Calle Cava Baja, which all of you O-Level Spanish students know means Digging Drop Street. Three hours later and I would simply refer to it as Heaven.

The street probably had a million bars, each one packed to the rafters with people enjoying their Sunday lunch. Every few minutes a big group would leave and continue down the street to the next bar that took their fancy and be replaced by a new intake that had arrived. The drinks were a commodity; it was the tapas people came for. Each bar had its own speciality that it gave away (yep, gave away) when you bought a drink. None of this "sharing a bowl of Aunt Bessie's Roast Potatoes" on-the-bar-type stuff either. This was a portion, or a "raciones" as I quickly learnt, each. We started tamely with a bowl of olives (me and olives don't get on, after an unfortunate incident with one becoming lodged up my nose when I used to work in Greece – long story and one for another day) in a rooftop bar with a view to die for of the San Francisco el Grande Basilica, and progressed through a full menu as we made our way down the street. Chorizo, squid, prawns, paella, chicken, more olives and finally, of course, tortilla. All washed down by the finest local beers known to man.

As we walked, Danny gave me a crash course in the etiquette of Tapasing, which is passed down from father to son. Of course I was sworn to secrecy, so I have changed the names below to protect their identity.

Tapas are as much a part of the fabric of Spain as Raul and even Enrique Iglesias. As with many traditions these days, they were rumoured to have been invented by royalty. Just as Marie Antoinette created "elevenses" by telling people to eat cake mid-morning, King Alfonso X, "The Wise", claimed to have named them after the small portions of leftovers he snacked on throughout the day with a glass or two of wine. Legend has it that when the cleaners came to take away his big dinner plate, he grabbed some remnants of his lunch and carried them around with him on the lid covering his wine. The word "tapa" means lid or cover in Spanish and thus the name was born.

Some more learned scholars will tell you that tapas originated as a snack for field workers during the long hours between meals, but that isn't as imaginative as the royal story. So what else can I tell you about the secrets of the Tapasnista? Well that would be telling and would take the pleasure out of hopping from bar to bar simply enjoying the experience.

Calle Cava Baja conquered, we pressed on. "There's one more place we have to visit," Danny said, as if I needed any further encouragement. Through Plaza Mayor, across Puerto Del Sol, the centre of the city in many people's eyes, and there it was. The Museum of Ham or Museo Del Jambon. Well, it is not really a museum unless you get your kick wandering around a huge delicatessen full of Spain's finest meats and cheeses. What it is is an experience. And it is the home of the €1 beer. I had you at beer, didn't I? Real Madrid fans were flocking to the bar to get their fill of cheap beer and bocadillos full of chorizo and Serrano ham. I was in heaven. This was a Spanish J.D. Wetherspoon but with more meat hanging up. Danny had to drag me away with the promise of "one final special treat".

Without a doubt the highlight of our afternoon of Iberian cuisine was a visit to La Casa Del Abuelo, or as Danny said, "Grandpa's House". The traditional tavern has been serving the best prawns in sizzling chilli and garlic in front of your eyes for over a century. It wasn't the cheapest round of the day but it sure was the best. Legend has it that Andy Warhol used to dine here when he was in town and he was inspired to paint his legendary Campbell's Soup image in 1968 while high on the heat of the chilli from his prawns.

I could go on about the pleasure of an afternoon in Madrid but it was time for a game of football. Real Madrid fans were milling around the bars circulating Sol, with chatter about what the new Welsh wonder would bring to the side. His opening two games had brought a draw (and a goal) away to Villarreal, followed by an impressive 6-1 win in Istanbul against Galatasaray in the Champions League. Tonight's game was seen as a formality, a walk-over, with odds of 11/10 on a home victory. Our final challenge of the day was to get our tickets.

Whatever you believe about buying tickets for clubs like Real, Barcelona and AC Milan, forget it. I still find it amazing that ticket resale websites are so popular. Well, actually, I do know why – because people take the easy option, even if it means they pay twice as much for the tickets. Real Madrid ticket tip of the day: be patient.

On their official website the clubs tend to list hospitality seats as the only one available (at a cool €200 plus) until a few days before the game. Don't be fooled into investing your hard-earned cash until they go on general sale. You can then choose your seat, pay by card and pick the tickets up in any La Caxia ATM machine in or around the city. Simple as that. Well, it should have been but for some reason every time I tried it during the day at various machines I was told my transaction was cancelled. But fear not. A swift visit to the ticket office and we had our tickets within seconds.

Formalities out of the way it was time to hit the Megastore to stock up on pictures of Real Madrid tat.

Unsurprisingly, they had gone Bale crazy. Gareth Bale shirt, Gareth Bale hats and Gareth Bale slippers. What more could a man want? The store was doing a roaring business, as too were the stalls around the ground, which were still happily selling their "The Special One" Mourinho scarves at €10. Shopping has a funny effect on Danny and I, so after 10 minutes we needed a sit-down and a drink. OK, a beer then if you are offering. We headed into the La Bodega, slap-bang opposite the stadium where Man City were demolishing another small club from the north-west of England. We only had time for the one, especially at an outrageous €3 a beer, before we bought our bag of sunflower seeds and headed into the stadium. One of our major topics during our afternoon of tapasing had been whether Real was the most famous club in the world. They are certainly the richest, with annual revenues of over €510 million and an estimated asset value of over €3 billion. Over 50 major domestic honours and a dozen European titles prove their pedigree on the pitch as well. We all know the stats like the back of our hands, but our task, apart from eating loads of fine plates of Spanish food and consuming copious amounts of cold beer, was to find the three killer facts about the club that would amaze fellow guests at a dinner party. So try these ones for size.

The British club with the most successful record against Real Madrid is not Manchester United, Arsenal or Chelsea. It isn't even West Ham United, I hear you gasp in surprise, but a team that currently play their football in the parks of South London. Let me take you back to the post-Great War years. The only people who really crossed the English Channel then were those dressed in military uniform. But one side decided to take the "English" game to the continent and so that is why the Civil Service FC found themselves lining up against Real Madrid in their Campo de O'Donnell ground, not once but twice. And on both occasions they won, 4-0 and 3-1. Quite what jobs the players actually did is a mystery, but in such a regimented occupation it is hard to imagine they weren't expected to "make their time up" later in the year.

Only two football sides in the world have been awarded the FIFA Order of Merit. There is no surprise that one of them is Real, but the other? Well, that would be Sheffield FC, of course. Back in 2004, to celebrate their centenary, the Gods of Football in their Swiss Mountain chalet decided to recognise the two sides that had shaped the beautiful game more than any other. Sheffield FC were the founding fathers of the game and shared a stage at FIFA's gala dinner with Real Madrid.

In December 2000, Real were voted the FIFA team of the century via a poll voted for by readers of FIFA's bi-monthly magazine. Over 42 per cent of the votes were for Real, with Manchester United a distant second with just 9.7 per cent of the vote. Unbelievably, Chelsea didn't feature in the top 20 – quite amazing for such a universally liked club.

If these facts aren't enough to gain instant street credibility then quite frankly you are living in the wrong neighbourhood.

So back to the main event. We were here to be entertained by the world's most expensive player. We had travelled over 600 miles just for the occasion – well, actually that isn't strictly true. The trip had been planned a good week or so before Gareth put pen to paper so we'd had no way of knowing that this would be his first game. And as it turned out, it wasn't. It seemed that attempting a Peter Kay-esque "'ave it" kicking competition with Ronaldo he had tweaked a thigh muscle. No matter how much his upper thigh was rubbed by some of the most exclusive physios in world football (I believe in other countries such activity is classed under the category of "extras"), it wasn't improving. Gareth would be a notable absentee from his own welcome party.

We could have had a strop at that point and thrown our sunflower seeds to the floor in anger, but we are bigger men than that (apparently) so we sat back in our luxurious surroundings and let the Real wave roll over us.

Bigger and better men (and women) have written more eloquent words about the Real performance that night, so it doesn't need my humble hand to write anything new about the game. Suffice to say that Real strutted around the pitch for the first few minutes, then conceded a goal in the fifth minute, scored by Lafita after Getafe's first foray into the Madrid half. Fifteen minutes later the new Pepe (one with almost a full head of hair) turned in a corner to equalise before Ronaldo converted a dubious spot-kick to put Madrid 2-1 up at half-time. Forty-five minutes in which we had hardly made a dent in our family bag of sunflower seeds. In all honesty I had actually given up trying to eat them, taking instead an approach of simply sucking the salt off the shell before cracking them in my teeth and spitting them out on the floor. I looked the part, just as 15-year-olds pretend to inhale when they smoke, trying to look all grown up (or was that just me?). Danny went off to explore and came back with a big cheesy grin that just spelt mischief. He had somehow got "caught up" in a party who were just going back into their executive box, and had managed to quaff two glasses of red and eaten a chorizo sausage roll before he had been rumbled, not for wearing shorts and a T-shirt when everyone else was suited and booted, but because he didn't have his sunglasses on, even though the sun had long since set over the stadium.

Back to the second half and Isco made the points safe for Real on the hour mark, meaning that the crowd could have a final 30-minute siesta. Real passed the ball around as if it were a training match. In truth, according to my new best friend, 19-year old Roseanne from Salamanca who was sitting next to me and had struck up a conversation about my sunflower-seed-eating habits, Real played like this in most matches only raising their game for the visit of Barcelona. They didn't win every game because they gave the ball away and made little effort to get it back. I offered her a job on *Match of the Day* straight away.

With most of the 70,000 spectators already heading for the exits, Khedira made a run down the left, crossed it and Ronaldo pulled out one of his tricks from the pocket marked "injury-time fun" and back-heeled the ball into the net. Full time and Real had eased to a 4-1 win. The La Liga table was already taking a familiar look after just six games, with Real and Barca occupying the top two spots, and sharing eleven wins out of a possible twelve so far. It was going to be a long season for the teams below them and we were still in September.

It was only 10pm, or "early evening" as it is known in Madrid, so we headed back to the city centre for a nightcap or two. Although the evening was young, Danny and I aren't, and with my ridiculously early start combined with his ridiculously late finish the night before, we were soon flagging.

"One more at Café Canada?" he suggested. Of course, a Canadian-themed bar complete with a bull-head on the wall wearing a straw hat at a jaunty angle. What a perfect way to end the day.

I've never been shy in professing my love for the real beautiful game. The one played in hundreds of ramshackle venues up and down the country every week, where players are playing for the love of the game and not the huge salary, and where fans genuinely mean so much more to clubs. But there is something about watching the game in the world's greatest stadiums. The ground wasn't full, and many of the seats in the middle and upper tiers were taken by people like us, football tourists, but there was something in the air, a kind of expectation that you were watching a performance rather than a simple football match. I know I am not alone in experiencing this – friends go back every year to the Camp Nou with the same feeling. Perhaps it is the fact you experience a match day here rather than just 90 minutes of football. To me, what made Madrid so special was the slow build-up during the day. The tapas, the sunshine, the senoritas, the museum of ham; even without the appearance of the world's most expensive player, it had been a trip to savour. But sorry Gareth, you had your chance to win us over and if you can't be bothered to put on a show for two of your most loyal fans, then you don't deserve our support. Well, at least for a month or two.

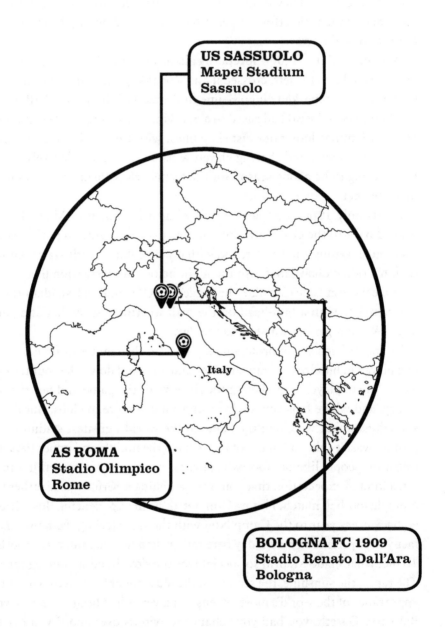

US SASSUOLO
Mapei Stadium
Sassuolo

AS ROMA
Stadio Olimpico
Rome

BOLOGNA FC 1909
Stadio Renato Dall'Ara
Bologna

Italy

Reggio Emilia was at least a little bit more racy,
being the home of Lambrusco wine as well as being
twinned with Fort Worth, Texas.

3. No Place Like Rome

Nearly 25 years ago we all went Serie A crazy. In fact I would go as far as saying that it was because of the James Richardson-fronted Channel 4 programme *Gazzetta* every Saturday morning that coffee was imported into our culture. Millions of football fans used to tune in to hear the latest gossip from James as he sat coolly at a table in a piazza somewhere in Italy, sipping a cappuccino (but only before 11am of course). But did you know that the programme title was actually in homage to Paul Gasciogne who, having just signed for Lazio, was due to front it each week, with Jimbo producing it? Alas, Gazza's time-keeping meant that Mr Richardson had to spend more time in front of the camera instead of behind it. And the rest is history.

Twenty-four hours after *Gazzetta* was screened, even more people would watch the Channel 4 live game, which somehow always seemed to be the best game of the season, every week. In the first ever live game they showed is still etched in my mind.

On a boiling hot September afternoon, Sampdoria and Lazio played out an outstanding 3-3 draw, with Des Walker lining up for i Blucerchiati. This was a time before live football from around the globe saturated our TV screens and thus it was something new, exciting, and even fearful. This was what it was like when Cheese & Onion became the second flavour of crisp to be launched, after decades of Ready Salted, to explode our taste buds.

We lapped up the games from all corners of Italy, quickly learning who the teams, the players and of course the stadiums were. We learnt more about Italian geography than would have had Catherine Zeta-Jones and Holly Willoughby been our teachers at school (well, maybe not). We marvelled at the pyrotechnics and visual displays the fans put on and wondered what had gone wrong with our own game. Everyone wanted to have a bit of Serie A, and us adventurous Brits slowly wised up to the fact that visiting Italy was easy, cheap and the Best Weekend Ever.

Italy was the destination for my first ever European Football Weekend. Two days in Milan, with a trip to the San Siro to watch one of the finest AC teams of all time. Paolo Maldini, George Weah, Zvonimir Boban, Andriy Shevchenko before he was Chelsea-fied, Alessandro Costacurta and of course Plymouth

Argyle-bound Taribo West. But it was freezing cold Sunday afternoon in the Stadio Giuseppe Meazza when I made a heavily pregnant Current Mrs Fuller climb up to the top tier to watch "the stars of world football". Of course, when the opponents Lecce took a 2-0 lead thanks to Cristiano Lucarelli she was very pleased with me and my "stupid, f'ing false expectations". To this day I have no idea whether she was talking about the disappointment of the Milan performance or me promising a romantic weekend in Milan that ended up at the football. I was hooked, even if she wasn't, and there wasn't a month that passed when I didn't hop over to Italia for a bit of Sunday-afternoon Calcio. A morning arrival into Milan Linate, train down to Bologna, up to Como or even, if I was hungry, Parma. Then football, food and a few Peronis before I headed back in time for story-time with the little Fullers.

But nothing lasts forever and as Jimbo disappeared from our screens 10 years later and Sky Sports took over the world, Serie A slipped down the popularity stakes behind La Liga, the Bundesliga and even Scottish football in TV coverage terms. New legislation in Italian football introduced to prevent escalating fan violence that had led to a number of football-related deaths meant that the days of pitching up and buying tickets from the stadiums on the day, or even from touts, was now a distant dream. For our weekend footballing treats we had to look further afield and Italy became a distant memory of the Football Tourist past.

So there was no real reason why I was now sitting on a cross-country train running through the Northern Italian countryside on a chilly Sunday afternoon. I can't even blame my arch nemesis, Danny Last. He was 700 miles away sitting on his sofa, enjoying a beer and a slice of Super Sunday no doubt. I could blame my current travel partner, Adam Lloyd, but that would be unfair. It was my fault. There, I've said it. I was once told that apologising is a sign of weakness but even I cannot wiggle out of this one. I admit that as soon as I saw the opportunity for a two-day, three-game Serie A extravaganza nothing was going to get in my way. Even the annual arrival of my mother in-law couldn't tempt me to stay. I put aside the disappointment of missing stories of "Mrs Jones's bunions" and concentrated on three Serie A games in 30 hours.

I'd merely hinted at a trip before Adam launched into logistics mode. Before I could say *"A caval donato non si guarda in bocca"* he had sorted train tickets, hotels and lunch. Well, when I say lunch I mean a Tramezzino (just like the sandwiches your mum made with the crusts cut off) and ice-cold bottles of Peroni Red. Our destination for the first leg of the Italian Tripod was the city of Reggio Emilia, 40 miles north-east of Bologna.

The main train line in these parts runs from Rimini on the Adriatic coast right up to Turin, nestling in the shadows of the Alps. Along this route there are footballing towns and cities almost at every stop. As the train pulled into the first stop at Modena, the floodlights of the Stadio Alberto Braglia came into view, home today of the Serie B side. It was worth paying the small premium to go first class on the 40-minute journey from Bologna to see the hulking lights leaning in over the action.

I'm sure the view wasn't anywhere near as good in second class. Of course we were too grown up to be leaning out of the window and taking pictures. That was the other English Football Tourists further down the carriage.

Reggio Emilia wasn't exactly brimming with life as we arrived. Our destination was the Mapei Stadium, which according to our good friends at Google Maps, was a brisk 2.1 miles away. We started on our journey and were soon joined by a fellow Englishman, who told us he was a scout for an English club he would rather not identify. A strange chap who swore blind that the stadium was next to the station, and had no idea which two teams were playing. His lack of laptop, notebook, tablet or even a basic pen and paper also raised our collective eyebrows. We told him there was no shame in just wanting to be at a game but he didn't seem ready to confess his Football Tourist tendencies just yet.

The Mapei Stadium – Città Del Tricolore, to give it its full name – is described by our good friends at Wikipedia as "multi-purpose", which is the functional phrase for "completely lacking in character, atmosphere or facilities for spectators". I hoped to be proved wrong but my experience of similar Italian stadiums in Piacenza, Bergamo (Atalanta), Modena and Ancona hadn't been good. In fact I always wonder how these small clubs can justify charging ticket prices for ordinary games. Ten years ago I paid over €100 for a seat at Brescia v Bari because it was raining and the seat was one of the few under cover. And when I say seat, I mean a bit of plastic with no back bolted onto concrete steps. Even Premier League clubs today rarely offer tickets over £90 and at least at those levels you get a degree of comfort. Heck, at the Emirates they even mute the atmosphere so as not to disturb you should you wish to have a snooze.

Unfortunately, with few stadiums privately owned in Italy, clubs need to get as much revenue as possible on the gate because commercial opportunities are so limited and the money taken in the bars (where they exist) goes directly to the municipality that owns the ground. Few clubs have the money to build their own stadiums – in fact since the redevelopment work carried out, and funded centrally, for the 1990 World Cup, only one new stadium has opened in the top flight of Italian football: The Stadium IS Arena in Cagliari. Others, such as the Olympic Stadium and the Juventus Stadium in Turin, have been rebuilt, but that is the extent of Italy's ambitions in terms of stadium modernisation. In the same period, eight brand new Premier League grounds have been opened and every one of the remaining eleven has had significant redevelopment work, bar Everton's Goodison Park.

We weren't here in the home of Italian cheese manufacturing to see the home side, the Teste Quadre (Square Heads), also better known as Associazione Calcio Reggiana 1919. The maroons could boast an alumni featuring Fabrizio Ravanelli, Paulo Futre and Cristiano Zanetti but today they were playing in the third tier of Italian football. We were here to see US Sassuolo. Cue tumbleweeds drifting across the page.

I had been asked the question "who?" every time I had mentioned the trip for the past couple of weeks. Even people who I would consider to be European football experts had expressed some bewilderment when I told them the first destination. The Serie A debutants had been playing in the third tier for the first time just five years ago. Last season they'd upset the form book by winning Serie B, thus taking their place along with the likes of Juventus, Milan and Roma for the first time. But their own Stadio Enzo Ricci with its 4,000 capacity wasn't deemed big enough for Serie B, let alone Serie A, so a deal was made with Reggiana AC to cohabit in their still modest 15,000-capacity Mapei Stadium.

There isn't really a lot I can tell you about Sassuolo. In fact there isn't much anyone who doesn't live and breathe Italian football can tell you about Sassuolo. The town itself is located just south of Modena and 20 miles from where we were today. As any ceramics expert will of course know, it is the home of the Italian tile industry. There, I told you I couldn't tell you much. Reggio Emilia was at least a little bit more racy, being the home of Lambrusco wine as well as being twinned with Fort Worth, Texas. Boom. I had you on . . . well, on nothing really.

So far this season i Nerroverdi (the black and greens) were keeping their heads above water . . . just. Two wins and four draws saw them sitting outside of the relegation zone, and with wins away at Sampdoria and in Reggio Emilia over local rivals Bologna in the bank already, they fancied their chances against the visitors today from Bergamo. Crowds up by 218 per cent on last season at the Stadio Alberto Braglia in Modena were flocking to the Mapei to taste the rare air of Serie A. In truth Adam and I didn't really care who won the game. We were the winners because we were back in the days of Mancini, Lombardo and Crespo, the face of James Richardson, the tones of

Peter Brackley and the awe of David Platt, Des Walker and Jay Bothroyd, all washed down with a double espresso and a Baci di Dama.

After what seemed to be an age of wandering around the nondescript roads of the Italian suburbs we arrived at the Stadio Mapei. Hardly eye-catching or built with spectator comfort in mind, plonked in between industrial estates, a motorway and wasteland. Apparently, there was due to be a metro line opening close to the stadium, but we saw little in the way of public transport options unless you count the practice of having four people riding on the same scooter. We passed through security with the stewards asking us if we had any flares and asking me to take my woolly hat off just in case I had hidden any under there. Apparently this was a very big no-no in Reggio Emilia. As we walked out into the bowl of the ground it was amazing to believe this was a top-flight stadium. Basic is not a word you can use too often for stadiums in major leagues, but this summed it up perfectly. No facilities except for one tiny coffee bar, concrete steps with numbers painted on for seats and open to all the elements. At the far end, around 1,500 Atalanta fans had made the journey eastwards from Bergamo, although the open-air nature of the ground was diluting their efforts to create an atmosphere. But we didn't care, we were Football Tourists doing what we do best, watching football, and it was bloody great.

SASSUOLO 2, ATALANTA 0
Sunday 24th November 2013 – The Mapei Stadium

Our "seats" were showing signs of dampness so we moved to the top of the stadium. We were marked out as Johnny Foreigner by the fact we hadn't picked up one of the free programmes outside that would act as a cushion. It seems that not only did everyone want to sit down, but they also wanted to do so in their correct small square of concrete.

The game wasn't a classic – the fact that there was on average a free-kick every 110 seconds gives you an idea that it was a stop/start game, and with just 10 shots on target it will not go down in the "classic" folder in my footballing memoirs (just call me OptaStu). The home fans in the "bullpit" at the bottom of our stand tried to create some atmosphere and a beat for their team, but in the first period nothing seemed to gel for Sassuolo. In fact the most impressive part of the first 45 minutes was the sunset behind us, which had us snapping away like loons and drew the attention of the stewards, who came to see what all the fuss was about over the back of the stand where we were pointing our cameras. "English," we said in unison. They understood.

As the temperature dropped we expected a similar battle of attrition in the second half. Despite Antei receiving his marching orders for a second yellow card, Sassuolo dominated the remainder of the game and were great value for the three points. The danger man was the holding midfielder (none of these "false nine" or "lazy ten" buzz words here) Luca Marrone, who set up both goals in a three-minute period just after the hour mark, scored by the two forwards Zaza and Berardi. Atalanta can have no grumbles at the end result, although the home keeper, Pegolo, was the busier of the two. Sassuolo appear to have built a team that the locals, well those from 20 miles down the road anyway, are rightly proud of. Eleven Italians started the game for them, which in any major league these days is unheard of. Many commentators wrote off Sassuolo's hopes of survival before a ball was ever kicked that season, but the three points meant they sat in the Serie A table above the likes of some of the bigger names in Italian football including Sampdoria and Bologna. They had earned their place at the top table of Italian football, and they were certainly enjoying the feast.

With the temperature dropping, the hike back to the station wasn't the most enticing prospect, but we were kept going by the thought of game number two, just a few hours away back in Bologna. Just a small matter of il Rossublu versus i Nerazzurri, one of Italy's greatest teams.

Let me take you back to 26 June 1990. England are one minute away from a penalty shoot-out in the second round of the FIFA World Cup against Belgium. Paul Gascoigne floats in a free-kick from the left-hand side which appears to be drifting over everyone's head. Everyone? No, not quite, because at the back post is 24-year-old Aston Villa midfielder David Platt, on the field as a replacement for Steve McMahon and making one of his first appearances for the national side. Platt follows the flight of the ball and connects with the ball perfectly, turning away as his volley hits the back of the net and takes England into the last eight of the World Cup. It could be argued that that one moment set Platt on to becoming one of the first footballing millionaires. Less than 12 months after that goal, Platt was on his way to Serie A side Bari for a whopping £5.5 million.

Fast-forward three years and Bobby Robson is long gone as England manager. The hopes of a nation that we would repeat our semi-final appearance at the 1994 FIFA World Cup have crumbled under Graham Taylor's reign as England manager. Three years of poor football, poor players and poor excuses is coming to an inglorious end. His last game in charge is against San Marino, the lowest ranked team in UEFA and one that was yet to record an international win. Bookies had stopped taking odds on an England win days before, despite Taylor's woeful reign and the failure of the team to reach the 1994 World Cup finals in the USA. While it was possible that England could still qualify for the finals, it would take a miraculous set of results elsewhere. The ask on the England team was simple: win by seven clear goals.

San Marino kicked off and hoofed the ball hopefully into the right-hand quadrant. Left-back stalwart Stuart Pearce picked the ball up and under no pressure at all played the ball back to the England keeper David Seaman. Unfortunately, Davide Gualtieri had guessed this was what the experienced full-back would do and nipped in and planted the ball past the Arsenal keeper. Just over eight seconds were on the clock -the fastest goal in international football and still the greatest moment in San Marino's history.

These two events are connected by one simple fact -both memorable nights had been played out on our TV screens live from Bologna's Stadio Renate Dall'Ara. Fat Town, as it is often referred to in Italian culture, is known for its hearty food rather than its footballing pedigree, but it was to be our destination for the second game of the day. After the magic in Reggio Emilia we headed back down for part two of our adventure to the most important city in North Italy. Bar Turin. And Milan, of course. Not forgetting Venice mind, and Genoa now I think about it. Well, one of the most important cities anyway. The almost completely open-air stadium would have been a beautiful venue back in June 1990, but in late November 23 years later, it promised to be bloody cold. Still, with Internazionale the visitors, we hoped the atmosphere created by Bologna's Tifosi Bulgarelli would keep us warm and entertained. Despite their winning the Italian title on seven occasions, and being the most successful Italian team outside of Milan, Turin or Rome, recent times have been very tough on the Rossoblù.

Despite being one of the founder members of Serie A back in 1929, which ironically was won by tonight's opponents Inter in their initial guise of Ambrosiana FC, Bologna have spent far too long in recent years outside the top flight, dogged by distractions regarding their ownership. I had been here once before, marvelling at the stunning architecture of the stadium rather than the football.

Ironically, that game too had been against Inter Milan, although in sunnier times. I remembered wandering the centre of the historic part of the city, marvelling at the buildings in the Piazza del Nettuno.

Only one thing is more important to Italians than football, and that is food. With a couple of hours to spare before the game we made sure we blended in with the locals by heading to an old-school Italian restaurant in Palazzo Re Enzo (aka one that didn't serve Spaghetti Bolognese -a dish created for those bloody tourists). This building, dating back to the thirteenth century, is the beating heart of the city. Amazingly, you are free to wander around it unchallenged, which is relatively ironic considering its history. It was originally built as a palace but became a prison for one man, Enzo, son of the Roman emperor Frederik II. It wasn't necessarily a hard life for Enzo as he had free rein of the place, and despite him being locked up at night in a cage hanging from the ceiling, he managed to father four children during his stay here. All of this history was explained to us by our waiter, who wanted us to enjoy not only the outstanding locally produced food but also the history of where we were eating it. It was no surprise that the food kept on coming – these Italians don't do things by half and we ended up eating our own body weight in local cold meats, cheeses, pasta (squid-ink tortellini filled with truffle carbonara, as you have asked), washed down with a couple of beers. But no ordinary beer. Oh, no. Being one of the centres of style in the country, Bologna serve their bottles of beer in a clear plastic handbag, filled with ice.

Adam had managed to remember his pedometer and as we washed down our feast with a double espresso, he told me that the 37-minute walk to the Stadio Renato Dall'Ara would burn off around 1,000 calories, or approximately half of the pasta I had just wolfed down. So we set off, hot footing it through piazzas and palazzos, dodging locals on scooters and gelato-wielding tourists. Fortunately the Italian footballing mentality isn't to pitch up at the turnstiles five minutes before kick-off so as the teams came out onto the pitch we breezed into the stadium and started the monumental climb up to the top of the Curva Ospiti. Ah yes, that was the slight detail I had omitted to tell Adam. The website was all in Italian and I simply picked the cheapest tickets, which just so happened to be in the middle of the Ultras. I'm sure 90 minutes of acrid flare smoke, bouncing around like a loon, was exactly what he was looking forward to on his Sunday night.

The Dall'Ara, beautiful as it may seem to many with a glorious tower sitting in the middle of the Poltrone stand, is essentially an open-air athletics stadium, with basic small plastic seats sitting directly on the concrete steps. It was certainly never built for comfort, or even with 25,000 or so spectators in mind but it certainly delivered joy in the bucket-full. We appeared to have taken a wrong turn somewhere on our way up into the Curve and ended up slap-bang in the middle of the Vecchia Guardia, one of the Tifosi groups. What to do in such circumstances? Simple, jump around, clap your hands and shout abuse at the referee. While our Italian left a lot to be desired (well, mine anyway), we quickly learnt the relevant gestures for us to be considered locals.

BOLOGNA 1, INTERNAZIONALE 1
Sunday 24th November 2013 – Stadio Renato Dall'Ara

In the grand scheme of things, this looked like a very valuable point for Bologna. The result actually took them out of the relegation zone for at least seven days. Inter will rue the two points they dropped, and the opportunity to go back into the top three of Serie A. They had over 60 per cent of the possession, 23 shots to Bologna's 9 and a staggering 15 corners, but it took a dubious goal from Brazilian full-back Jonathan to bring them back into the game just after half-time. Prior to this, Bologna strolled around the pitch with a unexpected smile on their faces, holding a one-goal lead thanks to Kone's 12th-minute goal, like a boy who has just discovered their elder brother's porn stash.

In truth we saw very little of the game. In between taking a million pictures of fans holding flares and looking a bit "Danny Dyerish", trying to blend in by jumping around like loons and discovering they served real beer in the bar by the Ultras entrance, there wasn't a lot of time for ball-watching. This was what continental football was all about, and what was missing from our own game. Yes, the stadium experience for watching a game was poor. Yes, the fans in Italy are treated more like criminals with the security, fences and moats around the pitch, and yes, the fans seemed completely oblivious to what was happening on the pitch, but even with 20,000 empty seats in an open-air stadium, the atmosphere was cracking. Deep down (or for some of us a little closer to the surface) we are all jealous of such atmosphere. There wasn't one policeman in the stadium, nor did we see any hint of trouble, despite Inter having around a quarter of the stadium for their fans.

Neither team would have been satisfied with the point at full time, although both sets of fans wandered into the night relatively happy. They had done their respective teams proud and could go to work on Monday with their heads held high. We piled onto the buses waiting outside the ground, rather than attempt the "brisk" 40-minute walk back into town, arriving back at our hotel on the stroke of midnight, just in time for a nightcap or three. It had been a long, enjoyable, day getting reacquainted with Serie A. Adam's pedometer informed us we had walked over 10 miles in the day, perfectly balancing out our excesses, although in truth you can never get enough of Bologna, whether it be food, drink or calcio. Gentlemen, to bed. For we rise at dawn for Rome.

The sun was streaming through our window to welcome us to the second day of the Calcio Italia adventure, and after the two games yesterday we were heading south on the ultra-swish new high-speed train line through Tuscany, Umbria and Lazio. Replacing what had previously been a seven-hour train journey up and over the Apennines, running down the spine of Italy, this line now cuts through the hills and has reduced the travel time from Bologna to Rome to just over two hours. These new express trains run three times an hour, linking cities in the south of the country such as Reggio Calabria and Naples with Milan, Turin and Genoa in the north. The fares are low (our first-class ticket had cost just £35), meaning that people are flocking onto them, a lesson I hope we take heed of in the UK when we eventually open up our High Speed lines (though I know we won't). We hardly had time to make full use of the free Wi-Fi, champagne and salty snacks (peanuts) before we were easing into Roma Termini.

Those who missed the first instalment of my adventures, *The Football Tourist*, will not be aware that Adam is a Roman. Well, sort of. Despite hailing from Basingstoke and working for many years in Guildford, he now lives in a villa in the village of Frascati, overlooking Rome. Work has been very kind to him in terms of living arrangements, but still he cannot sate his old pleasures of a good old afternoon out at football. So once a season I come and help him scratch that itch. Our final destination was where he had laid his hat (random Paul Young reference – kids, ask your dad).

Initially our plan had been to enjoy a leisurely long lunch in the Travestere area of the city, a few drinks and perhaps even a bit of sight-seeing. But then Adam got a call. Or should I say, the call. He'd struck up a relationship a few games ago in the Stadio Olimpico with a chap running up and down the front of the Tribuna Tevere waving a huge flag, professing the support of the Roma United Kingdom group. The flag waver was Marcello, a Joe Pesci lookalike, who actually worked for BT in Reading but whenever cash and time permitted, hot-footed it to the Italian capital to wave his flag.

He was a one-man PR machine for the group and had somehow managed to arrange some live airtime with Sky Italia as part of their build-up to the game versus Cagliari. Adam, appointed the group's official social media photographer, was to appear alongside Marcello on Italian prime time TV.

So our new plan was to meet Marcello outside the ground at 4pm, nearly FIVE hours before kick-off. I'd never been at a ground that early – well, apart from once in Bilbao when I turned up 24 hours early due to a late change for Spanish TV. So our relaxing lunch turned into a quick snack at a stand-up trattoria before we jumped in a taxi for the stadium. It appeared that the tram drivers also fancied a night watching the game on TV so they had gone on strike, meaning that even at 4pm, traffic around the stadium was building up.

Our meeting place was outside the Stadio dei Marmi, the stadium of marbles, the amazing arena surrounded by 59 statues of (almost) naked athletes next to the Stadio Olimpico, built in 1928 as a showpiece of the Academy of Physical Education next door. It was here that Sky Italia set up their match-day nerve centre and it would be here that Adam and Marcello would be interviewed by Angelo Mangiante, Sky Italia's equivalent of Geoff Shreeves and Chris Kamara all rolled into one, but with a much nicer tan and no bubble perm.

Us Englishmen had fallen into the trap set by Romans. When they say meet at 4pm, what they really mean is meet at some point between 4.30pm and 5pm. While we were waiting, a number of rather attractive young ladies appeared, went into a small hut, and came out minutes later with a big smile on their faces. We were intrigued. Finally, the door opened and out came a tall, smartly dressed young chap. "That's Kevin Strootman," Adam said, and I simply nodded, none the wiser. I secretly Googled the name and found out that Mr Strootman was in fact a Dutch international and a key part of the successful start to the Roma season; he who should have been tucking into his plate of pre-match pasta rather than flirting in a car park with hostesses (of the VIP hospitality kind), handing them their match-day passes. "Adam, I don't think that is Kevin Strootman," I suggested. Adam was having none of it and engaged him in conversation. His Dutch accent certainly seemed very Italian, and he appeared to have had his hand tattooed since the picture I was looking at from last week's match had been taken. Hmm. But our heated debate was interrupted by the arrival of Marcello, who briefed us both (yep, somehow I had now been roped into the interview) on what we should and shouldn't say. We couldn't help but giggle. Marcello, who worked for BT in an engineering capacity, was doing a media debrief with two Directors of Communication for major companies. We had to draw the line when he got to page four of his briefing document, which detailed what we should say if transvestites asked to join the UK Roma fan group.

After walking from pillar to post, stopping to have the smallest coffee in the world and freezing our butts off waiting for our moment, the gates finally opened and we were ushered into the ground. Angelo's English wasn't that good, but that didn't worry him as he fired questions at us live on Italian TV. We smiled, answered the best we could, remembering if we got stuck to simply say *Totti è il nostro leader, lui è il re* (Totti is our leader, he is the king). However, his final question threw me.

"Are you nervous?" Assuming he meant about being on live TV I answered, "No, not at all. I've been in this situation many times before." My answer got a strange look from Angelo, as well as from the lady back in the studio. Of course, what Angelo meant was, "As a loyal Roma fan, was I nervous that Juventus had now caught up with Roma and were actually above them in the table?" Simple mistake, I think.

The first of the media duties over, we headed into the fans village on the other side of the stadium and were immediately pushed in front of another camera, this time for Roma Channel, the official YouTube TV station for the club. Once again, with the autocue cards from Marcello, we handled the questions in English and Italian. The Totti rule once again proved invaluable, as you cannot do much wrong when being interviewed on TV by just saying "Totti" in different tones of voice. I could see the very attractive presenter was suitably impressed. Of course she was, Stuart.

It was nearly match time. Somehow we had spent over four hours walking around the edge of the stadium without actually doing much. We passed through the security cordon and were in. We had the choice of around 10,000 seats in the Tribune Tevere so, like Goldilocks, we tried a few, both right at the top of the stand, and down at the bottom, before settling on one in the middle just in time to see the Curva Sud explode into sound, colour and smoke to welcome the two teams.

AS ROMA 0, CAGLIARI 0
Monday 25th November 2013 – Stadio Olimpico

Once again, the gambling man would have been foolish to bet against AS Roma, who were 7/4 to beat the Sardinians. I mean, who would have thought that after 10 consecutive wins i Giallorossi would then only manage draws against Sassuolo and Torino. This game was a banker home win, despite the absence of a certain Mr Totti. But football is unpredictable and that's why we love it. Despite 19 shots, 19 corners and over 60 per cent of the possession, Roma failed to score for the first time this season. As the fans trooped off into the cold Roman night at full time, the point would have felt like defeat, especially as Juventus had gone top of the league after their win 24 hours previously in Livorno.

It is amazing how fast the expectations of the fans had changed. In the space of 12 months this team had gone from possible Europa League candidates to recording an amazing 10 consecutive wins at the start of the season. Not only had the media been talking of them being a shoo-in for the Champions League, but there had also been talk of the Serie A title whispered in the corridors of the Stadio Olimpico. It couldn't last, everyone agreed that, and now, after games 11 and 12 had ended in draws, they had lost their top spot to a rampant Juventus.

For me, throughout the game, it was a dilemma whether to watch the match or the Curva Sud. Roma started with all the intent they had shown in their first 10 winning games, with ex-Arsenal flop Gervinho pulling the strings in a front three that had scored goals for fun so far this season. But there seemed to be something missing. A spark. A Totti. Without their talisman the home side often looked confused about how to break down a stubborn defence.

It wasn't a night for watching a frustrating goalless draw. In fact it was bloody freezing. Despite throwing all they had at the Sardinians, the best Roma could muster was a late Gervinho header which hit the post. The frustration was clear to see on the face and in the actions of coach Mister Garcia (as he had been announced to the crowd). With 15 minutes to go he was sent to the stands for kicking a water bottle onto the pitch from his technical area and with his departure went any inspiration and motivation the team had to find a winner.

It wasn't the game we had come to expect, and by "we" I refer to the 40,000 home fans in the Stadio Olimpico. That is what such an impressive start to the season does to the fans. They expect teams like Cagliari to be put to the sword, but the opposition came with a (defensive) plan and left with a point.

Their 50 or so fans, high up in the Curva Nord, surrounded by at least a hundred stewards "just in case", celebrated like they had won the league, rather than a point that moved them up to twelfth in the Serie A table, although that was one place higher than AC Milan.

Our final challenge of the evening was to get back to Casa Lloyd in the hills of Frascati. The tram strike meant we'd spent the last two days walking everywhere, neither of us fancied the three-mile walk back to the city centre so we jumped on a bus, which went nowhere. Actually, that wasn't true. It tried to head north so that it could do a sharp right to head south (turning circles and all that), but it got caught in a swarm of scooters and Smart cars which looked as though they were trying to create the world's largest automotive scrum. Finally we reached Flamino metro at 11.35pm. The last metro had departed, or so we thought. The Roma fans weren't going to let the small matter of a closed metro or no more trains running stop them getting home. A gate to the metro station was "opened" and we all piled in. Faced with hundreds of annoyed football fans with no way of getting home refusing to move from the platforms of the station, a train was quickly found and we were soon on our journey back.

A very early start was the reward for a couple of days of excellent footballing escapades. Somewhere in the past few years I had fallen out of love with Italian football. I blame James Richardson for giving up on his Saturday morning café culture. But after this weekend the *amore* was beating in my heart once more. Ciao Italia, I will be back to understand that dark, beating heart of yours.

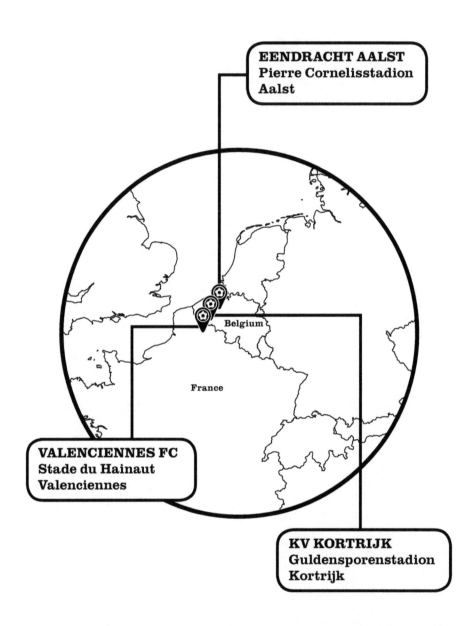

EENDRACHT AALST
Pierre Cornelisstadion
Aalst

Belgium

France

VALENCIENNES FC
Stade du Hainaut
Valenciennes

KV KORTRIJK
Guldensporenstadion
Kortrijk

What do you buy the man who already owns at
least two pairs of special non-league trousers?

4. Revenge of the Black Diamond

"You are going where?" That is the usual response I get from The Current Mrs Fuller when I float the idea of a weekend watching football somewhere in the far-flung corners of Europe. "It's never just Munich, Paris or Rome with you, is it?" I knew she was joking as I had been to all of those places already. Great woman, great sense of humour – well, at least I assume she was joking. Of course I always extend an offer that she can come with me but surprisingly she always declines.

Normally I blame the idea of these trips on Danny Last but this one was all down to French Television. F'ing French F'ing TV.

Let me take you back a few years to start. Danny and I don't do Christmas presents to each other.

I mean, what do you buy the man who already owns three (THREE!) non-league bags and at least two pairs of special non-league trousers? There isn't anything, so we put the money we would have spent on presents on one last hurrah for the year. Two years ago it was a trip to Poland, last year it was the Dundee derby via Arbroath and this year we had planned to visit warmer climes in the South of France.

Despite us having been to well over two hundred different grounds in Europe (probably – we don't actually keep a record), and half of France's current Ligue 1 grounds, there has been one large gaping hole in the list. Olympique Marseille, the Great OM. With a great fanfare, we announced to the world in October that our annual pre-Christmas trip this year was to be to the Mediterranean to watch Olympique take on Montpellier in the battle of the Côte d'Azur.

Stade Vélodrome is probably the most famous club stadium in France. Originally opened in 1937 as a cycling and football stadium, the open-air aspect has never diminished the red-hot atmosphere even on the coldest of nights in Provence. Despite having a capacity of just over 60,000, the club commenced on a redevelopment project last year that would see the capacity increase to over 67,000 in time for UEFA 2016 as well as the installation of a roof that will amplify the noise off the scale. Despite the ground having a reduced capacity due to the redevelopment, ticket buying these days is a simple job thanks to the internet, and before you could spell, let alone say, Bouillabaisse, I had two tickets for the game against Montpellier Hérault Sport Club in the bag. Perfect seats to the side of the Virage Nord to watch the Marseille Trop Puissant, the most notorious of the OM Fan Groups. After all, we weren't really going to watch the football, were we?

And then it went wrong. Horribly wrong. Those underpaid, overworked, stressed French footballers announced they were going on strike in protest about the amount of tax they had to pay. They argued that as they were "only" playing football, they shouldn't pay any tax at all. They would be barricading the golf courses and country clubs with their camouflage Lamborghinis until all of their demands were met. Our trip looked as if it would constitute one CFA2 game (think county league but with fewer dogs wearing scarves), lots of beer and buckets full of overpriced fish stew. And I hate fish stew. Two weeks before we were due to depart, somewhere in their collective brains, the French footballers realised it wasn't all about them, them, them. Someone told them about the fans, who, week-in, week-out, paid silly sums of money to watch them sweat for a few minutes, and they decreed to cancel their planned action. Or they realised that if they employed a very good accountant, they would only pay a tiny fraction of tax anyway. We were back on! France was the best country in the world and fish stew would become my favourite food, ever.

We were prepared, tickets in hand, hotel booked and French phrase-book in our pockets, with just one small obstacle to get over: whether this would be a Saturday or Sunday night game. No worries for us either way as we had both of them covered. And then it all went horribly wrong again. The French Football Association published their fixtures for the weekend and Marseille had been moved to Friday night. Friday bloody night. Around 12 hours BEFORE we were due to arrive on the Côte d'Azur. Despite OM playing in the Champions League at the Emirates during midweek, the French FA thought this would be a great Friday night treat for everyone . . . apart from Danny and me. We were screwed. Tickets, hotels, flights were all non-refundable. Thanks everyone. France was the worst country in the world, fish stew was the worst dish ever created.

Better men would have simply put it down to experience and given up, choosing to stand on the Jungle watching Lewes v Thamesmead Town when we should have been watching the Virage Nord in Marseille. But that's not what we do. So within 24 hours of the worst day of our lives, Plan B was signed, sealed and delivered in triplicate to our respective wives, complete with the biggest bunch of Petrol Station Flowers known to man. And for added value, Damon T, the brawn behind the Real FA Cup website, agreed to come and hold our hands and act as our translator.

We were off to the best country in the world, drum roll please, France!! Love fish stew, me. Well, technically, it was France and Belgium, which as you will know from an earlier chapter, is still the best European Football Weekend destination. What could go wrong?

Our plan was cunning, yet simple. Not one, or two, but three (THREE) new grounds in one 36-hour shift across national borders, including a couple of local derbies. OM's loss would be Valenciennes, Aalst's and Kortrijk's gain. The only downside was the fact that we would have to drive there. And of course by we, I mean me. I seem to be in the minority within the footballing blogging/writing community in the fact that I can drive. It seems that everyone else was far too busy watching football and talking about false nines and Christmas trees while I was learning to drive. I'm still positive it's some kind of conspiracy against me and that really they all can drive but don't dare admit it.

The journey was almost like clockwork. A leisurely drive down the M20, a little snooze as we travelled under the English Channel, and then a straight drive down the E15 and A21 to Valenciennes. Even torrential rain that reduced visibility to 10 metres on a foreign road wasn't a hindrance when you had the biggest game in France to look forward to.

When people asked me where I was going a few days before the weekend and I replied "Valenciennes" their immediate response was, of course, "Valencia? Spain?" That's right, I'm driving to Spain. Of course I am. A three-minute history lesson about the city and they were still none the wiser, and the topic changed to the weather. But Valenciennes is real, trust me. From our motel room we could see all the sights of the city: industrial units as far as the eye could see. After a 30-minute wait in the closed motel bar a taxi finally arrived and was soon stuck in a traffic jam that seemed to stretch to Paris. Someone up there didn't seem to want us to have a good weekend.

Finally, our Polish taxi driver – having learnt some new English swear-words and driven the wrong way down several one-way streets – got us to within walking distance of the stadium with enough time for some Leffe Ruby and a big bag of chips with Hannibal sauce, which turned out to be hot coronation chicken sauce. Two of the three vital elements of an EFW sated, it was time to sample the third: Le Foot.

Valenciennes FC are enjoying one of their longest stints in the top-level of French football after promotion in 2006. They are one of a few teams in France that could really class themselves as "mid-table". Their noisy fans haven't had much to cheer about in their history, with just one appearance, some 60 years ago, in the Coupe de France final, and they are still awaiting their first European adventure. There are few European top-flight sides that can say they have never had their passports stamped at some point in their history (a quick look at the Premier League suggests only Crystal Palace and Bournemouth have never played in a European competition). With a brand-spanking-new stadium dominating the skyline of the city, the infrastructure is now in place for the club, and Les Athenian fans will be hoping that one day soon they will have something to cheer and, who knows, perhaps even a little European jaunt.

The game was a local derby. In fact few games got the locals hotter under the collar than the visit of Lille Olympique Sporting Club from 50km up the A23. LOSC are enjoying a fair share of the limelight in the domestic game in France at the moment. Under First Team Coach Rudi Garcia, who has now departed to spin his magic at AS Roma, Les Dogues won a domestic double in 2011/12 and followed it up with another Champions League appearance the year after. And that was with Joe Cole playing for them. Coming into this game they were desperate to break the hold of the billionaires, AS Monaco and Paris Saint-Germain.

Despite the feelings of the Valenciennes fans, Lille have never seen this game as a "derby". To them they are keeping their powder dry for the eventual return of Racing Club Lens to the top table. In fact, many of the hardcore fans couldn't be arsed to make the journey down the A23 for the game, especially as they would be subject to a police escort down the motorway.

There are three things that you need to be prepared for before you enter the ultra-new, ultra-modern Stade du Hainaut in Valenciennes. Number One – take your sunglasses, as it is very red indeed. Headache-inducing red caused by 25,000 red seats, a red roof and red lighting. Do not risk experiencing this if you have a hangover or if you are taking any hallucinogenic substances. Number Two – as with all other French stadiums, no alcohol is served in the ground. Beer is over-priced, without alcohol and *sans* fun. That doesn't stop people queuing round the block to buy it. And finally, Number Three – the concept of hatching is alien to the French. The Oxford dictionary states that hatching is "an artistic technique used to create tonal or shading effects by painting closely spaced parallel lines", which in France is known as "hachure". Here, there was only an *imaginary* line which you could stand behind at the back of the stands, and woe betide anyone who stepped one inch over that line. Stewards marched back and forth, verbally berating anyone who was too forward.

Damon tried to reason with them, explaining that painting striped lines on the concrete would prevent such issues arising, but they just shrugged their shoulders "in that way".

As kick-off approached, the Valenciennes fans tried to make some noise to drown out the LOSC fans. Despite being small in number, they were big in voice, which at least took our minds off a game that failed to live up to the pre-match billing of "North France's biggest derby".

VALENCIENNES 0, LILLE OSC 1
Saturday 30th November 2013 – Stade du Hainaut

Nobody was surprised that that game was decided by one goal, although in truth it was quite a surprise that either team got close to actually threatening the net at all. If this was played on a Saturday afternoon in England it would be fighting Stoke City for the last game on *Match of the Day*. So here goes with the highlights as I wrote them down.

Big noise as the teams emerged. Kick-off. Half-time. Kick-off, Lille score, go down to 10 men when Béira is sent off for a second yellow. Full time. Four shots on target, a few corners and far too many niggling fouls. I bet the highlights DVD will be a best-seller at Christmas. The win moved LOSC back into second place, after AS Monaco had briefly taken that spot earlier in the day. However, with the firepower of Zlatan and Cavani and the billions of the Qatar Investment Authority, it would seem that Paris Saint-Germain will be hard to catch at the top so long as they don't get distracted by the Champions League.

Game over it was time to see what Valenciennes' night life had to offer. We went in with low expectations but eventually returned back to our small motel room at some point after 3am.

Quite what transpired in the intervening five hours is still a bit of a mystery to us. We started in the Ultras bar by the ground, drinking beer out of a glass horn with Ronaldo's body double, and it ended in a night club with Danny wandering around singing "I wanna dance with somebody" before a bouncer politely asked us to leave. In between we spent an hour or so in a bar where everyone except us was dressed as Superheroes, before paying a random couple €20 to take us home due to a lack of taxis. Just an average European Football Weekend night out.

Saturday was history. Sunday promised to be the Best. Day. Ever. That was if I could shake off that cloudy head feeling you get when you have stumbled home at some point well after midnight. You can never do enough research or planning for these trips. You need to maximise the short amount of time you have to sort out logistics before you depart. Fortunately Danny and I are good at this stuff. Very good in fact. Unfortunately, ending up at 3am in a night club in a very strange French town and consequently sleeping through three alarm calls ruins all of the homework.

Welcome to day two of our European Football Weekend.

We – which of course means I – had a short drive across the border into Belgium for what promised to be some spicy football. It remains a strange feeling crossing the border into Belgium on the E17 just outside Lille. There are still border posts on the road and you immediately slow down expecting guards to pop out and question you concerning why you would be leaving France on a Sunday morning. As we passed through the gate we felt a huge weight lift off our collective shoulders. I don't have anything against France, but Belgium offers so much more for the Football Tourist, and at 20 per cent less cost. Our destination was the town of Kortrijk, although if you are on the French side of the border you need to follow signs for Courtrai, as they are so scared of people going there, loving it and never coming back. We would be using Kortrijk as our stage post for the day of footballing delight.

Match one on our Super Sunday was a battle of East versus West Flanders in the town of Aalst. The home of the textile industry, Aalst isn't exactly known as a hotbed of Belgian football. In fact it is a relatively cool bed of most things, but we had been promised the best day ever so who were we to turn our noses up at the game against The Great Old, Royal Antwerp.

Confession time. I've only ever had two kebabs in my life. Once, back in 1989 when I pulled a legendary young lady on the Gravesend teen-scene who would do anything for a late-night dollop of chilli sauce (not true, as I found out after wasting £2.99 on her). Then, when I had a moment of weakness in Swansea after the 2006 FA Cup Final, but that was due to my friend Football Jo wanting me to ask the man behind the counter if he was single. But with just 10 minutes at Gent-Sint-Pieters station between trains, and having had no food since our bag of chips with Hannibal sauce some 15 hours previously, our only option was a kebab shop in the station. So we indulged in one, with all the trimmings, and I have to say, on a Sunday morning, it was wonderful. I can now understand what all the fuss is about. Sorry Current Mrs Fuller, a moment's weakness.

Aalst certainly wasn't rocking when our train arrived at midday. Perhaps it was the fear of the invading Royal Antwerp fans or the fact that time stands still in Belgium on a Sunday. We were due to meet Yves, known as "Mr Fix It" at Eendracht Aalst Football Club. With Antwerp being the visitors, this game had been designated as a "Combi" game (or a "Bubble" game in English speak), so tickets for three visitors from England would normally be difficult to get hold of. Danny reached out for help via the Aalst forum and the answer was clear from all directions: "Ask Yves". So he did, and three tickets were procured. All we had to do was meet Yves, shake him warmly by the hand, perhaps even treat him to a beer and enjoy the football.

Our chosen meeting point was, of course, a bar. One of the Aalst fans' bars, to be precise, which had all the right ingredients for a perfect pre-match warm-up. A number of decent beers on draught, dart boards, not one but two disco balls, and awash with football memorabilia. At the appointed hour, in walked a chap with a big camera and a bigger moustache. He looked like he had walked off the pages of an Asterix adventure. Judging by the back-slaps, high fives and kisses on each cheek, this was our man, Yves. Yves was a legend. He gave us our staples for life: tickets to the football and free beer. What more could we ask for? Well, how about a private audience with the Aalst mascot, a massive walking Onion?

We'd noticed the strange club motif on a number of the scarves and asked about "The Onion". De Ajuinen, as they are known in Belgium, are named in homage to the onion fields of Belgium. The club's fans used to turn up to games wielding large onion bulbs to frighten the opposition, until they were outlawed, just like the stick of celery was classed as an offensive weapon by Gillingham as far back as 1996 (and more recently by Chelsea), urged on no doubt by a chap who dressed every week as a half-man, half-onion.

It just so happened that a Belgian TV show was making a programme about the old chap who had undertaken the job of being Mr Onion for nearly three decades, so we were smuggled into the stadium on the pretence of being part of the media team following him around. We were ushered into a private room in the bowels of the main stand where in front of us, laid out perfectly like a school uniform on the first day of term, was the legendary outfit, including a pair of special onion shoes. Opportunities to slip into the shoes of someone famous rarely come along and so Danny tried to put one on. Alas, like Cinderella's ugly sisters, he couldn't get his foot in it. But it was a different story for me; and I would be marrying the Onion Prince. "How did it feel?" Danny asked me, disappointment etched all over his face. Cold and wet, as if onions themselves had been planted into those oversized shoes. We stayed for a few minutes to see the Onion-robing ceremony, and collectively agreed that this was the pinnacle of our football watching. We'd enjoyed World Cup Finals, Champions League, heck even scoring a goal on the hallowed turf of Wembley. Yet this was the one moment we would savour forever.

We floated from that room on a cloud of footballing euphoria. We had a game to watch after all, and despite lingering for a few minutes too long watching a very "fit" female riot police officer dress for action (football hooligan action, before anyone gets too excited) we made it onto the terrace in time to see our Onion hero lead out the two teams. The Royal Antwerp fans didn't seem to be too happy with their accommodation in a temporary stand and started throwing everything they could get their hands on across a makeshift barrier. A line of nervous-looking stewards were drafted in to keep the two sets of fans apart but they were no defence against the flares that were regularly exchanged. Our good friend Hans had travelled with the away fans to the game, but he was spotted hovering near the free buffet in the executive boxes above the far end of the stadium. For far too many years Royal Antwerp had been languishing in the second tier of Belgian football and their fans were growing weary of seeing smaller teams gaining promotion. They now had Jimmy Floyd Hasselbaink in the hot-seat but he hadn't exactly set the division alight so far.

EENDRACHT AALST 1, ROYAL ANTWERP 0
Sunday 1st December 2013 – Pierre Cornelisstadion

At the full-time whistle the home fans surged to the front of the perimeter barriers in our stand and joined in a spontaneous Zorba's dance with the Aalst players, as if they had won the cup final.

Ten years ago not only would this result have been unlikely, but the actual meeting of the two teams would only have been seen in a Belgian cup tie. After a decent first half, the home team had faded towards the end of the game, but hung on for all three points. The solitary goal, scored by Andy Carroll lookalike Glouftsis, was the difference between the two teams, although it was the home keeper, Verhoeven, who was the busier of the two.

Aalst took to the field with 11 Belgians in their starting line-up and came out of the blocks like a train. Glouftsis, his neatly trimmed stubble complementing his ponytail modelled on the crocked West Ham striker, had the ball in the net after a few minutes, heading in unchallenged after the ball had rebounded off the advertising boards behind the goal. Apparently, the rule about playing off the boards still hasn't been introduced by FIFA so the goal was ruled out. Fortunately the striker didn't have to wait long before his goal, taking the ball on his knee, swivelling and shooting in one flowing move to raise the temporary roof in the stand we were in. The away fans responded by firing a few more flares across the fence.

At half-time we headed into the bar. Being in Belgium we needed to buy our munts, the special cashless currency used across the land. The exchange rate is simple. One munt equals one drink, whether that may be a Shandy Bass, pint of Jägermeister or, as we wanted, a cup of Leffe. Danny hopped off to the toilet and quickly returned smiling his cheeky smile. Either he had accidentally walked into the cheerleaders' dressing room or he had found something "unusual". He urged us to look for ourselves and so we headed through the bar and through the door for the gents . . . which took us outside to a wall, completely open not only to the elements but also to the watching fans in the stands where the stand-alone urinals were positioned. People could die of exposure, and of the embarrassment of exposure, out here.

At the heart of Antwerp's midfield was a certain J. Bostock according to the team sheet, the "J" standing of course for John. Six years ago Bostock made his debut for Crystal Palace at the age of 15 and was the talk of SE20. A year later, with just four appearances under his belt for The Eagles, he was a Spurs player after a very heated and extremely public legal row on the subject of his ownership. Eventually, Spurs were ordered to pay £700,000 for his services, rising to over a million should such criteria be fulfilled as Bostock playing for England and winning *Celebrity Masterchef*.

But like many more before him, the "wonder-kid" never fulfilled his potential at Tottenham, playing just a handful of cup games before being loaned out to all and sundry, including a few months in the MLS with Toronto. In the summer Spurs released him, once again underlining the way in which promising youngsters are often simply warehoused by the top clubs, which will only get worse with the introduction of the Elite Player Performance Plan. One of the hottest young players at the age of 15 had played less than 50 first-class games in six years and was cast aside. Fortunately, Royal Antwerp liked what they saw and took a chance on him.

Alas, Bostock wasn't able to influence the result, as the home team held on for dear life to grab three valuable points. While there were only just over 3,500 people in the ground, the noise generated by both sets of fans was impressive. As a parting gesture the away fans sent over a few flares, and the home fans retorted with a few songs about the parentage of the visitors from Antwerp. But who were we to care? We were in the middle of the biggest conga since Zorba the Greek as the players, led of course by Mr Onion, were dancing across the pitch finishing off their celebrations with a run along the edge of the stand, high-fiving the fans as they went.

It had been a superb afternoon but the main event of the day beckoned. We just had enough time to stock up on Belgium staples of waffles, (more) chips and of course a few cheeky little local beers before we steamed back into Kortrijk. Our plan was to find a quiet little pub as our pre-match warm-up – despite this being a local-ish game, we weren't expecting much life in the town, judging by our brief tour of the place earlier in the day. On the way to Aalst we had passed through Waregem on the train. Damon had been there in May and suggested that it was a sleepy little place, akin to Hereford, and that he didn't think there would be much of an atmosphere for our final game of the weekend. "About 4 or 5,000 I reckon," he told us. Last season, the club had exceeded all expectations and for weeks looked like they might just give the likes of Anderlecht, Club Brugge and Standard Liège a kick up the Flanders by winning the Jupiler League. In the end they lost the title decider to Anderlecht, but they had done enough to make their mark on the domestic game, and consequently had earned a shot at Champions League qualification. Despite the town only being 10 miles down the road, it hadn't ever registered on our "European Derbies" index to warrant a visit before today. So when our train pulled into Kortrijk station two hours before kick-off, we had to pinch ourselves at the scene unfolding in front of us.

Thousands of home fans, dressed in red and white, were preparing to march to the stadium. And by preparing I mean firing flares into the air, throwing fire-crackers on the floor and twirling their scarves as though there was no tomorrow. It looked like being the best night ever. Danny and Damon aren't easily influenced but put a beer in one hand and the chance of holding a flare in the other and they are anyone's. As the sensible one in the group (i.e. the driver) I went and got the car, drove it to the Guldensporonstadion, and waited patiently for their three rings to say they had safely arrived after bravely integrating themselves into the home fans march to the ground. It is safe to say that any such attempt in England would have been met with the riot police's intervention.

Koninklijke Voetbalclub Kortrijk is a bit of a mouthful for any Euro sceptic, and so they are often simply referred to as KVK. They are another club that hasn't ever won a major honour. Their highest finish in the Jupiler League was fourth in 2010 although they did reach the Belgian Cup Final in 2012 before losing 1-0 to Lokeren. However, tonight was all about local pride and the crowds were flocking to the stadium, drawn to the towering floodlights like bees to a pot of honey.

The atmosphere in the ground was outstanding, with a couple of thousand home fans crammed into the big terrace behind the goal. Think Ashton Gate mixed with Griffin Park and then you have the Guldensporonstadion. Around six hundred away fans were crammed into a side stand and were being drowned out by song after song ("We all agree, Waregem fans are Wankers" was a firm favourite) from the crowd. As if the atmosphere needed any further stoking, the two teams emerged to a cacophony of fireworks, followed by a scarf-holding rendition of "You'll Never Walk Alone". Spine-tingling.

KV KORTRIJK 1, ZULTE WAREGEM 1
Sunday 1st December 2013 – Guldensporonstadion

Eventually the smoke cleared, the formalities were completed and we were off. The away keeper, Bossut, was welcomed at the home end with a shower of potatoes. Not once did he bat an eyelid or complain about the treatment. While none of them actually found their target, he must have been very wary that a baking potato would hit him at 50 miles per hour at any point. Three minutes into the game and he was called into action as the referee, perhaps influenced by the home fans, awarded a penalty to the home side. Standing on his line, Bossut was now a static target, yet although quite a few vegetables hit him, he pulled off a great save from Santini's spot-kick to silence the tuber-lobbers. But it wasn't long before KVK did take the lead when De Smet scored after some smart close control in the area, and unsurprisingly the fans around us went mental. We tried to join in, dancing around with two ladies who would be referred to in the current climate as "MILFS". When in Kortrijk and all that.

There wasn't a moment in the game when we weren't jumping up and down, linking arms and Poznaning across the terraces or swirling our scarves around our head. Occasionally we watched some of the game, with the home side being reduced to 10 men after a second yellow for De Smet in the second half, but the football was secondary. Despite our behaviour, some of the locals didn't think we were animated enough and suggested that we were actually Waregem fans in disguise. It could have got all Green Street, but Danny quickly broke into a chorus of "We all agree" and all of a sudden they were our best friends. However, deep down we wanted to see what would happen if Zulte scored at our end, and sure enough with just two minutes to go Habibou slotted home and cups of beer, mushrooms and tomatoes (they'd run out of potatoes by this stage) showered down from all sides onto the celebrating away players. A draw was the least the away side deserved based on possession and chances.

The full-time whistle saw both teams embrace and salute their respective fans. The atmosphere had been the winner and we had already got our diaries out to mark in when the reverse fixture would be taking place.

It was time for us to return home. For Damon and Danny it was a chance for a snooze, but for me it was a trip on the concentration highway. It had been a long, tiring weekend but one that had ultimately been more rewarding than the planned trip to Marseilles. Even the UK border guard who questioned us about our trip agreed. I mean, who in their right mind would lie about driving to Valenciennes and Kortrijk other than a group who really know their football. Rome, Copenhagen, Istanbul, Stockholm and Belgrade are without a doubt some of the best derbies in Europe we've experienced. Now add to that list, Kortrijk.

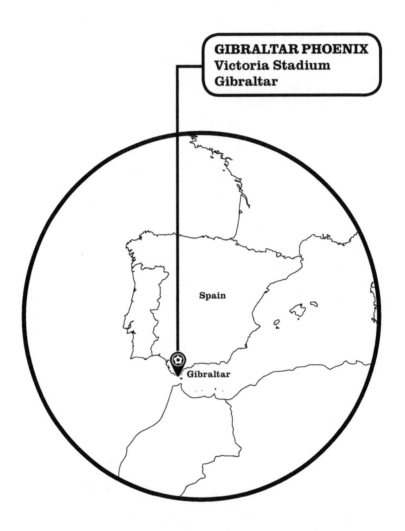

GIBRALTAR PHOENIX
Victoria Stadium
Gibraltar

Spain

Gibraltar

Spain was creating a problem over a 2.3-square-mile
rock that they hadn't owned for over 300 years.

5. New Kids on the Rock

Some years ago I came up with a brilliant idea for a TV show. It would be a six-part travelogue around the smallest nations in Europe watching football. On my way I would take in the local culture, local food and of course the local food. A camera crew would follow me from the airport as I experienced such cultural high points as Liechtenstein's false-teeth museum, San Marino's homage to medieval torture and the bar in Malta where Oliver Reed fell off his bar stool for the last time. A sort of cross between Michael Palin, Alan Whicker and James Richardson. It was a certain winner so I sat back and waited for the bidding war to start. Six months after my letters were dispatched I hadn't had a single reply. Not even UK Conquest were interested and they bought the rights to *Howard's Way*. But I wasn't going to be beaten and set off on a journey across Europe.

The Super Cup in Monaco, sitting next to Gérard Houllier as AC Milan beat Porto, arriving by helicopter from Nice Airport was nice. So was staying in the same five-star hotel as Sepp Blatter in Liechtenstein prior to their game against Turkey was good – so good that a few weeks later I was back with The Current Mrs Fuller for the game against Luxembourg. Then there was seeing San Marino come within 15 seconds of grabbing their first ever point in major tournament qualifying against Latvia and being the only member of the press there, which meant I had to lead the press conference in a language that neither coach understood. Next it was on to the national stadium in Malta and a treble-header with the over-amorous wives of some of the players. Andorra passed without any incident, which basically sums up the sleepiness of the principality.

So five down and one to go in the space of just a couple of years. But then I lost my mojo to complete the task. Every few months I sent off emails to production companies hoping to garner some interest. Occasionally I got a reply but it was never 100 per cent positive. "An interesting idea which we will consider when we next meet as a planning group" was the most enthusiastic response I ever got. Life then got in the way and the project was shelved.

But then interest in finally completing the mission peaked again in early 2014. I dusted down the file and prepared to finish off the job. One major footballing news story was the compelling event for me. Gibraltar were finally being accepted into the world footballing family and the British Overseas Territory would be number six on my list of the smallest footballing nations in Europe.

In mid-February the European footballing world officially welcomed its 54th member when Gibraltar were included in the draw for the 2016 European Championship qualifying. Their journey for acceptance on the world footballing stage has been a long and tortuous one, filled with inconsistencies and back-stabbing that has dogged the governing bodies for years. While territories such as the Faroe Islands (governed by Denmark) and Israel (not part of Europe) had been welcomed in by UEFA, Gibraltar's invite had been permanently lost in the post. There has even been talk of Greenland (also owned by Denmark) and Kosovo being admitted into the biggest football federation in the world. Yet Gibraltar had always been the last item on the agenda – the one that is always dropped to make room for a discussion on toilet facilities. Despite not being "at war" or even military-ready against any other nation, it has taken longer for Gibraltar to be allowed to compete than the former Yugoslavian states, Armenia, Azerbaijan, Russia and Georgia or even Greece and Turkey. And that has been because one nation has disputed their authenticity to be considered an equal member. One against 52 other nations: a no brainer? Well, it would be in most circumstances but when that nation is the most successful footballing country of the last 50 years then the rules change.

It wasn't as if the region had no footballing heritage. Formed in 1895 by British sailors, The Football Association of Gibraltar first applied to FIFA back in 1997 and, despite it not actually having a stadium capable of hosting an international game, the Swiss big cheeses said a big Yes in 1999 and passed the manilla folder down the road to Nyon and UEFA. Immediately, Spain started to throw their castanets out of the pram. While the rest of Europe was moving closer, forgiving not forgetting the conflicts of the past, Spain was creating a problem over a 2.3-square-mile rock that they hadn't owned for over 300 years. One of their arguments was that Gibraltar didn't even have a stadium that could host international football. Technically they had a point, but then again, Andorra had been moving their games against the likes of England, Netherlands and the Republic of Ireland hundreds of kilometres to Barcelona for a number of years. It seemed that Spain's lobbying worked, as in 2001 UEFA changed its statutes so that only associations in a country "recognised by the United Nations as an independent State" could become members. On such grounds, UEFA immediately rejected Gibraltar's application to become a member. Of course that ruling should have meant the immediate expulsion of England, Scotland, Northern Ireland and Wales, but that never happened. While the rest of Europe started qualifying for the 2004 European Championships hosted by Portugal, Gibraltar consoled themselves with a trip to Guernsey to take part in the Island Games Tournament.

There was still a hope that FIFA would allow them to take part in qualifying for the 2006 FIFA World Cup in Germany. Other British Overseas Territories such as Bermuda, British Virgin Islands and Anguilla were allowed to line up in the qualifying tournament but the invite to Gibraltar once again went missing. Instead of a shot at a trip to Bavaria to enjoy a month of football, fräuleins and frikadellen, Gibraltar headed to the Shetland Islands for another shot at the Island Games title.

Hopes were raised in 2007 when UEFA agreed that a vote would take place at its annual Congress. Unfortunately 45 members voted against allowing them in, with only England, Scotland and Wales saying yes, although they did allow Montenegro in. It took another six years for opinions to change in UEFA thanks to significant lobbying by Gibraltar, and to an extent by the English FA. The 2013 Congress vote saw Gibraltar finally accepted into the footballing family with just Spain (no surprise there) and Belarus (who thought they were voting whether to have a vegetarian option for dinner) voting against their membership. Woe betide anyone trying to cross the border back into Spain on that day.

With millions watching the draw for the 2016 European Championship live on TV and the internet, Gibraltar took their place in a pot with the likes of San Marino, Andorra, Luxembourg and Malta. They had arrived. And how the footballing world laughed as Gibraltar were initially placed in the same pot as Spain. Somewhere, someone upstairs quickly consulted the panic book and took control of the mouse, and the name of Gibraltar somehow miraculously popped into the next group headed by Germany and including Scotland, the Republic of Ireland, Poland and Georgia. The pub and bar owners on the Rock all let out a huge groan when the draw was made, knowing they would miss out on the Celtic-Nation tourist pounds and euros, as all of Gibraltar's home games will be played some 250 miles away in Faro, Portugal, since the current Victoria Stadium on the Rock is still not deemed capable of hosting international games.

Within an hour of the draw my TV show plan had been dusted off and was back in production. Heck, I wrote my first book without a publisher (and my next two) so how difficult could it be to produce my own TV show? I mean, judging by the production quality of ITV's *Splash!* I would be short-listed for the Sundance Film Festival. It did help that a former work colleague and all-round top chap Andy now lived and worked on the Rock and was more than happy to act as my chauffeur, chef, butler and tour guide as long as I brought him some PG Tips. Heck, despite preferring the oval-ball game he even agreed to come to a game with me.

Gibraltar has a population of just 30,000, about the same size as Lewes and Peacehaven put together. This makes supporting a football league quite difficult, but that is part of the entry criteria for UEFA. Add in the fact that there is only one stadium and you can start to see some of the problems they have to compete with. What it does mean though is that on any given weekend you will always be able to find a game or two at the national stadium, the 2,000-capacity Victoria Stadium adjacent to the airport runway.

This season, as part of the benefits package they get from being in UEFA, the winners of the Premier Division will get a place in the Champions League; well, at least the extra preliminary forgotten round of qualifying where they will probably play the winner of the Andorran Lliga de Primera in June when football is a million miles from everyone's thoughts. Unfortunately, it does seem that Gibraltar is suffering from "Scottish Syndrome" whereby one team simply wins almost every game and the league is done and dusted by Easter. That team is Lincoln Red Imps FC, winners of 13 of the last 14 Premier Division titles. Oh, and of this year's League Cup in which they beat "Manchester United" three weeks ago.

I have no idea what the association is with the Red Imps of Lincoln City. For a period in the last decade the team decided to rename themselves as Newcastle United, as you do, but it became more of an embarrassment locally with the goings-on at St James' Park so they quickly rebranded themselves back to Lincoln. Manchester United, on the other hand, can lay claim to currently being the most successful team of that name in the world this season. League Cup runners-up, still in the Rock Cup and third in the league. The club was given permission to adopt the name by the then United manager Matt Busby back in 1962 and they have kept it ever since. Quite what the army of brand managers and lawyers at Old Trafford thinks of that agreement today isn't clear but I am sure it won't be long before the branding police make a visit.

Six other teams make up the Premier Division, meaning that qualification for Europe, with a spot in the Champions League and Europa League, is possible for all of the sides. All except one it seems. With just over half of the season completed one side sit all alone at the bottom of the league with a 100 per cent loss record. Gibraltar Phoenix were promoted last season but are almost nailed-on certainties to go back to where they came from at the end of the season. In their last two games they had the displeasure of facing league-leaders Lincoln. The good news was that they did manage to score a goal, increasing their goals-for tally for the season by an impressive 33 per cent. Unfortunately they managed to ship in a total of 32 goals at the other end. I was sold – already heading out to see Gibraltar Phoenix play. The question was: should I take my boots?

Before I arrived in Gibraltar I contacted Chairman, joint owner, club captain and centre-back of the Gibraltar Phoenix, Garry Lowe, to understand a bit more about life at the bottom of the smallest league in UEFA. The club was founded in 2012 and had a dream first season that saw it promoted into the top division. Unfortunately, the club didn't have the funds to retain most of their squad and so they started the next season with a mixture of youth players and locals who wanted to play for the love of the game. Lowe is already planning for next year, fully aware that Phoenix cannot compete with some of the bigger clubs in terms of player recruitment or sponsorship. The promise of European football has driven a few to start paying serious money for their players, even bringing in some from across the border. Good news for the domestic game, but for the international side? Not really. Look no further than the fact they have tried to cast their net outside of Gibraltar in search of players who might qualify for the national squad, such as Danny Higginbotham (who had actually retired from the game), Bognor Regis Town's keeper Will Britt and Farsley striker Adam Priestley.

After weeks of torrential rain at home the prospect of a weekend in the sunshine was very appealing. So what odds would you have got on departing from Heathrow with 17 degrees of sunshine to touch down two and half hours later in the Mediterranean with lower temperatures and rain. Apparently it rains for two days a year in Gibraltar and this was one of them. Was that going to spoil the trip? Heck no – especially as we taxied down the runway with a clear view of the neat and tidy Victoria Stadium out of my window.

I was met outside Departures by a sign for a "Mr Tu Art Fueler of the Bell is Round". Andy had bunked off work for an hour to pick me up in his British Jag, imported from the UK to give me the 30-minute whistle-stop tour of the Rock. First up was a visit to Europa Point, the most southerly tip of Gibraltar and home to a bloody big gun and the Gibraltar Cricket Club. But not for much longer. If the Gibraltar Football Association get the funding, this will be the location of the new 10,000-seater national stadium.

It will certainly be spectacular, with vistas of the vastness of the Rock to the north, Spain to the west, Africa to the south and the huge expanse of the Mediterranean to the east. There is even a smart-looking mosque that will have a bird's-eye view of the action. But for now they have to make do with the Victoria Stadium and trips to the Algarve.

Andy used to call Cambridge home but he has now swapped that for the tax haven of Gibraltar. He lives in a flat with a view of the sea, overlooking the landing point where Nelson's body was eventually brought ashore, spending his spare time sitting on his balcony watching the ships pass by. Not that it is all relaxation and cruising the roads of the Rock in his British supercar. He sometimes has to work, wandering into the office in Ocean Village, overlooking the marina, O'Reilly's Irish Bar and Gala Bingo. Tax-free beer did I hear you say? Absolutely: £2 a pint if you please. Could life be any better? Well, throw in free Wi-Fi almost everywhere (which uses British IP addresses and thus you can use iPlayer and iTunes!), free car parking, free leisure activities and free football. Yep, that last one is correct but more of that later.

You would think that life there was idyllic but there was another side to being a tax-exile here. As Andy said, "Everything seems nice but if you take a closer look things are a bit crap." Projects around that time would be started and grind to a halt or never get off the ground at all. It also appeared that it was incredibly expensive to live here. Accommodation (both permanent and temporary) across the border in La Linea was abundant and cheap but the current strife with Spain meant it was impractical to commute across the border, when delays could be up to two hours each way depending on the day of the week, the weather or simply what had been on TV the night before.

The big story of the week had been a visitor to Burger King in Main Street. It seems that life was getting too good for the population of Barbary Apes that live on the Rock. They had started to recognise that Morrisons was the biggest supermarket in Gibraltar (one of the top five tourist attractions based on visitor numbers) and had been ambushing tourists who visited the top of the Rock with their bags full of food. The more they ate, the more they "partied", and so the population exploded. With less food available they had started to make their way down the Rock to feast on the waste food in the bins of the pubs and restaurants. When that became scarce they started paying visits to fast-food establishments. Hardly a recommendation that they could be proud of.

In Andy's office I met a number of his team, including the company lawyer. Most people look at me with a puzzled expression when I say I am in town to watch football, especially in a place like Gibraltar where there are a thousand other reasons above football to visit, but Peter didn't. In fact he even introduced me to one of his friends, another lawyer, Aaron Payas, who was one of the rocks in Gibraltar's best midfield, the Lincoln Red Imps, as well as being one of the Rock's most capped players at international level, which when you consider they have only officially played three games wasn't too much of an exclusive group.

A Friday night after work in Gibraltar is no different to that in other cities around the world. Workers head to the bright lights for some well-deserved rest and relaxation, the difference here being that the sun was shining. We took a few steps from Andy's office and found a seat in a restaurant with the water of the marina at our feet and discussed the pros (19 minutes) and cons (2 minutes) of swapping a daily commute from Cambridge to London with a leisurely walk along the seafront to Ocean Village.

GIBRALTAR PHOENIX 0, COLLEGE EUROPA 11
Friday 14th March 2014 – Victoria Stadium

According to the website, this game was supposed to kick off at 8pm. I say "supposed" because we arrived late (around 8.15pm) and thus missed the start. But we soon smelt something fishy when the game appeared to be entering its 60th minute in the first half. Perhaps they had different rules here or the referee was playing until the home side had a shot on goal. We eventually found a supporter who could shed some light on the delayed kick-off, or at least offer his opinion.

"Referee lives in Spain, doesn't he? So he got delayed at the border. Game kicked off at 8.15pm." Credible? Potentially, but then we heard that floodlight issues had caused the delay, so much so that one of the three qualified electricians had been called just in case they had further issues. So it appeared we hadn't missed anything at all when we arrived by the magic gate. It seems that football is free in Gibraltar and you can simply wander in as and when you want to take in some Premier Division action. Alas, it seemed that the idea was so alien to the locals that only 27 others had decided to spend their Friday night in the Victoria Stadium.

Fifteen minutes into the game and it was still goalless. While the home goal was being peppered with shots, only Phoenix keeper Tito Podeta stood in College Europa's way. You could see that Gibraltar Phoenix were out of their depth, even against a side who like themselves were promoted last season. However, they didn't do the simple things that would have led to them scoring.

It took a few words from the sidelines before Europa finally opened the scoring. And once they had done so, the flood-gates opened. One-nil (22 mins), two-nil (29 mins), three-nil (30 mins), four-nil (34 mins), five-nil (39 mins) and finally six-nil just before half-time.

While the home team sat in the dressing room wishing away the next 45 minutes, we headed down to the Wanderers bar for a swift pint. We wondered how many of them would want to swap places with us at that moment? Come to think of it, both Andy and I would have fancied a run-out in the second half. Perhaps the game would be changed by a Liverpool v AC Milan-style inspirational team talk or even an Al Pacino-like speech à la *Any Given Sunday*? Alas, it appeared it was neither as goal number seven was added within a minute of the restart.

Seven became eight and then nine, although there was an element of greed starting to creep in from the College players, who frequently elected to take the ball themselves when their five-man attack (everyone wanted a slice of the action) broke upfield. An injury to one of the Phoenix players gave them the chance to have a breather (and in one case a quick puff on an inhaler). Alas, our hopes that all Gibraltan football physios came from the same mould as Eva Carneiro (the territory's most famous woman apparently) were dashed when a chap with a scouse accent wearing three-quarter-length trousers ambled on. With 15 minutes to go, Phoenix made their final substitution, taking off one of the more athletic players on the pitch and replacing him with a chap who had gloves on and had to hand his inhaler to the coach. Sadly, it didn't do any good and, despite us willing them to score, all of the action was still at the other end as College Europa scored two more goals to make the final score Eleven-Nil. Quite what the score would have been if their keeper hadn't played a blinder I don't know, or if College had hit the target instead of striking the woodwork on six occasions.

Somehow, somewhere along the way, we appeared to have missed a goal as my notebook only showed 10 goals in the away column. The final score was recorded as 11-0, with Tostao scoring five, Toncheff three, Montovio two and Bakkari completing the rout for College Europe. Gibraltar Phoenix will be counting down the weeks until the season ends and they can start the rebuilding process once again.

Despite the final score you cannot fault the effort of the home side, especially the heroic performance of Podeta. It takes some bottle to take to the field every week knowing that you are likely to be on the end of another hiding. But as Garry Lowe told me before the game, "It's all about next season for us now. Starting the rebuilding work for the future." Quite what impact European football will have on the domestic game is unknown. In countries such as Estonia and Latvia, single clubs dominated the domestic game for years, using the UEFA cash from playing in the Champions and Europa League qualifying rounds to strengthen their squads. However, in other countries the central revenues have led to increased competition within the domestic game as new club owners invest their cash and gamble on success.

Saturday dawned with bright sunshine, so we walked down to Ocean Village for a spot of breakfast (£5.95 for the biggest breakfast I have ever tried to eat) among the cruise-ship tourists, workers and families. The bar had adverts for their St Patrick's Day celebrations (featuring Gibraltar's most loved Peter Kay impersonator, no less) and the live football being shown later via their Sky Sports feed. Yet just a few hundred yards away there would be free local football being played out in front of a few hundred souls at most. As we walked back towards Casement Square we passed the Victoria Stadium. The magic door was still open and so we popped in (Rule x.i of the European Football Weekends Rule Book concerning open access criteria). Two youth teams were enjoying the sunshine as they played out a competitive game that came to an end with a round of applause from a dozen or so fans. It was brilliant to see that the ground had a full schedule of matches throughout the day, starting with under-16s and finishing off with games featuring Manchester United and Lincoln Red Imps.

The walk back to Andy's apartment took us up a tourist-laden Main Street, all of them filling their boots with tax-free tobacco, tax-free alcohol and tax-free fake watches. But halfway up was a sports shop. Nothing too unusual in its window display: a Manchester United shirt on one side and a Barcelona one on the other. But taking pride of place in the middle of the two global superbrands was a red Nike shirt sporting the crest of Gibraltar. Football had finally arrived on the Rock.

So what will the future hold for them? Nobody is expecting them to shake up European football.

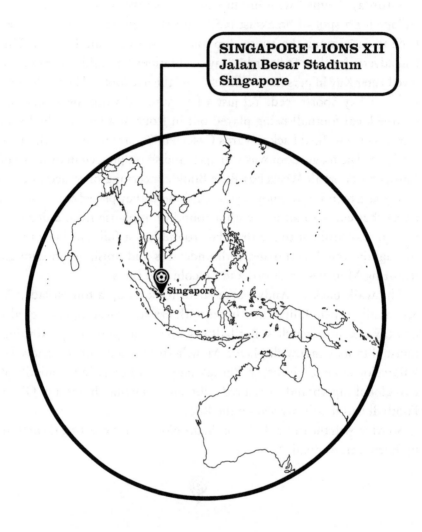

SINGAPORE LIONS XII
Jalan Besar Stadium
Singapore

Singapore

I expected to have to sell a kidney
to afford the 10-minute cab fare.

6. Into the Lions' Den

I would consider myself to be a seasoned traveller. I know my way around an airport executive lounge, can negotiate my way around even the most complex local transport systems and even hold a conversation in French and not completely sound like someone from 'Allo 'Allo. However, apart from a fantastic 10 days in South Korea for the FIFA World Cup in 2002, my adventures had been restricted to Europe and North America. That pales into insignificance against the global domination of Football Tourism that Stoffers could quite rightly boast. In the past year he had waved a virtual hello to us from Thailand, Columbia and, more recently, El Salvador. Occasionally he goes off the radar for days on end, worrying us sick, but then he reappears with a signature photo, sitting in a bar with a cold beer and looking very pleased with himself. By contrast, the most exotic place in which I had watched football had been Belarus. That had to change in 2014.

As luck would have it (of course, always blame it on luck), I had been asked to go to work conferences in the Far East with my colleague, good friend and regular travel buddy Ben. I let him plan the logistics for our first trip, a week-long conference in Singapore, where the future of the internet and all that we hold dear would be discussed in air-conditioned rooms all day and in swanky bars with fantastic views all night. While he planned our route to maximise our travel budget, and help us enjoy some of the best inflight luxury there is, I sorted out the football. That's the normal deal when we travel together. It wasn't all to be work, work, work, and as we would be arriving on a Saturday night there would be a few footballing options, I was sure.

Ben rang me excitedly to say that we would be travelling on an Airbus A380, the newest, most technologically-advanced aeroplane in the world. It did mean a stop-over in Dubai but it would be worth the extra travel time. I rang him a few hours later saying that we would be seeing football in not one, but two different leagues. I could tell he was still thinking about the A380.

Fast-forward a month and I was preparing to go. As I was packing my case, my daughter Lolly was helpfully reading out a list of things I should and shouldn't do when I was in Singapore. After providing me with a list of clothes and shoes she would "really like for an early birthday present" she got on to the big no-nos. I knew that the city of nearly 5 million people sitting like a perfectly groomed barnacle at the foot of Malaysia was strict but I didn't realise that they took things so seriously.

"You can't drive drugs," she told me as number one. "You mean traffick drugs." "Yes, that is what I said. If you are in traffic then you are in a car or bus." I explained to her the subtle difference and she then asked questions such as "What about if someone gives you a can of coke but really inside it is actual coke. Could you claim that you have brought it in by accident?"

"It is against the law and a public caning offence to not flush the toilet after using it. How can they tell you haven't?" I explained that in each toilet there was a special "pan" camera that could track your DNA. As she believed until she was 10 that you could use bacon as currency in Denmark, I think this one will take a number of years for her to question.

"If you drop litter on the floor you can be made to pick it up for three hours wearing a T-shirt saying "I am a litter lout" and fined $1,000,000. "I questioned the last part and she broke down under my intense interrogation and admitted it was $1,000.

"Chewing gum is banned." Now I knew this one wasn't quite true, but a common myth. You can buy chewing gum in most kiosks BUT you are not supposed to chew it on the streets. If you are caught you can be fined. If you are caught dropping it on the floor then you can be taken to the headmaster's office and caned, although they don't have to phone your parents first. I suggested to her that this was the sole reason why I wouldn't ever be taking her there as she gets through packets of the stuff every day.

"Pack plenty of pants." I stopped my packing and looked at her. Did she have concerns for my health, assuming I would pick up a bug from the water? No – she blushed red as she told me that I wasn't allowed to walk around my hotel room naked. "Can you imagine how embarrassing it would be for me if you were arrested for walking round naked?" Teenagers these days. I knew that pornography was illegal and even viewing, ahem, images accidentally appearing on your Twitter feed was against the law, but apparently the country thinks that nudity results in nasty, filthy business and will morally corrupt everyone. I also knew another fact relating to this law, told to me by a single friend who travelled to Singapore frequently about five years ago.

It is illegal to give or receive oral sex UNLESS it is part of foreplay. I am still not quite sure how they can enforce this or even check it, but that is what the law says. What about if it is at the end of lovemaking? What if you physically can't do anything else? No casting couches in Singapore then. I would love to see how a case is presented in a Singapore court. As the Current Mrs Fuller told me in passing when I read this out to her, "No happy endings for you then."

Next up was a sensible law. In fact one that we should have in place in the UK. It is illegal to piggyback off someone else's Wi-Fi unless they have given permission. Connecting on unsecured Wi-Fi hotspots means hacking in Singapore – and bearing in mind that you can be fined $1,000 for chewing gum I'd hate to think what you'd get for that!

"Oh, and Dad. No bungee jumping!" Again I assumed she was saying this out of daughterly love for me but no, it was another law concerning an activity that was deemed to encourage danger, and they don't like danger there. It is, apparently, fine though to have an infinity pool on the edge of a 63-floor tower at Marina Bay or to party at the top of 1 Raffles Place, the world's highest rooftop bar.

"You'll be fine," she told me, laughing at her own joke as she went to do something more important in her room.

Twenty-four hours later and I was sitting in the lounge in Dubai Airport. Ben had flown from Copenhagen and already set up base camp. It was 2am local time but that didn't stop us eagerly planning our week ahead. It was obvious that downtime would be at a premium and so just the two games were on the agenda. One in the Malaysian Super League and one in the Singapore Premier League. You wait over a decade to watch a game in Asia and then two present themselves in a few days – I know that is what you are saying to yourself and you would be right.

At this point I will make a small detour in the tale just to give a bit of background as to why we were going to see games in two different countries. Whisper it quietly but we weren't. As noted earlier, Singapore sits on the bottom of the Malaysian peninsula, like a plumb and prosperous barnacle. A small strait of water separates the two countries, with relatively strict border controls existing between the two. Malaysia is a big old beast, with 30,000,000 people spread across 128,000 square miles. In contrast Singapore has a population of just 5.4 million people squeezed on an island the same size as Manchester, making it the third most densely populated sovereign state in the world.

The issue, footballing wise, that small countries or territories have is the competitiveness of their domestic game. One or two teams will dominate the domestic game, leading to a growing imbalance as they win the honours, qualify for continental competition and share the significant cash pot that these tournaments offer. Scotland, Portugal, the Netherlands, Austria and

Denmark are examples of where one or two teams have dominated, creating a self-perpetuating widening gap between the top and the rest of the table. In some regions the bigger sides have even migrated to play in more competitive local neighbouring countries, such as FC Vaduz of Lichtenstein playing in the Swiss League, AS Monaco in France's Ligue 1 and Swansea City and Cardiff City playing in the English League system.

The same is true in Singapore. Up until 1994 a team from Singapore played in the Malaysian cup but for a number of political and financial reasons the team was withdrawn and a league set up in Singapore. But in 2011 the Football Associations of Malaysia and Singapore came to an agreement that a team from the peninsula would take their place in the Malaysian Super League from the start of the 2012/13 season. There were a couple of stipulations, namely that the squad would have to all be Singapore nationals, and the core of the squad had to be under 23 years old.

The team took the name the Singapore Lions XII. XII not XI, or should I say, for those who failed their Latin O-Level (kids, ask your dad . . . but it's nothing to do with certain acronyms I believe exist on certain adult websites), 12 not 11. Those clever marketing people wanted to recognise the impact the fans would have on the team, effectively functioning as the twelfth man. The motto fortunately was slightly better: "For Country, For Fans, For Football".

Back over in Singapore, the domestic league (aka The Great Eastern S League) continued as it was, although a number of clubs were unhappy that their best players were essentially press-ganged into joining the Lions XII. The Young Lions club was created to become the feeder club for them. To complicate matters even further, the league also hosted a team from an overseas territory, DPMM FC being based in Brunei, on the north coast of Borneo. The league has also welcomed teams from Japan (well, the feeder team of Niigata) and Haimau Muda B, which is basically the Malaysian National Under-21 team. As with football in some of the world's smallest territories such as Malta, Gibraltar, Andorra and San Marino, many clubs do not have the resources to own their own ground so they share the current national stadium, the 8,000-seater Jalan Besar Stadium in Kallang, a short cab ride from the business district of Singapore. This was also the home of the Singapore Lions XII at the time of our visit, until they moved to the very impressive new 55,000-all-seater national stadium in late 2014.

So our itinerary for the week would see us take in the Lions' home game with Malaysian side PKNS on Saturday night, just a few hours after arriving (Football Tourism Rule 7:1 subsection 3c – Jet lag cannot formally be recognised until after the match has finished or if the game is still scoreless after 67 minutes, at which point you are allowed to snooze in your seat), and then on the evening of our departure we would be back in the Jalan Besar to watch Home United FC take on Hougang United. Best-laid plans and all that.

The A380 experience was all that it promised and we were treated like royalty for six hours as we headed east from Dubai. As we walked out of Singapore's Changi Airport, memories of Korea came flooding back in the form of crippling humidity, made all the worse by stepping out of an air-conditioned enviroment. We had a car waiting for us and within 20 minutes (everything is no more than 20 minutes away in Singapore) we were checking into our hotel, shedding our formalities and diving into the rooftop infinity pool with a beer (not diving with the beer because that would be silly, up there with swimming pool no-no's such as no petting). We had been travelling for 17 hours. That is a long time to be wearing the same pants.

Our hotel was located next to the famous Raffles Hotel and just a short walk from the conference centre next door in the Fairmont. Once we felt we had washed the travel fatigue out of our bones we headed to the Fairmont bar where we met a number of familiar faces from around the world. The standard etiquette at these events is to ask (1) when they got in, (2) what route did they took and (3) when they would be going home. Repeat that to fade and you have an idea of what the first few hours were like. Surprisingly few of the people we knew fancied the idea of a Malaysian Super League game on a Saturday night in Singapore, one of the party capitals of the world. Some people! Ben was kidnapped by an old work colleague and given the option of a night at the football or a free steak dinner at Raffles. He chose the latter. Sometimes I do wonder where his loyalties lie.

I found the stadium on the map and had three options. I could walk it – it looked to be only about a couple of miles away – but as I had already spent five minutes waiting to cross a main road (oh yes, Lolly forgot to tell me that jaywalking is also illegal and punishable by 50 lashes or something equally harsh) in the oppressive heat I thought I would need to take a suitcase full of fresh clothes for the trip. Oh, and there was the fact I would be wandering around unfamiliar areas in an unfamiliar city with that pasty white 'just arrived' tourist look.

Option two was the subway. Once again it looked like it was a short trip but who could say where I might end up, so option three seemed the safe bet: a taxi. Having only been in the city for a few hours yet already having paid S$18 (about £9) for a small beer I expected to have to sell a kidney to afford the 10-minute cab fare. The taxi driver wanted to know my opinion on every Premier League team and footballer once he knew I was going to the game. As I would soon find out, they are Premier League crazy in Singapore and love nothing more than to talk about it. The final fare turned out to be less than £3 and my driver left me with parting words that Chelsea would be "stuffing the life" out of Arsenal in the early game of the day, which was being shown on prime-time Saturday night TV. We get Dale Winton and the Lottery, they get the Mourinho and Wenger show.

The stadium lit up the local neighbourhood, which was thronging (love that word) with football fans of all genders, shapes, sizes and ages all bedecked in red shirts. Loyal Singapore Lions fans? Some, yes, but there were hundreds in Manchester United and Liverpool shirts. A few Newcastle ones and even a Coventry City one. The story behind that one could have taken us deep into the night. I had already sorted out my media pass with the club so headed up to the top of the main stand to take my seat.

The stadium was quite full with over half an hour to kick-off. The two-tier main stand with its curved roof, like a little mini Galpharm/John Smith's stand from Huddersfield Town, was rocking with some synchronised singing and chanting. The stand opposite was almost full of the main Lions supporters, the "Hooligans", who may need to look up the meaning of that word. They took up three-quarters of the stand with the small spattering of away fans sitting behind a banner that said "We welcome away fans". It's touches like those that make you all warm and fuzzy inside.

With the north end of the ground being simply the wall to another building, the only other stand was a big temporary structure that was completely alien to Singapore. All of their construction projects are cutting edge with no detail left unfinished, so it was surprising to see something so ugly.

While crowds had been good during the Lions' Championship-winning season last year, there were around 6,000 in the house for this match. Quite what a crowd like that will feel like in the new state-of-the-art national stadium when it opens in the Singapore Sports Hub in October I do not know. Perhaps more locals will come to games – ticket prices are certainly not an issue, starting at just £6 for home games. But that 6,000 crowd generated a decent din. Not a Serbian or Rome derby type of din but an old Wembley Stadium schoolboy international din. Polite clapping, appreciative cheers and pantomime booing when the opposition team were mentioned. Our stadium announcer was whipping up the crowd into a frenzy, and then the two teams emerged, accompanied by the club anthem and the "hooligans" all raising their "Go Lions Go" banners. Showtime.

SINGAPORE LIONS XII 2, PKNS FC 1
Saturday 21st March 2014 – Jalan Besar Stadium

According to the Wikipedia page for the Lions, they have a great rivalry with PKNS. This would surely mean that those "hooligans" would be out in force, wreaking havoc in the area and then attacking all of the PKNS fans who had made the cross-border trip from Selangor in Malaysia. Based on my brief snapshot of life in Singapore so far I doubted that this would be the case, but then again I have seen Danish Cup games played in front of crowds of less than 50 in which it has all kicked off.

The away team PKNS, short for the memorable Kelab Bola Perbadanan Kemajuan Negeri Selangor Football Club, were in only their second season of top-flight football. Despite playing in orange and blue (with a change strip of green) they are nicknamed "The Red Ants", which I assume can only refer to their nasty habit of biting the opposition.

The question I asked myself (apart from wtf I am doing here after a 20-hour journey?) before the game concerned what the standard of football would be. Whereas the football last week in Gibraltar had been almost at my level (very ageing centre back whose golden spell had been in the last century), I had no reference point for Singapore. With over 5 million inhabitants, they had a bigger pool of potential players than countries such as Ireland, Norway and Uruguay, but then again they had never featured on the world footballing stage, coming from a region where the likes of Bahrain and Qatar had come so close to qualifying for the FIFA World Cup. So my expectation was Conference level at best.

The answer was that it was a very good standard indeed. The game was played at pace on an artificial pitch which allowed the home side to zip the ball around. The home fans, almost filling the stand on the far side as well as the lower tier of the main stand, made a din throughout the first half, the noise resembling a schoolboy international with rhythmic clapping, synchronised chanting and pantomime booing when PKNS had the ball. In the end it was two quality goals that sent the Man Utd-shirted fans happy into the night.

It was somewhat against the run of play that the away side took the lead on the half-hour mark, as the lad Faiz was given far too much space in the area to pick his spot, sending the hundred or so away fans into polite applause delirium. The Lions simply upped the tempo and just before the break their key man, midfielder Zulfhami, curled a free-kick over the wall and into the top corner of the net. Two minutes later he had exactly the same opportunity but on this occasion his effort struck the crossbar.

Half-time saw everyone in the media area whip a rice dish out of their bags. I think at some point I had missed getting my little goodie bag, although seeing what appeared to be something squirming around in the container of the chap next to me (introducing himself as "Joe Geordie" for his love of the Toon) I wasn't too fussed to have missed out. The Lions won the second half hands down, dominating from the first minute, and it was somewhat surprising that they only scored one further goal, an excellent strike from Faris that no keeper in the world would have got their hands to.

The game was incredibly enjoyable to watch. The fans around me were really getting into it and you could see one or two players were stand-out; as Joe Geordie told me, the team had a number of international players in the starting eleven.

With 10 minutes to go I started to flag. Two long-haul flights in less than 24 hours, eight time zones away and an incessant Mexican wave all took their toll on me. I headed out of the stadium and onto the subway for the short ride home. Singapore gets football and the locals have a team they can be proud of. My only comment would be that they need to look up the meaning of the word "hooligan".

The rest of the week was spent in big meeting rooms listening to people talking in acronyms, punctuated by some decent food and drink. We were invited to parties at the highest rooftop bar in the world, Altitude, with its jaw-dropping views of the whole city, and in the most fashionable club in Singapore on top of the "baguette" where the Grand Prix track was lit up in the midnight moonlight. And everywhere we went we encountered the infamous SPGs.

Singapore Party Girls. You cannot fail to notice the young pretty things everywhere you go in Singapore. Immaculately dressed during the day in the shortest of shorts and tiniest of tops, they transform themselves to super models in expensive designer dresses for the bright lights in the evening. Many of these girls simply want to shop in the hundreds of upmarket malls in Orchard Road all day and sip Champagne in the bars of the Marina Bay resort all evening. But to do that they need a sugar daddy, someone who will keep them in Gucci and Prada. That's where the wealthy middle-aged Westerners come in. While we waited in line to enter the Lounge at Skyline, the outdoor bar with an infinity pool some 63 storey above Marina Bay, a group behind us started to ask us questions. "You live here?" "You work for big bank?" "You like my pretty friend?" They soon lost interest when they knew we were simply misplaced Football Tourists and not Nick Leesons in the making.

Our last night saw us reflect on what had been a full-on week. Singapore was a great place to visit. The locals like to work hard and play hard, that was for sure, and we didn't see any sign of the strict controls the government imposes on its citizens. It seemed on every corner there was a shopping mall, an air-conditioned oasis in the oppressive heat of the Singapore sun, filled with locals fuelling an ever-expanding economy. Life here was good and they were certainly friendly and absolutely loved their football.

Our final day was spent writing up notes. It had been a hard week and we needed to give our colleagues value for money, while being able to enjoy our long flight home. We had two choices for our last night in Singapore. Option one was a trip back to the Jalan Baser to watch Home United in the Singapore League. Option two was a bloody big steak and a bottle of Malbec at Raffles Hotel. Sorry football fans but I hate to say we chose the latter option. I can talk you through the meal, tasty morsel by smooth velvety sip, but I don't think you will have the appetite for that.

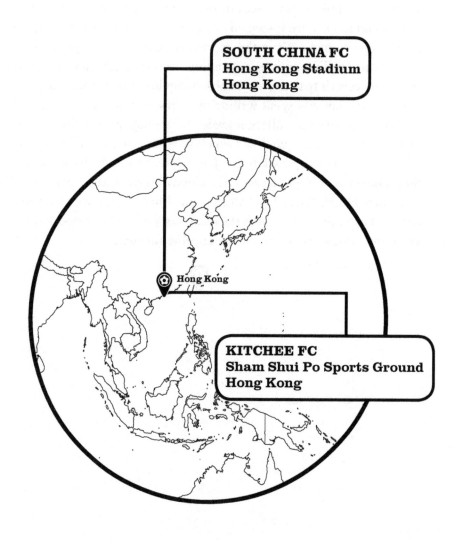

SOUTH CHINA FC
Hong Kong Stadium
Hong Kong

Hong Kong

KITCHEE FC
Sham Shui Po Sports Ground
Hong Kong

Not even a pair of South China FC slippers
would placate him this time.

7. Just a Mild-mannered Janitor

I've learnt a few things in my career from wise men who have made it to the top of their game. Never be late for a meeting with your superiors, always be the smartest person in the room and always surf the internet for "research" purposes on your own computer. But the best life lesson has to be never saying "no" when the Chief Executive asks you if you want to go on a business trip with him. That, and buy low, sell high, of course.

That was the situation I was faced with in early May. The good news is that it was to be an all-expenses-paid trip, flying in champagne class, staying in a five-star hotel and being wined and dined by business partners on some of the finest food and drink that Hong Kong could offer. The bad news was that he was coming too. Only joking Gary! You gain a lot of respect for a person when they decide to join you in that "one for the runway" extra gin and tonic, then add that "what is said on tour, stays on tour". He had also bought a copy of *The Football Tourist*, so I had a moral duty to be nice to someone who had indirectly given me some royalties.

While I went home from the office on that day in early May with a skip in my step, I had to think as to how I would sell the idea of another prolonged trip away to the ones I love. At the start of 2014 I had made a New Year's resolution to travel less. January went well, February saw me slip away to Europe for a few trips, but in March it all sort of went wrong when I headed off to Dubai and Singapore. April was a mini-tour of Europe before ending in New York and Boston, and now May would see me on foreign shores for over half the month. I could kid myself and say that the travel would be less in the second half of the year, or at least when the season ended, but it wouldn't have been true: 2014 looked like breaking all records for business (ahem) travel.

"So you are leaving me again, are you? Another weekend we will be apart! Don't you realise that it is Derby County away in the second leg of the Play-offs!" Danny was getting tired of my trips away. I was in the last-chance saloon in our relationship. Not even a pair of South China FC slippers would placate him this time. Thankfully the Current Mrs Fuller was more understanding and needed nothing more than a delivery of yellow roses from the petrol station for her to give me her blessing to go East. "Just don't come back with some strange disease this time!" she warned me. As if. It was only the once, returning from Slovakia with dysentery. Oh, and the trip to the Playboy Mansion, where I caught Pontiac Fever. But I've told you about that before, right? No? Well, let me tell you about the time I was invited to Hugh Hefner's house then. The house was full of women, wearing very little, and as soon as the drink started flowing they were shedding what was left of their underwear and jumping in the pool. I wandered into the grotto and was amazed to see a very famous face. There, in her birthday suit was [content removed by publishers for fear of prosecution]. And that was how I caught Pontiac Fever.

But back to the present. I was going to be spending five days in the company of intellectual property lawyers and attorneys. Over eight and a half thousand of them, squeezed onto the 30 square miles of Hong Kong Island. That's enough to get the pulse racing, right? Have you ever seen two lawyers from different firms try to split the bill at a restaurant? Funniest thing ever. They will argue the merits for hours as to why the other party should pay, before both conceding and agreeing to split the bill. This annual event is normally held in the USA and in the past my firm has organised events for our special legal friends to attend. Last year in Dallas it was an Executive Box to watch the Texas Rangers play in the MLB. A few years back, when it was held in Berlin, we had executive seats at the DFB-Pokal Final in the OlympiaStadion. This year we were going on a boat. Oh, how I laughed when I was given the job of organising that one.

Hong Kong was a new destination on me though. Of course the first thing I did when told I was going was to check the fixtures. The good news was that the weekend I was going to be there was the final round of games in the Hong Kong Football League. The bad news, due to the scheduling of the kick-offs, and the fact I was actually there to do some work, was that I could only get to two games. As in Singapore, Hong Kong's top-level clubs mostly play within a small area, meaning that you would never be far away from a game. The one real bonus was that I would be getting in a game at the fabulous Hong Kong Stadium, home to the annual Hong Kong Sevens Tournament during which over 40,000 pissed-up Brits wear funny shorts, even funnier hats (so they think) and fall asleep in the sunshine while an international rugby tournament takes place around them.

Since 2007 the South Stand, along the lines of the famous Western Terrace at Headingley, has been made officially accessible to over-eighteens only, due to various alcohol-fuelled jolly japes. Streakers are now arrested if they try and run across the pitch (alas, no leeway is given for the quality of what is on show, despite protests that some "criminals" should be shown leniency). In 2010, someone managed to scale the goal posts and sit on the crossbar, causing many fans to spill their drinks, so something had to be done and a new zero-tolerance policy was put in place in 2011.

That must be an amusing event to watch. Not the rugby side of things – the result of that will always be relatively the same, with a small number of nations ever winning the tournament (this year New Zealand beat England in the final, their third win at the stadium in the past 10 years). No, I mean off the pitch, when the fans fuelled by alcohol descend back down the hill and into the street markets around Causeway Bay, where every part of a chicken, goat or pig can be, and is, eaten. Who needs to play the biscuit game when you could do paper, scissors, stone to decide who will eat the chicken intestines or deep-fried pigs' willies?

My flight took me from an air-conditioned executive lounge at Heathrow to the desert-furnace of Doha. As our plane approached the runway in Qatar a simple glance out of the window confirmed the common belief that holding a World Cup here is simply madness. I'm sure that Qataris have more money than sense but even if we ignore the fact that the temperatures will be over 40 degrees in June 2022 when the games are on, what will the legacy be of building a bunch of shiny new stadia?

Even the then Lord High Admiral of World Football, Sepp Blatter, admitted in an interview with Swiss TV channel RTS, "Of course, it was a mistake. You know, one makes a lot of mistakes in life. The technical report indicated clearly that it was too hot in summer, but despite that the executive committee decided with quite a big majority that the tournament would be in Qatar." Despite admitting this error Blatter, who voted for Qatar, confirmed he will run for a fifth term as FIFA president in 2015. Great news all round for world football I am sure you will agree!

Qatar plans to build eight new stadia and redevelop existing ones to give a total seating capacity of nearly 600,000, or essentially one seat for every fourth person in the country. They would be the smallest nation to host the FIFA World Cup both geographically and population-wise. Qatar is the 164th biggest (or 76th smallest) nation in the world in terms of land area. Bigger than places such as Aruba, Gibraltar and of course our old friends Tokelau but still lagging behind the Falkland Islands, Svalbard and Kyrgyzstan. Heck, it isn't even half the size of Wales. Imagine holding a World Cup in Wales? Don't get me wrong here – I love Wales, love the Welsh, and love Brains beer. But could you imagine Brazil v Holland in Afan Lido, or Germany v Argentina in Rhyl. How would the nightclubs of Newport cope with an influx of thousands of Japanese fans?

A few major concerns were flagged at the time the decision was made to award the tournament to Qatar ahead of the USA, South Korea, Japan and Australia, such as the scorching-hot temperatures in June, which can reach up to 50 degrees centigrade, and the fact that the state observes Sharia Law, thus making the drinking of alcohol, as well as homosexuality, illegal.

But the organising committee have been unrepentant. Qatar bid's chief executive, Hassan al-Thawadi, said, "Heat is not and will not be an issue. The plan is that all of the stadiums will harness the power of the sun's rays to provide a cool environment for players and fans by converting solar energy into electricity that will then be used to cool both fans and players. When games are not taking place, the solar installations at the stadiums will export energy onto the power grid. During matches, the stadiums will draw energy from the grid." So that's sorted then. The fact that the big yellow ball of fire in the sky will still be sending harmful rays onto the people in the stadium is negligible, presumably.

My time in Qatar went like this (adopts a Jack Bauer voice about events being shown in real time). Land an hour late at 6am (outside temperature "just" 29 degrees), taxi to a remote part of the airfield. Wait for "executive buses" to arrive. Get on buses (executive as they have darkened windows). Drive around the perimeter of the airport for 20 minutes until we pull up outside the Premium Transfer Terminal. Get off bus, pass through security point, walk 30 yards to check-in desk, get back onto an executive bus (next to the one we got off) drive 20 minutes back around the airport perimeter, get onto a plane that was parked next to the one we got off. Put on Qatar pyjamas, drink gin and tonic, and fall asleep before we take off. Total time in Qatar – 41 minutes.

Fast-forward 9 hours 20 minutes and I open the window blinds on the plane. Brilliant cloudless skies have been replaced by darkness, punctuated by flashes of lightning and rain. Lots of rain. Fortunately our approach to Chek Lap Kok Airport is unproblematic and we land, despite the conditions, without an issue. Twenty years ago it would have been a different story, as we would have been trying to land at Kai Tak Airport on Kowloon, ranked as one of the most dangerous airport approaches in the world. Navigate through the skyscrapers, bank hard right hundreds of feet above Kowloon Bay and then avoid falling off the end of the runway into the water.

Hong Kong is a small place in terms of geography (even smaller than Qatar, so it must be small), but a massive one in terms of people and buildings. It doesn't seem humanly possible to squeeze any more buildings into such a small space as Hong Kong Island (30 square miles) but that is exactly what developers are trying to do. Cheap local transport, "exotic" food, people who speak English, the eleventh-smallest country in the world in terms of land mass – what could possibly go wrong?

Due to the size of the territory, there aren't many stadiums, with many teams sharing facilities. The national stadium, a fatter version of the John Smith's Stadium in Huddersfield or a slimmed-down Estadio do Dragao, holds 40,000, which, with an average attendance in the Hong Kong Football League of 931, means there are quite a few spare seats on any given game each weekend. Buying in advance, just in case, simply wasn't necessary.

After a decent night's sleep our work team met for breakfast in the comfortable surroundings of the 34th floor of the JW Marriott hotel, which, as I am sure all you tall-building aficionados will know was one of the first Western-brand skyscraper hotels to open in the Far East. While today it is dwarfed by other hotels around it, it is still a landmark on Hong Kong Island and the business update was made more interesting by the view of Kowloon Bay out of the window. We each gave an update of our plans for the day and I was dismayed to learn I had a meeting with a luxury car brand (I can't reveal any specific names but let's just say it is named after a 1970s American disco band, albeit with the first name slightly changed) at 4pm. "What else do you have on, Stuart?" my boss asked. He was off to do a bit of networking at the convention centre so I said I was going to explore the island, as it would be one of my only chances to do so. "Good plan. Here's what I suggest you do", and he gave me a list of must-see things, although I noted that a visit to watch Kitchee FC wasn't among them.

So after a trip up the Bank of China Tower, a trip up (and walk down) the Mid-Levels escalator (the longest covered escalator system in the world spanning a distance of 800 metres and a height of 135 metres) and then a wander around one of the markets, selling a range of fake branded goods, I headed for the Star Ferry. It was here that the dichotomy between the two sides of Hong Kong struck me. There was I with my HK$500 note (about £45) trying to pay for a ticket on the ferry costing HK$4 (31 pence). Despite the dripping wealth of the island, some things still remained cheaper than you could imagine.

A trip on the Star Ferry to Kowloon is one of the must-do things in Hong Kong. The views back across the water are outstanding and here you can see how the rich and poor rub shoulders. Old apartment blocks housing thousands of locals are now being joined at arm's-length by monuments of capitalism.

After a little wander around the bottom end of Kowloon it was time to head for my first taste of football in Hong Kong. My choice of game (in fact, the only game being played that day) was Kitchee FC v Yokohama Hong Kong at the wonderfully named Sham Shui Po Sports Ground.

The home side had walked to the Hong Kong championship that season, winning the league over six weeks earlier and with one game to go, they stood on the brink of going throughout the whole season unbeaten. The glory days were coming back to the Mong Kok area of the territory, following up on their domestic treble in 2012 and the Hong Kong FA Cup last season. The glory days were back and people (well, the driver of a taxi I had used earlier in the day) were talking about the current team in the same breath as the one from 10 years ago who had been the talk of the footballing town after beating both AC Milan and Juventus in pre-season friendlies.

In the last couple of seasons Arsenal and Manchester United had visited Kitchee, with the Gunners entering into a formal agreement to help the Kitchee Academy develop players, while obviously keeping a watchful eye on any outstanding talent that may emerge. They will then, of course, buy them, bring them over to England and farm them out on loan to the four corners of the Football League, never to be seen or heard of again.

Kitchee translates in Native American as "brave young men". Quite why a team formed on the other side of the world in 1931 is named after Native Americans is unknown to even the finest football scholar, but six Hong Kong Championships make them the third most successful team in football in the province. However, it has been their recent form that has had the Hong Kong Barca (as they are known) fans purring with pleasure. Building on their domestic success over the past few years, this season has seen them progress to the Quarter-Finals of the AFC Cup, the Champions League competition for Asian footballing nations, becoming only the third club from Hong Kong to do so. Alas, any hopes of a domestic double were thwarted by Eastern AA in late May in the FA Cup Final.

As I left the safe haven of the air-conditioned Mass Transit Railway (MTR) the humidity hit me once again, as though someone had opened the door of a giant sauna. Rain streamed down from the heavens, almost evaporating due to the heat before it hit the ground. I was looking for the Sham Shui Po sports ground, the 2,200-all-seater athletics ground that is home to Kitchee FC as well as Biu Chun Rangers and Eastern Salon, who were once managed by the late, great Bobby Moore. The ground wasn't hard to find, located as it was in the only area of greenery in the mostly residential Cheung Sha Wan district. Fans weren't exactly flocking to the ground despite kick-off being just 15 minutes away – perhaps it was the weather; after all I couldn't believe that football is not the Saturday afternoon entertainment of choice.

Watching football in Hong Kong falls into the "really!!" bucket in terms of cost, along with taxi fares, train tickets and fried chicken intestines. The admission for this game, and all others in the HKFL thanks to some sensible price fixing, was HK$60 – approximately £4.50 or slightly cheaper than a bottle of mineral water in my hotel (sitting in the "really??" bucket at HK$70).

This was to be the last ever Football League season in Hong Kong. The English influence was all too clear to see in the plans for the future, as in October 2014 a new 12-team Premier League would take its place. Concerns that there wouldn't be enough financially viable clubs able to take part seemed well founded when Happy Valley and Tuen Mun were kicked out of the league mid-season for failing to demonstrate their financial sustainability. The current rules around foreign players will also be carried forward for the time being, with each club allowed to field a maximum of five "foreign" players at any stage during a game from seven that they can have in their squad, one of whom must be Asian. The bulk of these foreigners are Brazilian, 25 players at the time of writing, followed by 11 Spanish nationals.

Kitchee's championship-winning squad had been built on workman-like performances from Hong Kong natives mixed with those of five Spanish players, a Nigerian and an Irishman – although with the latter being named Wan Chun, you would never have figured that one out. Despite the team's impressive record this season, the crowds haven't exactly flocked to the Sham Shui Po to watch the champions-elect. It wasn't supposed to be like this. Back in 2011, the government-sponsored Project Phoenix was supposed to revamp Hong Kong soccer from top to bottom, with over HK$20million being injected into the domestic game every year, although it seems that the majority of this cash has been taken by new high-paid administrative roles at the top of the game in the province, rather than being allocated to the clubs in trying to improve infrastructure, academies and facilities to encourage more fans.

Fans do not appear to be impressed, with attendance figures far from ideal. South China, the province's best-supported club, gets an average attendance of 2,200 at the 40,000 Hong Kong Stadium, while Kitchee struggle to break the 1,000 barrier for home games. None of the clubs in Hong Kong owns their own stadium, all of them instead renting sports grounds on a season-by-season basis from the local authorities.

One club, Citizen AA, spent HK$9 million in the 2012/13 season, including having to spend over HK$40,000 for the use of the Mong Kok Stadium for each home game. With crowds of less than 1,000, paying less than the £4.50

the league mandate, it is hard to see how they can make ends meet. The Chairman of Citizen AA, Pui Kwan-kay, has been very critical of Phoenix.

"Coupled with other expenses on players' salaries, administration costs, training and other support services, we are losing money season after season. And all this money comes from either our own pockets or sponsor support; nothing comes from Project Phoenix.

"If the government is really serious about Hong Kong soccer, it should at least do something to reduce our expenditure, such as waiving its charges for the use of venues. After all, the government owns these venues. If they want to help, this would be a good way to start." Couldn't agree more myself.

The visitors, Yokohama, as you would expect, had a backbone of Japanese players and an arrangement in place with the Japanese League side of the same name that saw a number of promising youngsters loaned out during the season to Hong Kong for match experience. While the season had ultimately been disappointing for the Blues, they had done enough to ensure they would be dining at the new top table next season.

The Sham Shui Po stadium is essentially an athletics track with one main stand set six feet above the playing field. Fortunately the main stand offered most of the 600 fans respite from the pouring rain. There were fans of all ages in the crowd, with more and more young families arriving during the afternoon to let their kids run riot in the stands. Everyone seemed to know each other, giving me a wide berth as if I were some strange foreigner. I don't think many tourists make their way up these parts, so a sweaty, slightly past his physical prime, camera-toting Englishman provided the pre-match entertainment. Lightning crackled overhead and with this being the only open space in miles there must have been some concern for the welfare of the players.

Opposite the main stand, huge high-rise apartment blocks offered some fantastic views of the pitch, although few window seats seemed to have been taken up. Quite what else there would be to do on a wet Saturday afternoon was lost on me, unless they were showing *Holiday on the Buses* on the TV – the 1970s comedy series is still a big pull in these parts. They simply cannot get enough of Butler, Harper and Blakey.

Both teams emerged to polite applause, lined up on the touchline and gave us all a big wave. A bunch of flowers was presented to the female assistant referee by a ball boy – not sure if that counts as trying to bribe an official but she seemed to appreciate the touch, gesturing that perhaps she should hold those aloft rather than the flag. Oh, how we all laughed.

As for the game itself, the league champions gave a display of clinical finishing which underlined their success. Despite having the lion's share of possession, Kitchee only mustered five shots in the whole game, scoring all four on-target opportunities. Their dominance was clear from the first kick although it took them 25 minutes to open the scoring when the Spaniard Diego Cascon was brought down in the area, dusted himself down and slotted home the penalty to send a small band of flag-waving and drum-beating Yokohama fans into rapture. Despite their season being long over, they still tried to muster some enthusiasm for their team. What was strange was that, despite their dominance during the season, Kitchee didn't look anything particularly special. A bit like Chelsea really.

On the stroke of half-time the visitors equalised through Yoshitake, sending the hundred or so away fans into drum-beating, flag-waving ecstasy. There were murmurings of a pitch invasion among the under-fives, but their parents soon called them to order with the promise of a bottle of milk. Parity lasted approximately 37 seconds before Christian Annan put the home side back into the lead. I had a wander, desperate for some food, but it appeared that nothing was on offer. Here was a captive market for all of those strange cuts of chicken (I knew only too well what normally goes into a half-time burger or hot dog), yet there was nothing on offer. It is at times like these that I thank my special pocket with the emergency Mars Bar in it.

The result was never in doubt once Kitchee had retaken the lead and a third goal mid-way through the second half by Annan put the result beyond doubt. A final strike from the brilliantly named Ka Hai Leung Robson Augusto (that'll be £23 for your name printing please sir) was the icing on the cake and, despite the incessant rain, there was plenty of dancing in the streets of Chung Sha Wan at the final whistle.

The game, atmosphere and attendance had met my preconceived expectations and it could be summed up in one word: "passive". In less than 24 hours I would be heading to see the province's biggest side, South China, but before then I had the small matter of a meeting back at base.

Sunday morning broke just as Saturday night had ended: more rain. Once again our daily briefing session over breakfast focused on the meetings for the day ahead. "Now Stuart, I want you to meet with xyz at 4pm" (name changed to protect the innocent although I can reveal that they did invent the light bulb and have their own works football team and played regularly in the Champions League). "Hmm, can someone else do it?" I asked, thinking of the game kicking off at 4pm. "No, it has to be you. They like you – heck, they love you." I am good at schmoozing, so I took it as a compliment and went back to Uncle Google to work out my travel plan for the afternoon.

I had planned a trip around the island in the morning, followed by a slap-up lunch, and then to take the MTR to Causeway Bay and the short walk uphill to the Hong Kong Stadium. Then I would have a leisurely wander back. Now it seemed I would need to try and find a taxi to get back to the hotel in time, meaning the walk would have to come first.

I couldn't pass up an opportunity to visit the biggest stadium in the country – that is what the Football Tourist rule book clearly states. The Hong Kong Stadium was opened in 1953 on the site of the old Government Stadium. After it was renovated and reopened in 1994, the contract to run the stadium was won by Wembley International, a subsidiary of the old Wembley Plc, which also ran our famous Twin Towers. It had been in the press a lot in recent years but not for good reasons. The pitch had been the cause of many a complaint from English Premier League managers in various pre-season tournaments including Sir Alex Ferguson, Paolo Di Canio and André Villas-Boas, although former Manchester City boss Manuel Pelligrini had no complaints when his side played here in 2013. Now, I am not one for conspiracy theories, but only one of those managers is still in their job.

If plans are to be believed, the stadium only has a short life expectancy in its current guise, as a new stadium is due to be constructed on the site of the old airport in Kowloon Bay. Quite why it is needed when the Hong Kong Stadium is more than ample for the province is another story, but that sums up Hong Kong perfectly well – just keep building.

Tenants South China are Hong Kong's biggest and most successful football club. Forty-one league titles, thirty-one Senior Shields, nine FA Cups and numerous campaigns in the AFC Cup, not to mention the patronage and sponsorship of some of the world's biggest brands and once the home of Nicky Butt. The club also have a "partnership" with Tottenham Hotspur, although it is unclear what that actually involves apart from losing three times a season to West Ham United.

Just a 20-minute walk from the hotel according to Google. Hong Kong Island itself is just 30 square miles yet somehow I managed to lose a 40,000-seater stadium. I say "lose" but technically it was "not found". I followed my walking instructions to the Happy Valley racetrack. But with data on my phone costing just the £6 per MB I was quickly up to my monthly limit and had to rely on my pocket map. When I reached the edge of that and was still walking uphill I should have declared I was lost and simply asked a local. But I am a man. Men do not cry, wear scented moisturiser, follow instructions when building flat-pack furniture or ask for directions. EVER. So I carried on walking. I remember seeing pictures of the stadium set on a hillside, so I headed north, trekking uphill. At some point, around the next corner perhaps, it would appear. I said that to myself for over 30 minutes, by which time I seemed to be following a road that went back down the hillside towards Kowloon Bay. Eventually, with kick-off long gone, pride got the better of me and I asked some directions from the best-looking girl I could find.

"Go down this hill until you reach the racetrack. Take first right, it is on that road in five minutes."

That would be the racetrack I passed over half an hour ago. I had taken a nearly 45-minute, five-kilometre, oxygen-starved detour around the peaks of Hong Kong and here I was almost back to where I'd started. My determination saw me through. Yes, I had missed 30 minutes of the game, but I was the real winner by beating the odds, the mobile phone company and DK fold-out maps. Take that, modernisation! This was a victory for proper men.

When I finally took one of the spare 39,500 seats I was relieved to see the match was still goalless. On either side of the stadium small pockets of fans banged drums and chanted "let's go xxx, let's go" (obviously inserting South China or Citizens for the xxx). Fans lethargically reclined in their seats, not seeming particularly interested in what was going on on the pitch.

The long walk had made me peckish and I was tempted by the fact they had a KFC in the concourse. However, when I asked for a chicken burger I was told "no chicken" but was then offered another deep-fried product, coated in the Colonel's special blend of herbs. Having seen the street food market offerings earlier in the day I passed, opting for a deep-fried pork bun instead (because you can be really sure of what's in that one!).

Two goals in no more than 45 seconds on the stroke of half-time by the Australian Barisic and locallad Lo Kong Wai for the home side gave the scoreline a flattering look at the break. In fact when the half-time stat sheets were issued in the press area, it appeared South China had scored the two goals without actually registering a shot on goal in the first 45 minutes.

The Portuguese player Joao Emir was their star player, pulling the strings in a tired midfield and he made the game safe on the hour mark with a third goal for South China, after Citizen had pulled one back. Despite a second from the away team it was a comfortable win to end the season for South China, although that final goal from Citizen meant Sun Pegasus finished the season above them in second place on goal difference, meaning both of them would have to contest a play-off for the AFC Champions League spot along with Kitchee.

Up against the clock I struck gold within 30 seconds of the final whistle as a lone cab sat outside the stadium. I sprinted down the steps, pushing the very old, very young and very frail out of the way to jump in. Ten minutes later I was pulling up outside the hotel with minutes to spare before my meeting. Mission accomplished.

The rest of the week passed by in a flash. Fine wine, fine food and even more rain couldn't dampen my spirits after seeing the two games. When it came to bidding a fond farewell to Asia (for a few weeks at least) I could do so with a proud smile on my face and another stamp in the Football Tourist passport. Hong Kong was certainly a stunning place in terms of the wealth on offer, yet it still retained that gritty Eastern outlook. Perhaps it hadn't been the most passionate of footballing welcomes but it was cheap, enjoyable and offered a welcome distraction to the heat, humidity and the workload. Zia Kan Hong Kong.

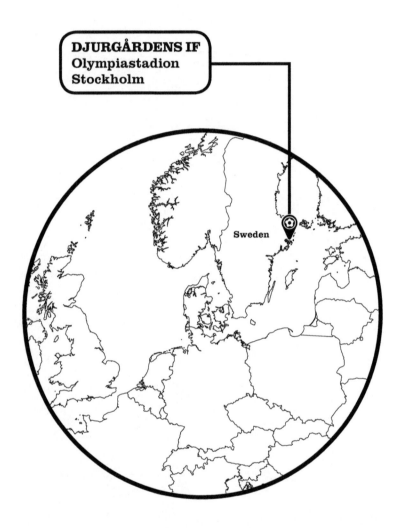

DJURGÅRDENS IF
Olympiastadion
Stockholm

Sweden

The eleventh-noisiest stadium in the world,
beating such stadiums as the Nou Camp,
San Siro and even the Dripping Pan.

8. Closing Time

The end of an era in Stockholm

───────────

**"Closing time . . . every new beginning
comes from some other beginning's end."**

Football fans hate change. We have our match-day routines. We take the same bus or train to every home game, park in the same street if we drive. We buy our programme from the same chap every game, even if we have walked past 10 others. We talk to people sitting around us who we have nothing in common with apart from the 90 minutes of shared passion every other week. We know every nook and cranny of OUR ground. But at some point things have to change. That's life.

As a lifelong West Ham United fan I dread the day that Upton Park will close, the final piece in the plan of our owners to rid us of any history or sense of perspective. The team will move a few miles to the north into Stratford, where the centrepiece of the Queen Elizabeth II Park, the Olympic Stadium and its 60,000 empty seats, lie waiting. Notice I said team and not club. To me the club is more than 11 overpaid, uncaring players who hoof the ball in the air each week. The club is the fabric around the stadium. It is the history, the heritage, the memories that the local community has offered up. The move to the new Olympic Stadium is all about money.

Many service industries use a term called ARPU. Average Revenue per User. It is one of the key metrics used by mobile phone operators; airlines look at yield per passenger, the amount that an average passenger will spend once aboard. Football clubs are no different. They may use different terminology, but their overarching aim is to increase the revenue they get from every fan on a match day.

Ticket prices continue to spiral out of control. Slowly but surely a generation of football fans are being priced out of the game. Many clubs are blinded by greed to notice this and will not see it until the number of empty seats becomes a major talking point on Sky Sports' *Super Sunday*. Clubs blame falling attendances on the influence of TV companies and their insistence on changing kick-off times, yet are happy to take their millions every time a new deal is struck.

When David Sullivan and David Gold stood in front of the media to announce that West Ham would be moving to the Olympic Stadium they made a wild claim that the club would be the cheapest to watch in the Premier League. Considering the club is one of the most expensive to watch today, with tickets costing up to £77, I doubt that claim will ever stand the test of time.

London is the home to some of the best football stadiums in the world. A common discussion on our European Football Weekends is what a major tournament in the city would look like. After all, if a city can host the greatest show on earth in the form of the Olympics, why couldn't it host the European Championships or even the FIFA World Cup itself? UEFA's idea for 2020 of having it spread across the whole of Europe is a step in the right direction, but how long will it be before London gets the honour of hosting a whole tournament?

By 2018 the city will be able to boast five stadiums with capacities over 60,000, assuming White Hart Lane's redevelopment is completed. Add in Stamford Bridge, still restricted by a railway line, cemetery and housing in the surrounding area - or wherever Chelsea end up playing - and you have plenty of capacity for a major tournament. Wembley is already demonstrating its position on the world stage by hosting two Champions League finals in three years, and being a regular venue now for NFL games and every finals in all codes of sport.

But London is not the only city experiencing such a change in its footballing infrastructure. Within the space of nine months the face of football in Stockholm has changed beyond belief. The story of urban development in the capital of Sweden is echoed in many cities around the globe. Football stadiums are today the key to such huge development projects, forming cornerstones in the planners' projects. New stadiums are rarely built nowadays in the traditional locations where access is poor and there is little opportunity for big brands to prosper through tapping into football fans' disposable income.

Look at some of the new, great stadiums around the world. The Amsterdam ArenA, Stade de France in Paris and almost every stadium in the USA. All located in areas away from the city centre, initially in the middle of a barren wasteland, but today in the middle of new cities of entertainment.

Restaurants, shopping centres, hotels and indoor areas are now as commonplace around football stadiums as rows of terrace houses and pubs were 50 years ago.

But likewise, while we might lament the passing of some iconic stadiums like Highbury, The Dell and Roker Park, how many Bolton Wanderers fans wish to swap The Reebok with Burnden Park, Swansea City fans Liberty

Stadium with The Vetch Field, or Brighton & Hove Albion fans their brand-new stadium at Falmer with the soulless charm of the Withdean? Progress is the only way forward for teams that genuinely want to compete at the highest level both domestically and overseas.

Is it any wonder that the "smaller" teams who are now making a real impact on the Premier League are those who have swapped cramped city-centre locations, with crumbling terraces, overflowing toilets and no corporate facilities? Southampton, Hull City, Leicester City, Swansea City and to an extent (in terms of longevity in the Premier League) Stoke City. In the Championship, four sides have enjoyed life in the Premier League since moving to a new stadium.

While Arsenal, Sunderland or Manchester City fans may have been up in arms about their respective moves to new stadiums, the huge increases in match-day commercial revenues and the subsequent improvements in the quality of the team has been all too clear to see. Well, certainly for Arsenal and Man City anyway. You only have to look at the constant talk coming out of Anfield, Goodison Park, Stamford Bridge and Tottenham Hotspur about their prospective stadium plans to know how important commercial revenues are in order to compete with one's footballing peers.

At the start of the 2012 Swedish football season, the three biggest clubs located in the capital city looked forward to a final season in their old stadiums. The Råsunda, Olympiastadion and the Soderstadion had each had time called on them and their respective clubs, AIK, Djurgårdens and Hammarby, would soon be moving to brand spanking new arenas (the word stadium is so twentieth century), thus giving them an opportunity to compete domestically with the new force in Swedish football, Malmö, Allsvenskan champions in 2010, 2013 and 2014 after four years since moving to their all-mod-cons Swedbank Stadion. It seems football across Europe is all about progress on and off the pitch these days.

The Råsunda was the first to close, hosting its last game in November 2012 when SCC Napoli were the visitors for a Europa League match. AIK's new home, just a few hundred yards to the east, had already opened and hosted its first game when England were humbled by Zlatan Ibrahimovic in a friendly against Sweden. A retractable roof, air conditioning, wide concourses, a huge TV screen hanging down from the ceiling and a perfect view from every seat is what fans today want, not cramped, uncomfortable wooden seats with poor sightlines. Heck, the stadium had even produced its own sausage. Welcome to the future of European football, welcome to the Friends Arena.

Six months later and as I passed the ground on the high-speed, high-cost train from Stockholm Arlanda I could see the development work continuing around the stadium at a pace. The Mall of Scandinavia will rival the shopping cathedrals of Westfield in London. Hotels are springing up, keen to take advantage of the Football Tourist and transport links are being improved to bring fans from the city centre.

In an all-too-familiar story, improvements off the pitch have led to a rise in fortunes on it. AIK, traditionally one of the Swedish powerhouses, had endured a torrid time in recent years after winning the double back in 2009. In fact, it is a common trait in Swedish football that Allsvenskan champions struggle to defend their title. That may be because the summer season means that by the time the campaign restarts each year, the best players have been poached by bigger teams in Europe.

The 2015 season, their first in the new Friends Arena, AIK finished as runners-up to Malmö FF. Their reward next season is a place in the Europa League. But most importantly for the club, attendances were up by 32 per cent at 18,900. Their 43,466 for the game against Syrianska in April was the biggest in the Swedish season by nearly 20,000.

Alas, the story hasn't been the same for their bitterest rivals across town. Hammarby IF are still fighting to climb out of the second tier of Swedish football after relegation from the Allsvenskan in 2009. Despite being one of the best-supported sides in the whole country, constant debate about the future of their ground has distracted their efforts. The Söderstadion, located in Johanneshov, always has the feeling of being an afterthought, shoehorned in between office space, a motorway and the ice hockey stadium, although it has had the honour of hosting the 1987 Bandy World Championship final – you can't get a much higher honour in terms of ice-based ball sports.

According to Setanta Sports (remember them, kids), the stadium was listed as the eleventh-noisiest stadium in the world, beating such stadiums as the Nou Camp, San Siro and even the Dripping Pan.

The move to the Tele2 Arena wasn't so much an upheaval as a minor diversion. For those familiar with the area in the south of the city centre you simply come out of the stadium, do a right, walk past the shopping centre, the world's biggest spherical building, and the shiny new stadium is right in front of you. Prior to their relocation in July 2013 they welcomed around 8,500 for home games at the Söderstadion; now that figure is around 40 per cent higher. Alas, it wasn't all champagne and roses after the move. On the 19th September 2013 the match between Hammarby IF and GAIS was suspended after 57 minutes following crowd trouble. About 50 home fans made their way up to the area above the away fans and started throwing objects down on them. The referee took the teams off as the security team tried to restore order. The game eventually finished, but GAIS filed an appeal for the game to be awarded to them, and although this was denied, Hammarby were heavily fined and ordered to play two games behind closed doors.

Hammarby wouldn't be rattling around the new place all alone. A deal had been done with Djurgårdens IF to join the "New Stadium Party" during the 2013 Allsvenskan. If there is a stadium that oozed history more than the Stockholms Stadion then I have yet to hear about it. Of course it is totally unsuitable for a club with lofty ambitions such as Djurgårdens IF, and finally the Swedish Football Association had given them notice to conform to new ground regulations, which is why they were finally moving south to share the Tele2 Arena mid-season.

But on a warm summer's night in late May with the stadium bathed in sunshine it was to be a perfect venue for my European adventure. The home side had spent far too long at the wrong end of the Allsvenskan. Ten years previously, in 2005, they made their last appearance in the Champions League and since then the closest they had come to any honours was a defeat on penalties in this season's Svenska Cupen final to Göteborg just a few days before I rolled into town. What made it even worse was that the Järnkaminerna were experiencing the season from hell in the Allsvenskan, propping up the 11 other teams with just two wins so far in the season.

Stockholm is like a fourth home to me, after London, Lewes and Copenhagen. Oh, and Zurich, Munich, Paris and New York. In fact anywhere where work pays for my travel, hotel, food and drink.

Wherever I lay my passport, that's my home. Work trips to Stockholm are always met with a big smile. Yes, the train from Arlanda Airport is an eye-watering £50. Yes, a decent meal here will set you back the best part of £50, and yes, a beer can be a wallet-busting £9. But just look around. The city bustles during the day with beautiful people going about their business with a smile on their faces. In the summer time there is simply no better place to be.

My excitement at being asked to go to Stockholm and deliver some consultancy was perhaps too palpable. Were the "woops" up and down the office, and high-fiving the Chief Executive, completely necessary? Perhaps not, but of course I had an ulterior motive. With each round of games spread over a weekend, the chances of getting an opportunity to see a Djurgårdens game during midweek was incredibly rare indeed. So as luck would have it, the fixtures had thrown up a Monday night game exactly when I was going to be there – what were the odds of that?

I delivered the best ever training session, full of passion, enthusiasm and knowledge about the dangers lurking in every corner of the internet for Brand Owners. I didn't need a round of applause as thanks (although I did of course stay for an encore); I had a press pass for the best stadium in the world. Five o'clock in the afternoon came and I was on my way, walking across the centre of the city to the ground, enjoying the beautiful sunshine. There is no finer city in the world than Stockholm in the sunshine. The water glistens, the nights are short and the beautiful people take every opportunity to de-robe. And the only thing better in the world than a semi-naked Swede is a group of semi-naked Swedes, enjoying an early evening dip in the water. Hard as it was to continue on my travels across the city from the waterside fun, I had a game to get to.

The crowds weren't out in force to watch the game as I approached the stadium. At the gate I was met with a big smile and a firm handshake from their press officer, who had been awaiting my arrival with anticipation. Apparently I was the first English visitor to the club for many a year. Not only did he place the press pass around my neck like an Olympic Gold Medal, but he also slipped me a free drinks voucher and pointed me in the direction of the neon sign that simply said "bar". I was already Djurgårdens' biggest fan. Despite my previously stated love for all things Himmelsblått (Malmö FF) and Gnaget (AIK), tonight I was an honorary Järnkaminerna. I was here to pay my respects to the Grand Old Lady of Sweden, the most historic football stadium in the whole of Scandinavia, the Stockholms Olympiastadion.

Everywhere you looked around the stadium, you could feel history oozing out. Grand entrances, century-old turnstiles and two iconic towers at one end of the ground. The canopy that once protected the Royal Family and dignitaries at the Olympic Games and the original steps that led up to the Olympic flame were all still here, although their uses were more functional these days.

Stadion, as it is known to its friends, already had its place in history assured long before DIF were due to depart in May. Built for the Games of the V Olympiad in 1912, very little in the design of the stadium had changed in the past century. The wooden benches, the gothic-style brick entrances that would look more in keeping with a castle, the elaborate entrance to the arena at one end – all remain as they were. The games weren't the most memorable in history, although they did have their moments. Alas, it is doubtful that anyone who witnessed the drama of the 1912 Tug of War competition is alive today. The event, which is still the shortest ever held in the Olympics' history, was completed in the Stadion from start to finish in less than five minutes when Sweden beat Great Britain 2-0, these being the only two competing nations, to take the Gold medal. The stadium is also famous for being one of a few in the history of the modern games to have held events in two separate Summer Games when in 1956 it hosted the equestrian events for the Melbourne Olympics due to quarantine regulations concerning the transportation of the horses.

Although the football club would be saying goodbye to the stadium, they hoped that the move to the south of the city would give them an upturn in fortune. The last golden period for DIF came a decade ago when the team won three Allsvenskan Championships in four years, including the domestic double in 2002 and 2005. With the expansion of the Champions League they had hoped that they could build on the domestic success in Europe. Once again, however, the Swedish summer season timing meant the champions had to wait a full eight months before they could play in the competition, by which time any momentum they had was broken, and key players had been snapped up by the time it started. In 2003 they fell at the first hurdle to Partizan Belgrade while three years later they lost to the Slovakian side MFK Ružomberok, proving the catch-22 nature of the competition for the Swedish League – no progress means no prize money or TV revenues to keep their best players or invest in the squad, meaning they cannot challenge for the title to keep their place on the gravy train.

Since their last honour back in 2005 the club have floated around the lower mid-table in the Allsvenskan. There have been far too many false dawns, the appointment of various new coaches (eight since 2004) having failed to make any progress in waking the sleeping giant. Seeing arch-rival AIK win the double in 2009 was a bitter pill to swallow, but perhaps the move to the Tele2 Arena may well see the rise of the blue half of the city once more.

Despite another disappointing start to the Allsvenskan season (read "crap") which had seen them take only eight points so far, seven of which had come in the past three games including a point in the first ever Stockholm derby in the Friends Arena, the club nearly had something to cheer just a few days prior to my visit. Out had gone coach Magnus Pehrsson to be replaced by Norwegian Per-Mathias Høgmo, and he had steered the club to their first Svenska Cupen final in eight years. Despite going into the game against IFK Göteborg as underdogs, DIF had fought tooth and nail to take the game to extra time and then penalties. Unfortunately, the Änglarna from Göteborg took the title after spot-kicks, but the contest gave the fans reason to believe that they would lift themselves out of the wrong end of the table, especially as the majority of sides were separated by just a few points and so a win or two could take them up into the European spots in just a week or two.

Of course the other reason to be here was to enjoy the Djurgårdens Ultras in action (in a positive sense) and with 15 minutes to go before kick-off against Kalmar FF they didn't disappoint, putting on an excellent pre-match display that saw them all swap flag designs mid-act in a move that Paul Daniels would have been proud of. How on earth they get these sorts of thing right on the night is beyond me, especially as the extent of our "tifosi" displays in England involves holding up bits of coloured cards at an unspecified time, which invariably looks a bit shit compared to what we see on the continent.

Any Football Tourist will tell you that Swedish football is the best in the world. Why? Because when all other football travelling options are exhausted at the end of the season in May, the Swedes are just getting going. Despite coming into this game against Kalmar propping up the rest of the league, The Iron Stoves wanted to give the fine old stadium a final few weeks to remember. The visitors from Småland in the south-west of Sweden came into the game just one point outside the European spots, although having scored only 12 goals in their opening 10 games didn't really suggest they were the most attacking team to watch.

With hope in their hearts the home side began the game with some purpose, having discovered their mojo with the first real appearance of the Stockholm summer a few weeks ago. With some cool, calm defending that belied the fact they had shipped an average of over two goals per game so far this season, and some good movement from the pacey front two Fenzullahu and Jawo, the home side looked the ones challenging for a European spot rather than Kalmar. Fifteen minutes into the game and they had their reward for their new-found belief. Midfielder Martin Broberg's ball over the top of the Kalmar defence saw Amadou Jawo outpace his markers and beat the keeper with ease from 10 yards. The Gambian was a constant thorn in the side of the visitors, playing on the last defender, looking for the ball over the top. Kalmar came back into the game, with the Brazilian Romário pulling the strings and forcing the home keeper Kenny Höie into action on frequent occasions to clear his lines.

The second half saw the teams welcomed back onto the pitch with a display of flares from the Ultras on the far side of the pitch. Laws introduced in Sweden back in 2011 decreed that the game couldn't restart until they were all extinguished which just encouraged them to light a few more throughout the half, resulting in a stern PA announcement that probably said something like "don't go back to fireworks once they have gone out" or "don't gargle petrol when holding a flare".

Despite forcing some early corners, Djurgårdens didn't have that cutting edge needed to build on their first-half lead. Although they managed 14 shots in the game, less than half were on target.

What they needed was a play-maker, a false nine to coin a modern phrase, someone who could dictate the rhythm of the game. A player like Teddy Sheringham in his prime perhaps. Now funny you mention Teddy, because young Edward, as Cloughie used to call him, had a very productive season in these parts back in 1985 and enjoyed his time in the Swedish capital – and who wouldn't? Stockholm is a fantastic city to relax in and I am sure Teddy made full use of his Saarf London persona in the bars and clubs of Gamla Stan.

With 10 minutes to go, Martin Broberg should have doubled the lead when he headed over from six yards and then broke the offside trap to surely seal the victory but blazed high and wide. It hadn't been the best night for him, but for the team as a whole it had been a performance that would give them confidence for the battles ahead. Relatively assured at the back, positive going forward. No Bayern Munich but certainly no Allardyce-confused West Ham United.

When the clock hit 90 minutes the fans on the far side of the stadium unfurled a banner: "Djurgården – we're gonna live forever" [Vi kommer att leva för evigt]", accompanied by a rousing verse of the club's hymn: "Sing for old Djurgår'n. Sing for old Djurgår'n now, sing by heart sing! Only club in the world that is forever as young!"

The three points won't give them immortality but it did take them up five places in the table, which on a beautiful Stockholm night is about as good as life could get for the blue side of the city. I headed down to the side of the pitch, using my access-all-areas pass to walk on the track that was seeped in so much history. As the players left the pitch they seemed almost blasé about their surroundings. To them, football is a job, a pay cheque, a way of life. Today the Olympiastadion, tomorrow the Tele2 Arena. History to them is all about appearances and goals, not stadiums.

I stayed in the stadium until stewards started yawning and tapping their watches. With the sun only just setting over the stadium I doffed my proverbial cap to all those who had gone before me and wandered off to see if the beautiful people were still skinny dipping in the cool waters.

"Closing time. So gather up your jackets, and move it to the exits. I hope you have found a Friend."

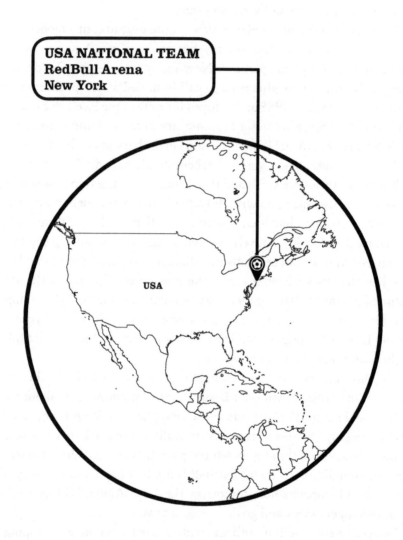

USA NATIONAL TEAM
RedBull Arena
New York

USA

I was very disappointed not to see anyone
dressed as Uncle Sam, Bill Clinton
or The Statue of Liberty.

9. Field of Financial Dreams

"Stu. I've got an idea."

That's how it always starts. Dave was keen for this book to break a few boundaries. Being a Football Tourist who is guided by a work schedule means that on occasions I end up in the same places time and time again. I'm not bemoaning my good fortune but there are only so many times you can see the same teams in Copenhagen, Stockholm or Munich. And New York, so it seemed.

My twice-yearly trips to the Big Apple tend to occur in the "soccer" season (funny that) although there is little option apart from a trip across the Hudson into the wastelands of New Jersey for a game at the RedBull Arena. That will change in 2015 when New York finally gets a team it can really call its own with the expansion of the MLS. Although many have lobbied for the New York Cosmos to be allowed to take their place again at the top table of American Soccer, it's actually a new franchise that will be joining Orlando City Sporting Club in the 2015 MLS: New York City Football Club.

The expansion rights for the franchise were purchased in a joint bid by Manchester City's owners and the New York Yankees. The world's richest football club and the world's most valuable sporting brand. That's one hell of a partnership. Initially playing at the Yankee Stadium, the club will no doubt gain favour through their association with major commercial partners in bringing some of the biggest names in the sport to town, both in terms of opposition in exhibition games but also in "marquee" signings such as the deal to bring in David Villa from Atlético Madrid and Frank Lampard, released by Chelsea at the end of the 2013/14 season. While every club has to work within a salary cap, this season being a maximum of $3.1million, they are able to offer a "Designated Player Rule" or the "Beckham Rule" that enables a team to pay whatever they want to certain players, although the first $387k counts towards the salary cap. This enables teams like New York City to bring in a maximum of two "designated players" such as Big Frank and Villa.

But back to the present and Dave's plan. My work trip had bizarrely coincided with the very weekend when the US national team would be playing their final FIFA World Cup warm-up games before heading down to Brazil. The first of the two games versus Turkey was being hosted at the RedBull Arena. Could I go? Should I go? Of course I would, with my permission slip duly completed by my wife, boss and publisher. Dave sensed that me simply copying and pasting the chapter from *The Football Tourist* on a trip to New Jersey wasn't really what JK Rowling would do, so he gave me some publishing insight.

"What about if you also take in a baseball game while you are there and do a bit of comparing and contrasting?" You can tell his daughter has started nursery with language like that – next up he will ask me to send him the match programme as part of Friday's Show and Tell over at In Bed With Maradona Towers. Who was I to argue with him?

The last time I was over in New Jersey to see a game, I watched the RedBulls lose to SC Kansas along with a few hundred other fans. Less than a thousand others had bothered to make the journey to the wastelands of Harrison. As kick-off approached, ticket scalpers were literally giving their wares away. Unfortunately, despite all of the marketing dollars of the RedBull machine, a small matter of the New York Yankees playing across the Hudson and up into the Bronx was more important. Despite playing over 75 games at home every season, an average of over 40,000 fans head for the home of baseball for each game. Soccer in America may be the fastest-growing spectator sport, but it still has a long way to go to get the same spectator engagement as the MLB (or ice hockey, basketball and American football). However, this time around it promised to be so different. Americans are the most patriotic bunch on earth, immensely proud of their nation, and so any opportunity to show their support for Uncle Sam and they are all over it.

With that in mind, it did beg the question why they chose to play the game in a 25,000-all-seater arena while just a few miles to the north sat the 82,500-capacity MetLife stadium, empty. Tickets were like gold dust and my hopes of getting a ticket in normal circumstances were as likely as John Terry keeping his civvies on when there was an award ceremony. But I knew a man who knew the system and within minutes of the tickets going on sale, Andy Mack had procured some prime tickets. Andy Mack, Mr Team USA. Along with everyone's favourite Englishman in New York, Luge Pravda, our plan was to take in a few of the drinking highlights of Harrison (and trust me, there aren't many) pre-match before we marched to the ground, chanting "USA, USA, USA" all the way.

However, the beauty of social media played its killer hand once again. Within a few minutes of announcing my arrival plans, a fellow owner of

Lewes FC's worldwide community got in touch and invited us to a tailgate party and then a march to the ground. It appeared I had stumbled upon on the American Outlaws, one of the two main grounps of supporters of the national team.

Once again the US team head into a major championships with their heads held high. With the development of US players and their continuing export to European leagues to play at the highest level, it is only a matter of time before they make their mark on the world stage. Under the legend that is Jürgen Klinsmann, they have a coach who has not only played at the highest level of the game, but has also managed the German national team back in the 2006 FIFA World Cup. While qualifying performances were good, and optimism was high, the brutal axing of fans favourite Landon Donovan has divided public opinion on the German in a similar way to Fabio Capello's decision four years earlier to exclude David Beckham from the England squad for the South African FIFA World Cup.

Although Beckham was one of the biggest brands (since when did they stop being just players?) in world football in 2010, he had peaked as a player in 2010 and public sentiment was the main driver behind the emotion for his inclusion on his fourth World Cup. However, in the case of Donovan, his impact on the US game can never be overlooked even today. He's got 156 caps, 57 international goals and has scored as often at World Cups as Ballon d'Or winners Lionel Messi and Cristiano Ronaldo combined, as *FourFourTwo* magazine observed. There has been previous between Donovan and Klinsmann which stemming from his unsuccessful spell playing for Bayern Munich when the German was in charge in 2009. In his place, Klinsmann drafted in 19-year-old Julian Green who had been playing for the past few years for Bayern Munich reserves. That's reserves . . . not first team. Armed with these facts you can perhaps understand the outcry even more.

My plan had been simple. Arrive in New York at 10.30am, taxi to hotel, walk across the street to the PATH train at the World Trade Center and 15 minutes later I would be joining the American Outlaws at their tailgate party and march to the ground. Simple. Alas, two things got in the way. First, I was distracted by Nicole Scherzinger in the arrivals hall at JFK. A baseball cap and dark sunglasses were supposed to dumb-down attention but the fact she was wearing what could only be described as a ripped body stocking covered only with a pair of hot pants sort of gave the game away. That and the fact she was with Lewis Hamilton. A moment's distraction caused me to miss my case going round the carousel, meaning by the time I got out of the terminal all the taxis were gone. Finally I got to Manhattan, dropped my bag and went to the PATH. No trains at the weekend. WTF? There's a major sporting event on and one of the main transport links is closed for engineering work. Obviously been taking lessons from London Underground on that score.

I met up with Luge and Andy for a swift beer in the shadow of the Empire State Building before getting a train from 33rd Street. We were joined en route by Andy's mate Alexi who had come prepared for the short journey with a Starbucks cup full of Sambuca, as you do in these parts, and were soon making the short walk from Harrison station to the RedBull Arena. Now, I have been chastised in the past for being rude about Harrison, New Jersey, home of Daisy Fuentes, everyone's favourite Cuban (or is it just me), but it really is a desperate place on the eye. I'm sure it has some nice bits, but it's no Hoboken. For now it is simply the alighting point for thousands of football fans.

I was very disappointed not to see anyone dressed as Uncle Sam, Bill Clinton or The Statue of Liberty as we entered the stadium, nor being given big foam hands with "USA, Number 1" on. Instead we were faced with queues a mile long for beer on the concourse. The US population is wising up and their palette is maturing. We could have bought our two pints of Coors Light (with ID of course) without any queue at all but who wants that these days? It's all about Goose Island, Honkers Ale or Patriot Ale. Twenty minutes, and three Nathan's hot dogs later we had our beers and headed up to the seats just in time to see the teams emerge at 2.03pm (once again, kick-off time in the US simply means what time the teams may come out of the tunnel).

USA 2, TURKEY 1
Sunday 1st June 2014 – RedBull Arena

In the grand scheme of events this was just a win in a friendly game against a team significantly lower in the FIFA rankings. I'm sure Turkey fans or observers would point out it was the end of a long European season, it was a hot day and they had flown thousands of miles across the world to play three games, of which this was the last. In other words, could Turkey actually be arsed? But that would be hard on the US, who tried to take the game to the visitors but were often frustrated by their delaying and unsporting tactics.

The US team had pace, played good football to feet and used the modest strengths of certain players. None more so than Jozy Altidore up front, who has had a relatively disappointing spell at Sunderland with just one goal in 30 performances, yet put him in a US shirt and he is a world beater. "Like a good Emile Heskey?" suggested Andy Mack. I'd probably not go that far but the Turkish defence had no idea how to handle him. He had a goal disallowed for a non-existent foul on the keeper and created havoc when running at the defenders.

But it wasn't the physical approach that led to the opening goal. A smart one-two between Fabian Johnson and Michael Bradley in the 26th minute saw the ball bounce kindly to Johnson and he volleyed home. Cue some wild celebrations, fist pumping and "Turkey, you suck my balls" shouts from the fans around us.

At the far end Everton's Tim Howard was rarely troubled and had to deal with the continuing threat of Turkey players throwing themselves to the floor in the area rather than shots on target. Before he collapsed with boredom he was replaced at half-time by Villa's Brad Guzan. At the other end, the Turkish keeper Onur Kivrak seemed to be flapping at everything and was at fault for the second in the 52nd minute when he failed to intercept a ball across the six-yard box and the ball hit Clint Dempsey rather than the other way round and rolled into the empty net.

We made the call to go and get a final beer. Perhaps we delayed our venture downstairs by a minute too long because "beer marshals" had been deployed to stop anyone new joining the queue. I didn't know whether to laugh or cry at the need to have such people. I could rant on here about how it is harder to buy a beer than a handgun in some places but that's for another time.

Turkey did get themselves a consolation goal in the 90th minute, although to me the decision to award a clear penalty for handball on the line by Jeff Cameron summed up the ridiculous performance by the referee. Since when has deliberate handball on the goal line not been a sending-off offence? Since when did the excuse "well, it is only a friendly" become a new FIFA rule? Denying a goal-scoring opportunity is still a straight-red-card offence, yet it seemed the referee either didn't know the rules or couldn't be arsed. That probably explains why he was refereeing this game and not on the plane to Brazil. Selçuk Inan converted the spot-kick but it was too little, too late for everyone as we had already made our excuses to the fans celebrating around us as though they had already won the World Cup and made our way back to Hoboken to hustle.

This may come as a shock to you but I am not bad at pool. Heck, I will go as far as saying I am bloody good. So turning up in a pub in a small town in New Jersey with a pool table was too good an opportunity to miss. Luge and I stood to attention as we sung "God Save the Queen" before we purposely lost a few games to Andy and Alexi. Lull them into a false sense of security. Best of three? Let's make it five . . . oh hang on, seven. We kept our powder dry, waiting for the shark to bite our English bait. And sure enough a confident couple stepped forward. We had been joined by a friend of Alexi from college (Katie, Katy, Katherine – I can't remember) who was all over our English accents and the fact we went to school with Hugh Grant, lived in thatched cottages and went to Buckingham Palace for a BBQ every year. She taught us how to say phrases in local dialect, we reciprocated, teaching her to say "jog on, sunshine" just like Ray Winstone, before teaching her the difference between the various English swear-words. We let our opponents win two games, at $5 a game, before we pulled out all the stops and went back on the midnight train to Manhattan $7.50 up EACH! Eat your heart out Newman and Cruise!

Part one of my assignment completed, 24 hours later I was exiting a train at 161st Street Station. Look to your right from the platform and you have the view over the cramped neighbourhoods of the Bronx, the poorest of the five New York City boroughs and home to 1.4 million New Yorkers. Turn your head the other way and the shining cathedral of American sport towers over the houses, casting a very long shadow. Crowds of families were heading to the ground, all decked out in their (Derek) Jeter T-Shirts and the famous NYY caps.

The Yankees are one of the biggest sporting brands in the world – in fact *Forbes* magazine last year calculated that it was the third-biggest brand in the world behind Manchester United and Real Madrid with a value of $520million. Sporting organisations in the US publish attendance statistics that are optimistic to say the least. I'm not calling them liars, but given the fact that so many tickets are available on ticket resale, with a fair percentage at less than face value, I would say they reflect the number of tickets sold rather than the actual attendees. For many sports, many "franchises" and many games, the two figures correlate, but it is the outliers that leave you scratching your head. The Yankees' average attendance is just over 41,000, while over in the MLS at the RedBulls it is just over 19,000. In reality those actually attending games is half or even a third of that number. In my last visit to the Yankee stadium, the official attendance was announced as 39,143. Looking around the stadium at vast swathes of dark blue seats, I would hazard a guess it was no more than 20,000.

But let's go with the official numbers for now. The Yankees play approximately 80 home games in a regular season, with an average attendance of over 41,000 (the fourth-biggest in Major League Baseball) and an average ticket price of $63, meaning that their revenue through the gate every season is close to

$300million. Compare that with the situation over in New Jersey with the RedBulls. An average ticket there is $42, the attendance is around 19,000 (cough) and they play 17 MLS games at home per season – making their gate receipts in the region of $13.6million. In terms of comparison with English football, they would be on a par with a club like Reading or Ipswich Town.

American sports stadiums have the most complex pricing structure known to man. For virtually every game you can buy tickets on the gate although you can end up paying silly money for a view that is no better than someone who has paid a few dollars. While I like the game, I'm not what could be called a fan, so our choice of seats was the cheapest. In baseball terms, these are commonly known as the Bleachers.

The Bleachers are the cheap seats for a very good reason: they aren't seats at all. While some people will have paid $575 for their seats for the visit to the Seattle Mariners, we could have paid $14 for a spot on a bench. In the case of a new stadium like the Yankee Stadium, they are cold metal benches. They are cheap because (a) they are uncomfortable, (b) they are uncovered and (c) they are the furthest away from the action. I have now heard two different stories as to why they are called Bleachers. The first is because they face the sunshine in most instances (as they are opposite the batter) and so the sun bleaches the wooden benches. But I prefer the second one, which is that they are so called because of the amount of bleach used to wash away vomit, as these seats are where the rowdiest and drunkest fans typically sat.

If you are sitting in the Bleachers now, you can only buy one beer per person (at an unbelievable $13 per pint) and they stop serving after the fifth innings of a game. For that reason we "upgraded" our viewing pleasure to the Upper Grandstand for a grand total of 45 cents. Our tickets, bought at 3pm on StubHub, had cost me $14.50 each with a face value of $20. Two weeks earlier back at home, BBC's *Watchdog* programme had run one of their trademark exposés on ticket resale sites, singling out StubHub and Viagogo for selling tickets at a far inflated price in the UK. In the USA you can more often than not pick up tickets on StubHub way below face value.

But back to the beer. Looking around the Yankee Stadium, about a third of the people had a beer at some point during the three-hour game. Let's assume that they had a couple each, as we did. Ten thousand pints of beer at $13 each; that's $130,000 in alcohol sales alone. Serving stopped in other sections of the ground at the end of the seventh innings. I'd say that alcohol sales were dwarfed by the amount of hot dogs, burgers, nachos and all manner of cholesterol-loaded fried food sold. Yesterday, a beer at the USA v Turkey game had cost $10, and there they had curtailed our drinking pleasure as early as the 55th minute. In addition, you had to provide ID (irrespective of how old you looked) and could only buy or "own" two beers at a time.

Still, it could have been worse. The date was almost 40 years to the day after the infamous Ten Cent Baseball Game. In their game against the Texas Rangers on 4th June 1974, Cleveland Indians came up with the idea of offering beer at 10 cents per pint, instead of 65 cents. However, many of the fans over-indulged and during the final innings a pitch invasion led to a riot that led to the game being forfeited due to *"the crowd's uncontrollable rowdiness and because the game could not be resumed in a timely manner"*. At $13 a pop tonight, I doubt that is going to happen again!

The official attendance was 41,529. The unofficial, best guestimate attendance was 15,000, still not bad for a Monday night. However, out of that number, half of the fans aren't watching the game at any one point. "Build it and they will come", so we are told, and that is the ethos adopted in the USA. No country in the world has more stadiums with capacities of 100,000 or more (six at the last count) and in many cases, such as the Michigan Stadium in Ann Arbor, it is full to the rafters every time an American Football game is staged there. There are a few old stadiums still used for major events. Fenway Park in Boston, home of the Red Sox, is one of the oldest but also most treasured. Stadiums seem to have a short shelf-life in the USA, often being torn down and built bigger to match the egos of their owners. They are built with the best of everything and facilities coming out of their ears. But that is the danger – too many facilities and there is so much choice concerning what to eat and drink and so forth that you miss parts of the game while you are queuing for your bucket of garlic fries, foot-long hot dog or dozen doughnuts. This also means that people are constantly moving up and down the aisles, annoyingly blocking your view. Interestingly enough, *Forbes* calculates that the average spend per spectator is $51 at the Yankees, which seems high but is actually just the equivalent of three beers and a couple of hot dogs!

What might surprise you is the revenues the Yankees derive from their iconic logo, which seems to be plastered on so many items across the world. In 2013 the club received revenues of $461million, although the merchandising element was a small fraction. That was a real surprise to me until I understood that all MLB clubs only receive licensing revenues from the metropolitan borough they are located in. I'd assumed they had a global retail network and superb marketing channels, but any sales of Yankees products outside of New York State are shared between the whole of the MLB teams.

Point a camera in front of a fan and they will do anything. Throughout the game we saw things like "Best Dress Fan Cam", "Best Muscles Cam",

"Give Us a Kiss Cam" . . . you name it and the camera zoomed to the crowd to spotlight someone unlucky enough to be caught picking their nose. These distractions are only needed because of the huge number of commercial breaks they have during the TV coverage of the game. It is hard for the players, who have to stand around waiting for play to resume. The game had lasted nearly three hours. In truth, they had probably played for just over an hour. Thankfully, although the brains behind the MLS have tried to find ways in which to make soccer more attractive to megabucks advertisers, even they haven't been able to put ad breaks into the beautiful game (so far).

Now here is a strange rule. There are two divisions of baseball which have different rules. Say that again? They have two divisions that have different rules. Earlier in the season the Yankees were away at the New York Mets across the East River in Queens in the Subway Series. When the Yankees travel to the Mets they have to play by the National League rules, which include the stipulation that all players on the team have to bat (including the pitcher) – similar to the concepts of cricket, yet when the Yankees are at home they play American League rules which means the pitcher doesn't have to bat and they bring in a designated hitter, who doesn't have to field (like a twelfth man in cricket but he can bat). So they could bring in the unfittest, biggest slugger in the game just to hit the ball a few times and do nothing else. The only comparison I can make is if a Premier League team played a Championship side and the rules said that they could have rush goalies when playing at home, but not away. Strange.

With another break in play and a few beers inside of me, I thought of how I could improve the game of baseball. I know my American friends will treat what I am about to propose as tantamount to treason, but perhaps they should ask themselves why only a handful of countries play the game to a decent standard. By adopting these slight rule modifications, I am sure we would soon be seeing Major League Baseball franchises up and down our green and pleasant lands. So here goes . . .

1. Do not allow any fielders in the outfield during the first three innings.
It is highly unusual for a batter to hit the ball at all, let alone into the outfield and not be either caught or run out at first base. So many will not try to strike the ball long, preferring the tactical approach to getting to first base. Bringing some excitement into the game as early as possible by keeping all the fielders "infield" would encourage the batters to hit the ball over the top and run. More hits = more runs = more excitement for the fans. This change was introduced into

limited-over cricket some years ago, with the fielding side only able to have a certain number of players in the outfield, and that is why some teams put their most aggressive strikers of the ball at the top of the batting order.

2. Ban fielders using gloves. Apart from the catcher, is there any reason why the rest of the fielders wear a glove? Surely it eliminates any risk of catching the ball when it's hit into the field. It discourages batters from trying to hit the ball. And it's not as if it's a really hard ball, is it? Once again, take a much heavier cricket ball being smashed around a pitch; all of the fielders have to try and catch the ball with their bare hands. At the moment in baseball, more than 90 per cent of balls hit in the air are caught. Take away the glove and these odds fall to around 50 per cent, thus making games higher scoring AND highlighting the fielding abilities of the players and teams.

3. **Make home runs worth two points.** The ultimate shot in baseball is the home run, the strike of the ball that sees it sail over the perimeter fence and into the crowd. Cue crowd going wild – after all it's what they've paid to see (well, from the home side anyway). Yet such an achievement gets the batter exactly the same as someone who takes 20 minutes stealing bases behind the pitcher's back. Where's the justice in that? So make a home run worth double. Celebrate the achievement, reward the brave.

4. Get rid of the foul line, the line that runs from the batting plate to the corners of the field. Sometimes the difference between success and failure in life can be a matter of millimetres, let alone the inches that Al Pacino waxed lyrical about in *Any Given Sunday*. In baseball the difference between a "play" and a "foul" can be the ball sailing 60/70 yards and then passing an inch over the foul line. That's crap. The ball is still rolling around in the outfield, so bloody play on! Cheated, that's what we are, cheated. So get rid of the foul line in front of the batter so they can swing freer.

5. **One-innings games.** Now this will sound very radical. About the same level of radical as when whichever genius it was first proposed the concept of Twenty20 cricket to the world. Today, the very short form of cricket is the most lucrative one across the globe, making

millionaires out of the best players. Due to the huge distances involved in the US (the distance that the Mariners had travelled for this game was over 2,800 miles) baseball matches tend to be played in a series of four games over four days. So my final idea is to reduce these to three games in three days. Then on the fourth day the game is played as a single-innings competition. Each team simply bats until all of the players are out and then the other team chases down that score. Games could last an hour or several – that's the beauty of it. And instead of counting towards the regular season league places, it would count as a separate competition. This is the next big idea, trust me – Big Bash Baseball.

If you are interested, the Yankees were absolutely stuffed out of sight by the Seattle Mariners. The unofficial 15,000 people in the crowd represented a cross-section of New Yorkers. To our right were two girls and a boyfriend of one (although having seen where his hand/fingers went during the game I would suggest something was going on with both) who were covered with tattoos and ate their own, considerable, bodyweight in every conceivable item that was on the menu. Behind us were two chaps, one who really smelt of urine, who had the most unusual relationship. Joe, the elder one, didn't appear to like anyone, including his friend, John, who had arrived with a bag of three double cheeseburgers, bought from his favourite McDonald's on 121st Street. He couldn't bring him a soda though as Joe hadn't given him enough money. We knew this because he said it every couple of minutes or so.

At one point John said to Joe, "You know I told you Dave was dead last week? Well he isn't. I saw his friend on the subway." Joe's answer was, "Why are you telling me that? I hate Dave, haven't spoken to him for 20 years." "Well, I didn't want you seeing him somewhere and thinking he was a ghost and had been sent to haunt you."

As the game entered the final death throes for the Yankees, only the die-hards and tourists were left in the stadium. It was a fitting moment to end my assignment here. Because this time next season I could be sitting in this very seat watching Big Frank and Dave Villa playing on the hallowed Yankee turf. As a spectator the experience of watching football in the Yankee Stadium will be awful. At least half of the stands will be further away from the action than at the Olympic Stadium.

Assignment completed, filed in triplicate Mr Publisher. I await your next instruction.

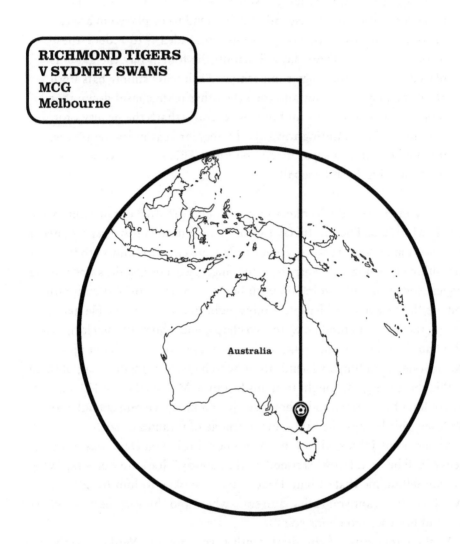

**RICHMOND TIGERS
V SYDNEY SWANS
MCG
Melbourne**

Australia

**No dramas re. lack of sport. Forgot that there
is AFL on at the G on Friday. Swans will be
kangarooing the Tigers.**

10. Men in Tight Shorts

For the past seven years I have enjoyed a fair bit of work travel. Copenhagen, Stockholm, Zurich, Munich, Paris and New York have been regulars on the agenda. While I can never complain about being given the opportunity to travel, and even live abroad, you get to a point where you have seen and done everything in these cities. And by "everything" I mean watching sport, specifically football. In my two years living in Copenhagen, I managed to get to over 30 different Danish clubs. I could tell you which grounds have the best sausage, the cheapest beer and, of course, the best-looking fans. When the football wasn't on during the long winter break I tried handball, ice hockey and Swedish long ball. Needs must sometimes.

Then in the space of a week we acquired two new companies. The powers that be had got out the cheque book and found a couple of bargains. Not just hop-on-a-plane-for-a-day-trip companies either. We were talking Business Class, champagne-fuelled, chauffeur-driven travel. Goodbye Paris with your confusing Metro system and Zurich with your ridiculously priced vanilla Lattes; (adopts Leslie Philips voice) hello Singapore and Melbourne. The Current Mrs Fuller was very excited. "Wow – the two street circuits in the Formula 1 calendar. When are we going?" She rarely raises an eyebrow these days over my work trips, knowing the hardships I have to endure by only travelling around Europe in Economy and sleeping in four star hotels. But these two are game changers. "If you even suggest to me you are travelling out there when the Grand Prix are on then I will block access indefinitely to the bottom drawer." She knows how to make a man weep.

When I was asked, I reluctantly agreed to spend a week with our new work colleagues on the other side of the world, introducing them into our company ways, warning them who they should not upset, and explaining how to use the internal phone system. That would warrant a 21,000-mile round trip to the other side of the world I'm sure.

Our HR Manager was worried that I might get lost on the way so the firm provided a chaperone for the trip. Haydn is Mr England. Not in a tattooed, jumping-on-tables-singing-"No Surrender"-in-an-Irish-Bar sort of way, but in your shoot-anything-that-moves-on-his-farm-and-then-cook-it sort of way. A former chef, he likes a nice drop of red, will eat any part of a dead animal and once dated royalty. In a nutshell, you can never get bored of spending an hour in his company, let alone 27 hours flying 40,000 feet above the earth.

We were relatively restricted by the dates and times we could travel, only being able to spend a week away from our respective families. I'm never particularly good with jet lag, and with a World Cup taking place on the other side of the planet it was bound to be a difficult time in adjusting to what day of the week it actually was. But the main problem I found when trying to plan our week was the simple lack of sporting action in Melbourne.

Sport and Melbourne go together like Great White, Funnel Web and shrimps on the barbie. The city boasts the world's biggest cricket stadium, the 100,000-plus capacity MCG; a 56,000-all-seater stadium, the Etihad, with a retractable roof; an inner-city Grand Prix circuit which hosts one of the few Formula 1 road races every year; one of the four Grand Slam tennis complexes; and a further 30,000-seater stadium, the AAMI Park, which is used for football and rugby. You can't walk very far in the compact city before you stumble upon a stadium. There aren't many times of the year you can arrive in the state capital of Victoria and not find a game or event. That is except in the third week of June, when we were there. Bonzer, as they say in these parts.

Just 48 hours prior to our arrival the Wallabies had hosted the French in the second of a three-test Rugby Union series in the unpopular Etihad Stadium, no more than a Wilkinson drop-kick from our hotel in Bourke Street. Less than 28,000 watched one of the dullest games of rugby ever seen in these parts as the Wallabies won 6-0. The low attendance wasn't particularly surprising considering the background to the stadium.

The Etihad Stadium has been controversial since it first opened in 2000, not only due to issues with the pitch but also due to the relationship the owners, a fund management company, have with the major tenants, the Australian Football League (the oval-ball variety). Although the original deal was to see ownership transfer to the AFL in 2025, numerous lawsuits have seen a rather large wedge driven between the two parties. The owners are certainly getting their money's worth out of the stadium at the moment, in a similar way to how the FA are prostituting Wembley Stadium at any opportunity. The stadium hosts five home clubs in the AFL, the occasional Rugby League and Union games including matches in the 2003 Rugby World Cup and British Lions test matches, international cricket (it was the first stadium to host an "indoor" international back in 2000) and concerts galore. However, the record attendance was for a sport of a completely different kind when over 70,000 squeezed in the stadium to praise God at a Catholic mass in November 2000.

Still, there would be time for a tour of the Melbourne Cricket Ground, or the "G" as they refer to it. Every four years on Boxing Day, England walk out onto the pitch for their ritual humiliation in front of over 100,000 fans. When full, it is as close to the Coliseum in Roman times as you could get. Now here is a lesson for the ECB back home. The reason why it is full is not just because the Aussies take any advantage to rub our noses into the dirt, but because they sell significant numbers of tickets at reasonable prices. For instance, a ticket to see England v Australia at the MCG in the 2015 ICC World Cup set you back £20. A ticket to see Essex play Kent in Colchester (not even their main country ground) is £29 when bought in advance. Want to see England play in a One Day International this summer against India? Well, that would be (a minimum) of £55 sir.

But back to the woes of being sport-free. A tour of the best cricket ground in the world was little consolation for our efforts and quite frankly we blamed Tyron and Ed, our new work colleagues from Melbourne. I mean, we would move heaven and earth to get some sport on for them if they pitched up in London. We did of course have the World Cup to console us, and plans were quickly drawn up to watch both the Australia v Netherlands and England v Uruguay games at silly o'clock in the morning.

As we sat in the Emirates lounge at Gatwick we discussed the agenda for the week and the realisation as to how bonkers the schedule was hit home. We were to be away six nights, three of which would be spent on aeroplanes. We would visit four countries in three continents before we arrived back home in 145 hours time. Our strategy was to put our watches in the pocket and simply assume that if we were awake, and not in the office, then it was time for a drink.

Our first stop was in Dubai, a chance for some more food and drink and a catch up on emails. One, among the offers of erectile dysfunction drugs, secret stashes of cash in West Africa and the most comfy trousers I will ever own, was an email from Ed in Melbourne. Ed, despite being born in England, and still having a fair amount of his family still living there, is Mr Australia. So the following email should be read with a suitable Shane Warne-style accent:

"Mate. No dramas re. lack of sport. Forgot that there is AFL on at the G on Friday. Swans will be kangarooing the Tigers. Will sort the tickets, you sort the pots and pies."

I showed it to Haydn, who had spent a few years in Australia in his younger years. He was none the wiser but we were rescued as we sat in our seats for leg two of our journey, from Dubai to Singapore, by an angel in crème and red. Our "personal" stewardess was from Melbourne and as she poured the Lanson Black she translated our missive from Ed.

"He has said that he has got tickets for you to watch Australian Rules Football on Friday night at the MCG. The Sydney Swans, who are quite good, are playing the Richmond Tigers, who aren't. You need to buy the beers and pies."

Our spirits were lifted, and not just because she was leaning right over us. We would we going to the ball after all. Five days to learn the rules, the etiquette and the fan behaviour of a brand new sport. Bring it on. It had the word "football" in and thus it counted as an adventure of a Football Tourist, right? After all, I have a moral obligation to explore all different varieties of the global game and walk away knowing that our version is the best in the world.

Before we arrived in Australia we had the small matter of a day of meetings in Singapore. We arrived in 90 per cent humidity and 34 degrees at 11pm in Changi Airport but the heat and jet lag had to be put aside as we had a match to watch. Our hotel was opposite the famous Raffles Hotel, just around the corner from where I had stayed a few months previously. We needed to find a bar open at midnight that was going to be showing the Germany v Portugal game. One of the most anticipated games in the World Cup, yet here in the wilds of Asia at midnight it was hardly likely that we would find anywhere showing it.

"What about that place there?" Haydn pointed at a bar literally across the road. "Deutsch Fußball-bar – where all those people are standing outside wearing German shirts?" He was right you know, and while the pints of Franziskaner Hefe-Weissbier were almost £15 we were going to the ball, Cinderella. Alas the only spare seats in the house were on a table with a group of young German female students, dressed appropriately for the heat. "Why are you crazy Englishmen here?" (adopt a Heidi Klum accent to get full effect). Before I could answer, Haydn waded in and told them: "We are making a film about the World Cup. We are travelling to a different city every day of the tournament to watch a game and then making it into a documentary." Of course they were smart girls and soon realised that neither of us had a camera. But all of a sudden a real film crew arrived. "There they are. Let me go and do my bit." So off he went, had a word in the female presenter's ear and before you know it Haydn's ruddy face was being beamed across Singapore.

Suitably impressed, the girls bought the next round (and the two after that), buoyed on by the rampaging start by their team against the Portuguese. The girl next to me asked if she could be in our film. I remembered the words of Danny Last at this point, who once said to me "If a girl ever asks you to take her photo then ask her to sign something, then say YES." I could see a whole world of trouble on the horizon here so I made an excuse about not having the right release form on me. She seemed crestfallen. On the next table another girl promised to remove an item of clothing for every goal the German's scored. As Thomas Müller scored his second, and Germany's third just before half-time, she didn't have much left on. "Will she be on your film?" my new friend asked. "Alas, no. We are trying to get a 12 certificate so we cannot show any nudity." "But she has, as you say in England, nice charlies?"

A 3am finish wasn't exactly in the plan, especially as we had a 7am alarm call, but we are consummate professionals and so the following day we put in a sterling performance on behalf of the company before we slumped back into the Business Class lounge at Changi Airport, less than 24 hours after arriving. The thought of another eight-hour flight was made all the better by being greeted by the same air stewardess as we had on our first flight out.

"Hey boys. I didn't know you were staying in Singapore last night. We could have come out with you. I'm sure we could have shown you some sights" (add suggestive wink here). "I bet all you did was go and watch the football with a few beers, right? Shame." We shook our heads and looked at our Emirates slippers like guilty schoolboys.

We should've sensibly tried to get as much sleep as we could on this leg of the flight as we were due to arrive in Australia at 7am, with a full day of work ahead. But the food was too appetising, the wine too full-bodied and the service too attentive so we ploughed on through the night, helped on by the fact the flight had live TV and just happened to be showing Brazil v Mexico and Russia v South Korea. There was always tomorrow night to sleep, after all.

Fast-forward to 7am and we touched down at Melbourne's Tullamarine Airport. We had gone from temperatures in the high 30s to the low 10s. Our perception of Australia was of hot, sunny weather, everyone wearing shorts and having that funny white face paint on. This was therefore a major culture shock. It looked more like mid-winter in Dudley. They never show you that on *Neighbours* do they?

After a short taxi ride to our hotel where we miraculously transformed ourselves from Phileas Foggs to extras from Wall Street (the '80s version) in less time than it would have taken any of the female Fullers to choose a pair of shoes to wear, we headed to meet our new colleagues. First order of the day after some mutual backslapping and sledging (the insulting of each other's mother, not the flying-down-a-hill-on-a-tea-tray-type) was some strong coffee. We have a fair contingent of Aussies in our office in London and when they knew I was heading to Melbourne they all enthused about the coffee. Quite how times have changed. Paul Hogan would have turned in his grave if he heard that. Not that Crocodile Dundee is actually dead although he did turn down the lead in the film *Ghost*, allowing Patrick Swayze (who *is* dead) to gain global fame for his pottery skills.

Melbourne is also the home of the fictitious suburb of Erinsborough, the location of *Neighbours*, which began its TV history back in 1985 (at the same time as *Eastenders* no less). The show was part of my childhood and adolescence – hardly surprising when they thrust Kylie Minogue, Natalia Imbruglia, Holly Valance and Annie Jones (Jane Harris) at you twice a day. Just like when tourists arrive in London, thinking it is like *Eastenders* (where everyone works either in the local pub or on a fruit and veg stall, sleeps with their immediate family and then is a victim or culprit of murder), we obviously assumed that we would be drinking in Charlie's Bar every night and eating in Lassiter's.

As part of our long journey out to Australia, Haydn had devised a true-or-false game based on famous people who may have appeared in *Neighbours* to get us in the Australian mood. I got a crap 3 out of 10. Our stewardess got 8/10 although she was from Australia so that is basically cheating. Go on, have a go yourself . . . answers somewhere near the back:

Emma Bunton or Victoria Beckham
Martin Clunes or Neil Morrissey
Dale Winton or Julian Clary
Matt Lucas or David Walliams
Lilly Allen or Cheryl Cole
Alesha Dixon or Paula Abdul
Shane Warne or Rodney Marsh
Clive James or Michael Parkinson
Tiffany or Sinitta
High 5 or The Wiggles

"So boys, what do you want to do while you we're here?" Ed asked us. Haydn had a list of restaurants he wanted to go to and I had a list of beers I wanted to try in the absence of any sport. I'd already mentioned about wanting to watch the World Cup games somewhere and Ed had already done some research for us, visiting bars close to our hotel and drawing up a short-list of the best places to watch a game. Factoring in that the England v Uruguay game would be kicking off at 5am his list included the Crown Casino, O'Flanagan's Irish Bar and two establishments he was reluctant to expand on called Goldfingers and Xplicit. "They will make sure you come out smiling even if you pommies lose." I assumed that he meant the beer was cheap and the location was perfect to see the sun rise at 7am when the game was finished.

"Typical that the first time I visit Sport City and nothing, NOTHING is on!" I told Ed and Ty, the other owner of the business, over lunch on our first day. "I know . . . well apart from the AFL on Friday." I stopped mid-bite of my burger and asked him to rewind. "Yeah, every Friday mate. AFL is THE sport in these parts". It turned out that the whole city was mad for AFL, with everyone you meet having an allegiance to a team, primarily based on which part of the city you came from.

The current Australian Football League has 18 teams in it, with nearly half of the clubs being based in Melbourne : Collingwood, Essendon, Melbourne, North Melbourne, Footscray, St Kilda, Hawthorn and Carlton. This meant that there were games every week in the city as the teams shared the two main stadiums – The Etihad and the Melbourne Cricket Ground. Two minutes after first telling us we might be able to go to the ball, and with me still holding my burger close to my mouth, Ed delivered the earth-shattering news.

"Yep, looks like we are in luck boys. Friday night, Richmond Tigers are playing Sydney Swans at the Melbourne Cricket Ground." That news made Australia the best place in the world. It turned out that a mutual friend had corporate seats at the MCG which he wouldn't be using, so not only were we going to one of the biggest stadiums in the world but we would be sitting there free of charge with access to unlimited beer and pies. Tough life you may think, and you'd be right.

Because of the logistics of the trip we would only be spending two nights in Melbourne, arriving on Wednesday morning and leaving in the very early hours of Saturday morning, heading to the airport directly after the game at the MCG. It probably wasn't the best idea then to try to work a full day, then have a few beers, some food and stay up for the World Cup games, which kicked off at 2am, 5am and then 8am.

After a superb meal on our hosts at a restaurant called Red Spice Road in the Central Business District and more than a couple of beers I hit the pillow about 11pm, setting my alarm for 1.30am on Thursday morning for the Australia versus Netherlands game. Despite feeling like hell when I woke from two hours sleep, this was a once-in-a-lifetime opportunity to immerse myself in true Australian culture. My plan was to go to a bar and watch the game with some of the locals. Wandering around the centre of Melbourne in the early hours of the morning was a surreal experience. I found Goldfingers, as recommended by Ed. It was a "Gentleman's" Bar. Admission was $20 but for that I would get a free beer, and apparently a free half-time personal show. Hmm, not quite what I was looking for in this instance, so I headed back to the hotel to watch the game in my room just in time to see Tim Cahill score one of the best ever goals in the World Cup.

It was a great performance by the Australians but one that saw them eliminated from the World Cup after just two games. Of course we would be sensitive to the fact when we went into the office. I mean it wasn't as if we had walked in there on our first day with a signed picture of Sir Jonny Wilkinson's drop-kick in the 2003 World Cup Final for the wall or something . . . well, OK we had.

Day two flew by as we trained the team on everything they needed to know and they lapped it up. The evening plan was to meet an old friend of Haydn's, dinner, early night, then up for the England game. Of course the early night bit didn't happen. Drinks followed a trip to one of Melbourne's most famous restaurants, Chin Chin, famous the Southern Hemisphere over for one particular dish. Mention the name to any Japanese person and they will giggle uncontrollably, as the name roughly translates to cock, but there is nothing funny about the Scud City Jungle Curry. Yes, it was the most expensive dish on the menu, but as Haydn's friend Celeste pointed out, that was because it included an insurance policy to indemnify the restaurant in case you sued them for third-degree internal burns. The Scud Chilli hits up to 1.4 million on the Scoville scale, about four times as hot as a Scotch Bonnet. It is fair to say you really should eat this dish with gloves on. An hour later and two sweating Brits were reduced to tears, crying for jugs of iced water.

No alarm clock was therefore needed to get up for the England game. The effects of the dish meant I was fully awake long before kick-off time, although I didn't feel too comfortable in venturing out to find a bar. The pain I was suffering was compounded by Luis Suarez's double strike and England were 99 per cent out. Not that the 1 per cent stopped the chaps in the office from rubbing it in. We were in good company was all that I could say, returning home early with the Spanish.

Excitement levels were rising in the office on Friday. We had two client meetings and at the end of both, talk turned not to the World Cup, or the final game in the Australia v France Rugby Union series, but to the weekend's

AFL (and England's crap performance in the cricket against Sri Lanka). The consensus was that the game we would be seeing would be so one-sided that it almost wasn't worth the home side, Richmond, turning up. The visitors, Sydney, were top of "the ladder", as they called it, while Richmond were just a few points off the bottom of the league. Around 35,000 were expected at the MCG for the game, which we were told was poor, with some games between the likes of North Melbourne or Collingwood attracting double that. But over 30,000 for any sporting event is impressive in my book.

Work done, we obviously headed for a bar. Here's a little tip for you if you haven't ever been to Australia. Don't go up to the bar and ask for a "pint". They look at you blankly. Remember, you are in a different hemisphere, let alone country or continent. Although English is the language of Australia, they have their own metric system which is based around being able to drink the equivalent of a boat (a Schooner) or for the tee-totallers one that is the size of a cooking vessel (a Pot). Doesn't quite have the same ring to it though when bigging up a night out:

"Heavy night last night. Had nine and a half pints" is the right way, rather than "Heavy night last night. Had five Schooners and four Pots."

Three Schooners to the wind (see what I did there), we headed along the Yarra River to the Olympic Park. It was here in 1956 that the Summer Olympic Games were held – well, all but one event anyway. As mentioned previously, because of quarantine regulations, all equestrian events were held five months earlier in Stockholm. The MCG hosted the athletics and a number of the bigger sporting finals, while next door the swimming and cycling were hosted. Today, all the facilities are still in use, along with the tennis stadium, The Rod Laver Arena, that hosts the Australian Open every year. The new kid on the block, the AAMI Park Stadium, replaced the old Olympic Park Stadium and is now home to Melbourne Victory FC and the two rugby teams. Basically, Melbourne has stadiums for everything.

Haydn and I seemed pretty underdressed for the evening, wearing just T-shirts. While this was the middle of winter for Australia, to us a balmy night where the temperature was hovering around the 10 degree mark was warm. We resisted the urge to buy a scarf from one of the unofficial sellers on the way up to the stadium, who hadn't let a simple matter of space affect his pitch. Richmond Tigers was one character too long for his scarf so he had simply dropped the "r" in Tigers.

You approach the MCG from the waterfront, and sitting on top of a hill all lit up it could be one of the seven wonders of the modern world. The stadium is one that not only the Australians can be proud of, but also the sports world. Biggest cricket stadium in the world; hosted the first ever test match in 1877 when England were the visitors; hosted the first ever one day international in 1971 when the West Indies were the opponents; one of the very few stadiums that has hosted an Olympic Games and a Commonwealth Games; the floodlights are the tallest at any sporting venue across the world. The list goes on. While my journey as the Football Tourist was all about the round-ball game, a visit here could never fail to be counted right up there with Wembley Stadium, the Westfalenstadion or The Dripping Pan.

Loaded up with pots and pies (apparently you cannot have one without the other at an Australian sporting match), we settled down to watch the action. About 50 people were running in all directions across the pitch as we sat down. Each team has 18 players, who all have to wear shorts that look like they have shrunk in Stuart Pearce's weekly wash, and those vest -tops that Brits abroad wear in Magaluf. There were eight officials, including the ones dressed as butchers behind the goals, and then there were various coaches and medical people constantly patching up people. In one word, it was BRILLIANT.

I'd been sceptical before I arrived, thinking it would be a cross between Rugby Union, in terms of the kicking game, and American Football in terms of the sheer needless violence. In some ways it was, but with a few little twists that made it all so appealing to watch. So, without spending thousands of words describing all the rules, here are my five highlights of watching an AFL game:

1) There are few sports in the world where at the start of the game you do not all have to be in your own half. In AFL you can basically stand where you want from the first second, meaning anything can, and does, go off in the first seconds of the match.

2) The umpire starts the game by bouncing the ball in the middle of the pitch. And when we say bounce, we actually mean throw it down on the turf and stand well back to see the carnage ensue. If the ball goes out of play then the side umpires throw it in, back to the field of play and over-their-shoulder style.

3) The goals are marshalled by umpires wearing white coats and butcher'-style trilby hats. Their job is to make funny hand signs and wave flags when the ball passes through the posts.

4) You cannot throw the ball – you have to fist or slap it to an opponent. You can kick it and they love a banana kick or two in the game.

5) While we have silly names for positions in our most familiar sports

such as Sweeper, Libero, Silly Mid-Wicket, Flanker and Fly-Half, you have to get your head around Rovers, Ruckmen and Back Pockets in AFL.

The game started with Richmond having all the possession and racing into an early lead, scoring the first goal (a kick between the middle posts that resulted in the umpire waving two flags) in the fifth minute. We were sitting with some passionate Tigers fans, and by passionate I mean completely blinkered in their view. One particular lady, if the referee had listened to her screams (and I mean screams), would have had Sydney reduced to 10 men within the first quarter. Every tackle made by a Richmond player was fair, yet if a Sydney player even looked at a Tigers player it was "illegal", "immoral" and "violent". With less than 10 minutes left of the first half Richmond led by 26 points. An upset was on the cards. But Sydney showed their Championship form with two late goals to reduce the half-time lead to 14 points.

After the obligatory interval refreshments the second half started with the Sydney Swans in rampant form. They scored four goals in the third period to reduce the deficit to one point going into the final quarter. With five minutes to go they took the lead for the first time in the game and never looked back. This was their ninth successive game and while they won ugly, it is all irrelevant when you look at the league table, sorry ladder.

The post-match summary on the AFL website said it all:

"The disappointing crowd of 34,633 was another vote of no-confidence from the Tigers faithful in their team, which battled manfully. Last week's turnout of 22,074 for the clash with Fremantle was the first indication that Richmond supporters were protesting with their feet, with that crowd down more than 18,000 on the same match-up in 2013. The Tigers were handed Friday night matches because of the excitement they generated in 2013, and the meeting with the Swans was as least close on the scoreboard. In the stands, the committed few couldn't create the atmosphere the tight contest deserved."

Sod that – where do we sign up to watch this every week!

Our time in Australia was coming to an end. As we walked back along the bank of the Yarra with Ed we were hatching a plan for a return visit (Asia Cup in January 2015 by any chance) as well as the reciprocal exchange visit to London in December. Our mission was complete – we had integrated the team, the company and the culture in just three days. We were tired beyond belief with just a 27-hour journey in front of us. But it had been a brilliant trip.

We still had the small matter of three World Cup games to watch on our journey back. France v Switzerland and Costa Rica v Italy were enjoyed as we flew at 40,000 feet across Asia on our way to Kuala Lumpur, washed down with some fine wine and fine food.

My initial disappointment at potentially missing out on a game on my first visit to Australia had been replaced with the joy of discovering AFL. I'm sure you will forgive me one chapter where I wander from the path of the beautiful game. Normal service will be resumed in Stockholm next month.

Answers to Neighbours *quiz: Bunton, Morrissey, Clary, Lucas AND Walliams, Allen, Abdul, Warne, James, Sinitta and The Wiggles.*

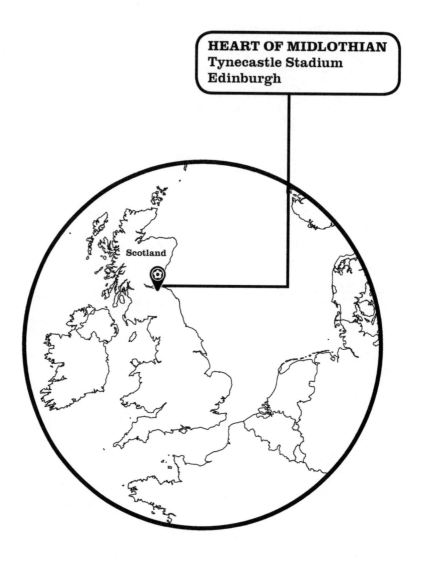

HEART OF MIDLOTHIAN
Tynecastle Stadium
Edinburgh

Scotland

Asking for a pint of Belhaven was like the scene
from *American Werewolf* in London where the two
backpackers enter the pub in the Yorkshire Moors.

11. Community Service

Six years ago I had no idea about the concept of fan ownership. I'd read about the creation of FC United of Manchester, a protest club at the way Manchester United were being owned by the Glazers, and was aware of the huge levels of support that were driving AFC Wimbledon forward from the County Leagues. But I was sheltered from all that – I was in the Premier League bubble after all. Clubs never went into meltdown at that level. Well, bar Leeds United, but if one can believe the media stories that was all down to a fish-tank and mortgaging their future Champions League revenues so that David O'Leary could build a new golden generation of English talent. O'Leary hasn't worked subsequently, ever since the financial realities finally came home to roost and Leeds fell to the third tier of English football.

But football clubs never seem to be in real trouble. Once or twice a season a club would go into administration but the only losers would be those hard-working staff who gave their all to keep the clubs afloat every day long after the players had departed from the training ground in their camouflaged Bentleys and neon Bugattis. The players whose wages had sent clubs like Crystal Palace, Portsmouth and Leeds United to the edge of bankruptcy still got their six-figure salaries every week and if there was any hint they wouldn't get all of their cash they would run to the newspapers and bleat about the hardship of not being able to heat their swimming pool or valet the car every day.

Football fans can be divided into a number of groups, such as the "die-hard fanatics" who believe everything written about their club, the "forum trolls" who will slag off everything their club does, or the "pessimists" who pour scorn on every transfer deal, but as the internet and the number of excellent analytical writers on club's finances has grown – Swiss Ramble or Anders Red for instance – we now have more of an insight into how clubs are being run. Financial governance is the new buzzword. Knowledge is power, the age-old adage goes, and a more in-depth understanding of what types of people are running our clubs, and how, has driven many fans into the newest bucket of fans: owners.

Twenty years ago, fan ownership in English football was almost unheard of. The first club to be owned by the supporters was Northampton Town back in 1992, although it was really Enfield Town that created the model we are familiar with today when they split from Enfield FC in 2001 after a disastrous attempt by a local businessman to push them to the Football League had failed, leaving them penniless and almost homeless. Dismissed as a fad by the football fraternity, fan ownership struggled to gain traction in England, despite its popularity and success overseas. After the 2006 FIFA World Cup we all raved about the German model for footballing success. Tired old stories have since been trotted out when something either goes wrong with football in this country (frequently) or goes right in Germany (frequently):

"World Class modern stadiums."
"Safe standing."
"Highest average attendances in the world."
"Season tickets for less than £100."
"Nice sausages."

All the above are true. You can also add in a strict licensing system which ensures that only clubs that demonstrate financial compliance and governance can take part in the Bundesliga. Any club that over-commits itself financially will find itself plunged down the leagues.

While England has seen one or two notable financial crises, the plight of Portsmouth and Crystal Palace in recent times pales into insignificance compared with the headlines recently in Scotland. The spectacular demise of Rangers and Heart of Midlothian has had a profound effect on the shape of Scottish football, both in positive and negative terms.

For nearly 30 years prior to 2012, Scottish football had been dominated by two clubs: Celtic and Rangers. Since the foundation of the Premier League back in 1975 they have won all but four league championships, 26 Scottish FA Cups and 26 Scottish League Cups. They essentially created a vacuum, with the honours every season realistically being decided in the four or so games the two clubs played against each other. While neither really set European football alight, bar a couple of campaigns such as the 2003 UEFA cup when Celtic lost to Jose Mourinho's Porto in the Final in Seville, the cash from every game they played simply strengthened their domestic position.

Unfortunately, in the case of Rangers, that cash was used to try to control the club's spiralling debts, built up in the footballing equivalent of the arms race. One of the competitors in the two-horserace was lame and had to be put down, starting again at the bottom of the Scottish League pyramid. Local derbies would now be against the likes of Queens Park and Clyde. European football meant a trip across the border to play Berwick Rangers.

The Rangers fans didn't desert the club. While they would hang their head in shame at the brazen attitude taken by the owners in dealing with the financial side of the club, they still supported the team. Home games at the modern Ibrox, built for European nights against the likes of AC Milan, Real Madrid and Bayern Munich, were now hosting the likes of Annan Athletic and Peterhead in front of up to 50,000 fans. Every week a club would essentially be playing in their cup final against Rangers, effectively ensuring their financial survival for another year through those home games. Under the management of Ally McCoist the team simply got on with the job of climbing back up to the Premier League. Two seasons on, two championships claimed, having won 58 of their 72 league games, they are well on the way. However this season they face their sternest test in trying to get out of a division that includes three other old Premier League rivals.

The loss of Rangers from the Premier League has made it easier for Celtic to win the league but on the flip side it has given some of the other teams an opportunity to compete. It is no coincidence that some of Celtic's most impressive European form in recent years has come since Rangers disappeared from the Premier League. They have concentrated their efforts on retaining their title and thus Champions League football, seemingly taken their foot off the gas in the domestic cups, meaning recent domestic cup winners have included Kilmarnock, St Mirren and Hearts.

And there we have the second dilemma in Scottish football. How do we start to solve a problem like Hearts? If any club were positioned to fight for the title of Scotland's second team then it should have been Heart of Midlothian Football Club.

Two years ago life looked good for Hearts fans as they took the field for the Europa League Play-Off against Liverpool at Tynecastle. They had finished the previous season in fifth place but had taken the silverware and city bragging rights by destroying their local rivals, Hibernian, at Hampden Park in the Scottish Cup Final in one of the greatest moments for the fans. A win over your local rivals is one thing, but to demolish them in a cup final with millions watching on TV takes it to a completely different level. Understandably the DVD of that game soon became a popular item in Secret Santa sacks for Hibs fans a few months later.

Talk around Tynecastle was of a push for second spot in the Rangers-less SPL. Dreams were of repeating the 2006 feat of reaching the Champions

League Qualifying Rounds, and nights of hosting more European greats at one of Britain's oldest used football grounds.

Instead, a series of "unfortunate events" off the pitch saw the club lurch from one financial crisis to another in a short period of time. Lithuanian owner Vladimir Romanov, having failed in attempts to buy Dundee United, Dundee and Dunfermline, had taken majority control of the club in 2005, making bold statements about breaking the monopoly that Celtic and Rangers had on Scottish football. On the field it seemed that things were going in the right direction as the club got off to a flyer in the 2005/2006 season. However, Romanov couldn't help but transfer his advice from the boardroom to the dressing room. He underlined his knowledge of the game by sacking manager George Burley after the club had won their first eight games of the season and were top of the Premier League.

This wasn't to be the last time that strange things happened in the dressing rooms in Edinburgh. The Lithuanian's time in charge would see nine managers appointed in just seven seasons, with many of those being ejected through the revolving doors in a similarly brutal way to Burley. All the time Hearts' objective of breaking the Old Firm monopoly on Scottish football was forgotten in a mess of rumour, strange decisions and walls of silence.

During Romanov's control of the club, debt mounted and the complex ownership structure of Hearts failed to deliver any reassurances to the authorities or the fans that it had a viable future. It appeared as if the Lithuanian had absorbed the club into his complicated structure of businesses including Lithuanian Basketball League club Žalgiris, FBK Kaunas, Partizan Minsk and one of Lithuania's biggest banks, UKIO Bankas.

In the summer of 2013 the club, saddled with a debt close to £25 million, and with Romanov absent without leave and his business affairs overseas in tatters, had no option but to file for administration. Their penalty was a 15-point deduction and a transfer embargo. Once again, the playing side (and ultimately the fans) was being punished for a lack of good governance on the administrative side of affairs. Although questions were obviously asked about the owner, many pointed fingers at the Scottish Premier League for failing to get involved sooner. Even the most ardent Hearts fan knew that avoiding relegation from the 2013/14 Scottish Premier League would be akin to climbing Arthur's Seat with both legs tied together while playing the bagpipes.

Football fans are a strange breed of people though. The demise of a football club is not like the collapse of any other business. When liquidation was the only viable option for retail chains like Woolworths or Comet, "fans" of the brand didn't protest or try to form a rescue mission. People saw that there was no future for their business, damaged irreparably by new competitors with more efficient and cost-effective business models. Football clubs, on the other hand, send us all back to times when everything was better. We hanker for moments when money wasn't the sole objective of a club and all we wanted to focus on was the team. But the reality is that most football clubs are not run as a business at all. They are run in an emotional way, in most instances at a loss, with one (or if they are lucky, a few) benefactors putting their hand in their pockets every year. That is all well and good as long as the benefactors do not lose interest or decide that there are better ways to invest their money.

However, this is where fan ownership comes into its own. Legendary Rugby Union coach Clive Woodward once said that he didn't think he could ever improve the England Rugby team by 100 per cent but he did think he could improve 100 things by 1 per cent. That's what fan ownership is all about. It is about 100 people investing £1 rather than one person investing £100. Not literally those figures, but the principle is the same. Shared ownership of football clubs is the future. Sharing the risks, the pain, the opportunity and the satisfaction.

Currently in British football we have a number of clubs that can demonstrate the successes of fan ownership. FC United of Manchester, AFC Wimbledon, Portsmouth, Exeter City, AFC Telford and of course a club close to my heart, Lewes. I know the pain and despair that only a club in serious financial distress can inflict on its fans. Not knowing that your club will be able to play again next weekend, or even if they can, what players the club will be able to call upon. Seeing the dread in the eyes of the club owners as the postman every day delivers more terminal news.

But I have come through the other side, seeing the realisation involved in a club of a different future, one free from crippling debt and a hand-to-mouth existence; a future that is now growing on and off the pitch. That was the emotional roller-coaster that Hearts fans went through in 2014, seeing their team in apparent financial free-fall and enduring relegation before the Foundation of Hearts finally were able to take control of the club. The spectre of administration and the painful memory of the Romanov decade officially ended on the 11th of June 2014 when the Foundation took control of the club. While the road ahead would be tough, the future of the club was finally secure. Fans raided savings accounts, kids broke open their piggy banks and local businesses called in their creditors to invest in the Foundation of Hearts, enabling them to start building for a better future.

Fast-forward six weeks and Tynecastle would be hosting its first ever Petrofac Training Cup game. As they say in the East End of London, "just like my dreams, they fade and die". Instead of welcoming the likes of Gerrard, Suarez, Sturridge and Andy Carroll onto the pitch again it would be the likes of Swinglehurst, McNiff and Carcary who would be lining up for Annan Athletic, currently plying their trade in the fourth tier of Scottish Football, at Tynecastle. This was to be the first meeting between the two sides – an event of such historic proportions that I simply had to be there. Well, the fact I was already in town for the Commonwealth Games was just pure coincidence.

This was to be my first visit to Tynecastle, long overdue having done every other major club in Scotland in the course of my weekends away. It was fair to say that emotions were still running high in Edinburgh about the takeover of the club, not knowing still what the future would hold.

The weekend was the traditional Fuller Family trip to Scotland, with a visit to the Commonwealth Games on the cards to take in the Rugby Sevens tournament, ironically being held at Ibrox. While the girls headed to spot Yuang Guang and Tian Tian at the Zoo, I planned to head down the Dalry Road to find Tynecastle. Yes, it was a cup competition that few of the fans really cared about. Yes, it was still firmly in the cricket season, and yes it was a game that few would ever care about. But for me, it was a new stadium, a chance to see how a fellow club in distress were doing, and the opportunity to immerse myself back into football after a break of some 10 days. I decided to walk down from Haymarket station, following a chap in a maroon scarf, who of course turned out to be wearing a Barcelona trinket rather than a Hearts one and ended up in the shadow of "Auld Reakie", the Caledonian brewery.

GPS coordinates realigned I found Dalry Road and a smattering of proper Hearts fans heading for the game. Thirsty from my long walk I decided to have a spot of refreshment in the Tynecastle Arms. Despite my feeble attempts at trying to disguise my English accent, asking for a pint of Belhaven was like the scene from *American Werewolf in London* where the two backpackers enter the pub in the Yorkshire Moors. I was saved by a man coming in, wearing a pair of Stuart Pearce's Italia 90 shorts, shrunken in the wash, who diverted most people's attention long enough for me to disappear into a dark corner.

A quick trip round the club shop revealed a complete lack of Heart-shaped merchandise or even any jam tarts, although I did manage to boost my collection of football socks with a natty pair of maroon ones. Littlest Fuller would also be impressed that the biggest seller in the shop was club-coloured loom bands that had sold out. My five-minute trip around the retail empire had seen the brilliant sunshine replaced by storm clouds. Welcome to Scotland.

The greeting at the main reception was heartfelt and warm. I was introduced to club officials left, right and centre before being taken on a mini tour of the historic ground. With an hour still to kick-off I wandered around the edge of the pitch, soaking up the history of the ground. Tynecastle today is a mixture of the old and new. Three modern, uniform stands provide comfort and excellent views for the fans, while the Archibald Leitch-built Main Stand where I would be sitting, dating back to 1914, still reminded the fans of former glories. In fact, just a few days prior to my visit, the English Premier League Champions had been in town to play the home side in a celebration of the old fella.

Fans were slowly taking their places in the stands, hoping for a much less dramatic season than 2013/14, starting with a first-round Scottish Challenge Cup game against Annan Athletic. This was to be a new experience for the Hearts fans, having been brought up on a diet of Scottish Premier League football.

The Scottish Challenge Cup, sponsored by Petrofac Training for the 2014/15 season, is an interesting concept that is akin to the Johnstone Paint Trophy in England. Few other leagues in Europe have such a competition that is only open to those clubs who play below the top tier of clubs. All clubs below the Premier League enter the cup at the first-round stage in July, with "wildcard" entries this season in the form of Brora Rangers and Spartans adding some Scottish Junior League spice to the competition. With Hearts, Hibernian and Rangers all in the Scottish Championship (aka the old First Division this season) it may well be the most competitive competition yet.

The odds were firmly in the home team's favour in the local bookmakers shop on Dalry Road. Visitors Annan Athletic's biggest claim to fame was beating Rangers two seasons earlier when they were bed-fellows in the Scottish Third Division. Elected into the professional leagues after the demise of Gretna in 2008, they had made themselves firmly at home as a mid-table club in the fourth tier of Scottish football. They couldn't have asked for a tougher draw in the Challenge Cup, although with both clubs sharing the gate receipts, they would at least get a nice windfall from the game.

HEART OF MIDLOTHIAN 3, ANNAN ATHLETIC 1
Saturday 26th July 2014 – Tynecastle

When Hearts opened the scoring in the eighth minute the only surprise for the crowd was that it had taken so long to arrive. Billy King's pile-driver into the roof of the net was their fourth shot on target in a game that appeared from the first few seconds to be a complete mismatch. It was good to see the PA announcer also taken by surprise by the goal while he was tucking into his bridie, having to ask the press box who scored – people don't realise what a tough job the announcer's is especially when you are playing Scrabble on your iPhone and drinking a beer at the same time. (I knew this, having taken on the job myself at Lewes just two weeks previously.)

Hearts looked like they meant business from the first minute. While they did have a couple of pre-season run-outs under their belt, this was still an early game in their campaign. Their very smart deep maroon shirts, free from a sponsor's logo (tick) swarmed over the pitch, manager and former playing hero Robbie Neilson looking equally immaculate on the touch line in his Barbour. One became two in the 20th minute when Osman Sow was allowed to overlap on the right and placed the ball into the corner of the net, then almost added a third seconds later. The group of vocal Annan fans (well, children) positioned at the top of the away stand, who had been so vociferous about their hatred of Edinburgh 15 minutes previously, were now silent.

The third arrived in the fortieth minute when full back Callum Paterson headed home unmarked from a corner. Paterson's happiness would turn to tears just five minutes later when on the half-time whistle he fell awkwardly after a challenge and was stretchered off the pitch.

Fair do's to the stadium announcer. He was obviously under orders to slip in the sponsor's name at every opportunity and he didn't waste the chance in a break in play to remind us where we could find all the latest Petrofac Training news, Petrofac Training reaction and even Petrofac Training Instagram pictures. My attention though was caught by the number of birds in the stadium. They were everywhere, sitting ominously on top of the stand opposite, waiting for their chance to swoop and head one in. A lone duck-like creature (sorry, I have no idea on ornithology) patrolled the Annan penalty area in the first half and could well have had the last touch on Sow's goal.

The second half didn't quite have the same storyline. Hearts continued to attack, using pace to get to the byline, but the Annan keeper, Alex Mitchell, was in inspired form. Then in injury time Scott Davidson gave the 50 or so away fans something to shout about when he scored the goal of the game for Annan, striking home from distance.

Just over 6,700 had come out on a sunny, then windy, rainy and sunny again afternoon to see the "New" Hearts. While it was only the Challenge Cup, the fans cannot complain that the team hadn't taken it seriously. With huge images on the sides of the stands of bygone heroes such as Tommy Walker looking down on today's players, there is a sense that the club is once again starting to build for the future. Game one of the future was successfully negotiated. Now there was just the small matter of league games away at Ibrox and home to arch-rivals Hibernian to open the season.

Ironically, less than 24 hours later, I was sitting in Ibrox. The stadium was rocking, but not to the sound of the Rangers fans singing the praises of Ally McCoist; instead they were cheering on the exploits of the Malaysian Rugby Sevens team as they took a lap of honour around the famous turf. We love a loser in Great Britain, and here were 40,000-plus fans of sport in general acting like they had just witnessed the most polished performance ever. Malaysia had lost every single one of their games in the Commonwealth Games Rugby Sevens, being convincingly stuffed at every point along the way. Yet almost to a man the crowd were standing to applaud their efforts. Grown men ran to the front of the stands to grab selfies, the autograph of the twenty-first century, with players like Muhammad Danial Noor Hamidi, Mohd Syahir Asraf Rosli and of course Wye Wong.

The Malaysians suffered 50-point defeats by Wales and Samoa in their group games and registered their only try in a 36-7 loss to Papua New Guinea. They were then thrashed 35-0 by Uganda in the Bowl Competition before almost registering a first win in the semi-finals of the Shield, only to be denied 15-10 by Trinidad and Tobago. But that didn't stop them getting a fine send-off.

Glasgow was having a bad day. The skies were grey (no surprise there – after all it was the height of the summer) and the transport network was struggling to cope with an estimated influx of 700,000 visitors, the equivalent of the whole population of the city, here to see the Games. With the marathon being held in the city centre, the start of the athletics at Hampden Park, the final day of the Rugby Sevens and of course, Lawn Bowls, people were trying to get somewhere, without any luck. We arrived at Partick station from Edinburgh, hoping to make the two-stop journey south on the "Clockwork Orange" to Ibrox. Unfortunately, it seemed that a few thousand others had the same idea and the authorities had taken the decision to close the station for safety reasons. Buses had been ordered to try and relieve the situation but it would have taken a few hours to get anywhere so we took the decision to walk, using our old trusted friend Google Maps, to direct us across the Clyde and down to the stadium.

We arrived just as the first game started. The rain hadn't dampened the party spirit, only the strange outfits, with a number of fans turning up in fancy dress. I'm going to share a secret here of my billion-pound business plan. Pop-up Fancy Dress shops. I came across the idea when I was at the darts at Alexandra Palace a few years ago. Fancy dress is not conducive to use when travelling on public transport. Pockets aren't handily placed, or even present at all, and then there is the issue of how do you wear a coat over the top of a giant banana costume. So what about setting up a shop at the venue? People can arrive in normal clothes, rent the outfit and then return it straight afterwards. No fuss, no hassle, less chance of Tinkerbell's wand going missing AND you can charge a premium for the convenience of it. It's a win/win/win situation but keep it under your hat.

Any Americans in the crowd would have hated the tournament. It was constant action, with a two-to-three-minute changeover between games. Hardly any time at all to go and get the Pie Deal, which actually cost 50 pence more than if you bought the items separately. Most of the games during the four-hour session (FOUR HOURS of sport for £50 as a family of four – take note football!) went to form. Wales came within seconds of upsetting the applecart and beating Australia, conceding a try on the last play of the game, while England fell one point short to Samoa much to the enjoyment of most of the 40,000 in the stadium.

We returned to Edinburgh in the early evening having thoroughly enjoyed our little slice of the Commonwealth Games. Glasgow is often hard to love but they had excelled themselves in trying to put on a party. Putting aside the transport problems (and the city centre is small enough to negotiate on foot) and the weather (well, what did you expect anyway!) everyone shared the same objective in trying to put on a good show.

Two very different sporting events in 24 hours gave me something to think about. One notable observation was the fact that alcohol could be consumed in the seats at the Commonwealth Games at Ibrox, yet if the ball being used was of the round variety it would be banned. The profile of the fans wouldn't be that different yet it is deemed that a man dressed as Snow White is able to handle his beer better than your average football fan. In terms of entertainment, you cannot complain at the ticket pricing for either event, although the Hearts game was heavily discounted from normal league prices. The concept of Rugby Sevens simply works for fans who either want to bring a family or have a few beers. Perhaps football could learn a lesson from the short-game format and event-nature of Rugby Sevens. Business idea number 2: bring back the International Football Sixes. With fancy dress mandatory.

I'll get my coat.

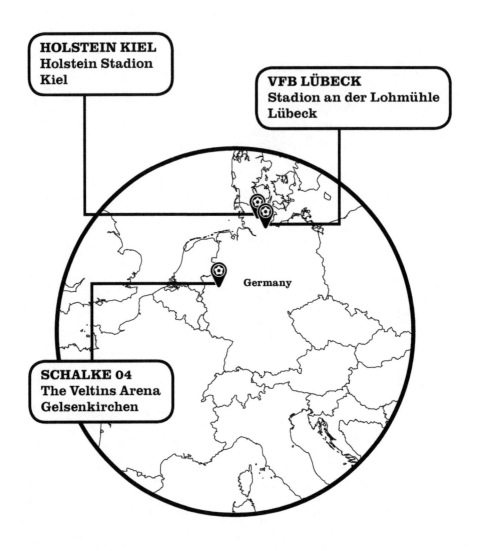

HOLSTEIN KIEL
Holstein Stadion
Kiel

VFB LÜBECK
Stadion an der Lohmühle
Lübeck

SCHALKE 04
The Veltins Arena
Gelsenkirchen

Germany

A chap walked past with a pair of home-made
trousers made out of old Kiel football shirts.

12. Kiel-hauled

It's 11am and with four pints and brandies inside him, Malcolm, the most nervous of nervous flyers, is asleep as our flight crosses the English Channel. Probably a sensible move in normal circumstances. Although the hop over to Dortmund with Ryanair is only an hour, it is an hour he's dreading. Unfortunately, the alcohol has put him in an almost coma-like sleep and with him being the only Newcastle United fan (and the only one wearing a football shirt) among a group of nine West Ham fans the temptation to "pimp" him is too much. First the empty cans of beer and bottles of spirits are piled on his head. Seven is a record, according to our stewardess, who takes a quick snap on her phone, undoubtedly planning to send it in to *Record Breakers*. Then a Dutch lady, wanting to get in on the action, donates her lipstick to the cause. What Newcastle, or any football fan, wouldn't want West Ham written on his forehead and ICF on each cheek?

At this point I'd like to apologise to the 70 or so other passengers in the front half of that flight for the drinks trolley never making it past row 5. Just as they had finished serving one of us with a round of 15 Heinekens, a double Jack Daniels and a bottle of Merlot then another round was in order. This was going to be the longest 24 hours of my life. Scrub that; with two out of the three next weekends being spent in Germany, August 2014 would undoubtedly be memorable for three things: beer, sausages and football.

Let me rewind to explain the why, where and who. In early June West Ham announced they had been invited to play in the 'prestigious' Schalke Cup. By prestigious what I really mean is that it was the first time it had ever been played, but it sounds better than inaugural. Newcastle United, Malaga and of course Schalke 04 would make up the numbers in a weekend of football in Gelsenkirchen. A subsequent conversation with an Everton fan in the know suggested that West Ham's involvement only came after their team turned down the opportunity.

My brother, with far too much time and money on his hands these days, decided this could be an ideal opportunity for some fraternal bonding. Back in the day he used to look after me when West Ham played away. I got to know the outsides of pubs up and down the country very well, armed with a bag of Salt 'n' Shake (kids: ask your mum) and a can of Shandy Bass. "You *will* look after him, Nigel?" my mum would ask him before we left the house. "Go straight to the ground, and don't go into any pubs." The price of my silence was a fiver, as, without my compliance, he wouldn't have been allowed to go himself. The stories from some of those trips would fill a whole book itself and I can now look back and laugh at being chased through Liverpool city centre, hiding in bins in Leicester or putting on a pretty good fake West Midlands accent to get out of scrapes.

It seemed that every other day another new name was added to the guest list for the trip. Nigel would regale me with their nicknames (Noise, Elvis, Gob, Nob, etc.) and where he knew them from, which was in every case "from the George", one of his many local pubs. The thing with living in a village as he does is that everyone knows everyone else, so soon news of the trip spread and everyone wanted in. Nick, one of the few on the trip without a pseudonym, decided we should do the trip in style and upgraded our Ryanair tickets to Priority Q ones. Oh, and rented an Executive Box at the Veltins Arena for the first day of the cup. After all, it's not every day West Ham play in a European competition, albeit one with absolutely no value at all.

There is always something appealing about watching the team you support playing abroad. Fans of the big clubs, and Tottenham Hotspur, have become blasé about seeing their teams play at the biggest stadiums in Europe against the best players. The policy of not taking the FA Cup seriously by many of these clubs has also given others, like Swansea City, Wigan Athletic and Hull City, the opportunity to have a European tour of their own. For the most part these teams treat the competition with respect, understanding the importance and value it can deliver to their image and standing, and its importance to the fans, who are often forced to pay ridiculous sums of money to travel on official club tours, the only way in some instances they can get access to tickets.

As a Lewes and West Ham fan the opportunity to see either of my teams overseas is limited to our away games in Canvey Island and Swansea City respectively. I was too young to have travelled in the West Ham golden period of the late 1970s and early 80s when we reached a European Cup Winners Cup (kids: ask your dad) Final in 1975 and then a Quarter-Final in 1981. I did see all of our home games on our way to winning the much-maligned Intertoto Cup in 2000 (kids: ask your dad again, although I doubt he will remember it); then in 2006 I travelled to Palermo to see us get embarrassed by the Italians in the UEFA Cup first round (you know the score now kids).

I've been travelling to watch football all over Europe for the best part of 15 years, seeing hundreds of games in 30-plus countries. I've learnt Football German, Italian, Spanish and a host of other languages by navigating around club websites, looking for the relevant information about forthcoming games I was going to attend. I'd say I have earned my Football Tourist passport through these trips, understanding how to get to games easily and as cheaply as possible. Heck, I've even devoted hundreds of hours to building a website to share the information with others. So it pisses me off no end when football clubs think they should have the monopoly on how fans can see them play in Europe. That trip to Palermo back in 2006 is a case in point. The official day trip, managed by the club's official travel agent (of course), was a snip at £399. For that we got our flight, a coach to/from the airport to the city centre, and a match ticket. Oh, and a police escort to the ground four hours before kick-off where we were then put in a pen with a small kiosk selling ice cream as our only entertainment. Some fans, acting as soon as the draw was made, booked flights themselves only to find that they couldn't then buy any tickets for the away end. So they had to buy home tickets and as they entered the stadium, they were escorted in small groups around the edge of the pitch to the away pen. Absolutely farcical.

Fortunately, there were to be none of those ridiculous rules for this trip. Although it was just a short hop across the Channel, with plenty of travel options available and tickets sensibly priced, less than a thousand West Ham fans would be making the trip. Complete apathy with the way the club was being run? Lack of faith in the so-called promise of a new dawn in "expansive" football? Or simply, despite how anyone might dress it up, that this was still only a pre-season game or two? Probably a mixture of all three, with heavy weighting on the latter.

Pre-season friendlies used to mean a visit to Buckie Thistle before a home friendly against a South American team as part of the testimonial celebrations for a long-serving player. In modern football, it is rare to see a player last five years playing for a club, let alone ten. The last West Ham player who reached that milestone was Steve Potts back in 1997 – so long ago in fact that his son, Dan, is now part of the first-team squad. In recent years clubs have looked further afield for pre-season friendlies, nearly always lured by a pot of gold. After taking in China in 2009 for the Asian Cup, and North America a year earlier as the opponents in the MLS All-Stars in Toronto, this year West Ham went to New Zealand and Australia, failing to win in the two games played there. In fact, add in the draws at Ipswich Town and Stevenage and you can see why media speculation was already building with regard to Sam Allardyce's days being numbered at Upton Park. The two games in Germany, irrespective of the result, wouldn't sway Sullivan and Gold, although good performances would perhaps sway a few of the fans sitting on the fence over his future.

West Ham had been regular pre-season visitors to Germany, most recently in 2012 when they took on Mainz 05, Rot-Weiss Erfurt and Dynamo Dresden. Back in 2005 I'd been lucky enough to watch the Hammers play 1860 Munich in one of the first games in the Allianz Arena.

The club, or to be more precise, the owners and management team, seemed to be going in different directions. Reading the official and unofficial communiques coming out of Upton Park was a daily giggle for fans of other clubs. Allardyce was to be sacked, then he wasn't. Sullivan and Gold took to social media to promise a new style of football, finally realising that the fans were fed up with a reliance on Allardyce hoof ball. Allardyce questions the value of Ravel Morrison in his squad, then the next day Sullivan tweets he should be given a new contract. Morrison reacts by getting himself arrested then put on remand for an alleged assault at 3am.

Andy Carroll was to be the saviour again. After missing over half of previous season's campaign through injury, his absence from the first friendly at Stevenage was due to a slight knock. Three weeks later, Gold tweeted he was to have surgery but would come back "fitter and stronger". Shades of Dean Ashton all over again and a repeat of the preceding season when our survival eggs were all put in Carroll's basket. While you cannot deny he does bring something to a team, especially for one who prefers the aerial route to goal, he has had a number of significant injuries for someone just 25 years old, which makes the £50 million that clubs have spent on transfer fees for him even more baffling.

With England once again basking in summer thunderstorms and torrential rain, our short flight saw us transported to Dortmund, a sunny utopia of beer, bratwurst and hopefully some decent football. Despite the sniggers of passers-by and the compliance of the border guards, Malcolm still had no idea about his make-up. He finally found out when he went to get changed at the hotel, swapping his "everyday" Newcastle home shirt for his match-day one, which was identical bar the Ba missing on the back.

For some of the grounp, this was a rare excursion to a new country, which of course meant an opportunity for a few wind-ups. One of the group, no names mentioned here Elvis, was convinced Germany still used the deutschmark and then got into a disagreement with a chap in the currency exchange booth about trying to give him euros instead. Another bought the fact that "dummkopf" meant thank you, rather than donkey or ass, and proceeded to use it at every opportunity. I should reiterate that the average age of our group was over 50.

A 30-minute taxi ride later and we were at the Veltins Arena, one of UEFA's jewels in the crown of European stadiums. Retractable roof – tick, retractable pitch – tick, fußball tables in the Executive lounges – tick. What more could you want? Well, one look at our Executive Box and our hostess Lisa certainly put that question to bed. Within minutes we were tucking into the free beer, free food and free football on offer. As we all know, 90 minutes of football often spoil a good day out but we were hopeful that this time West Ham would step up to the occasion and prove us all wrong.

SCHALKE 0, WEST HAM UNITED 0
Saturday 2nd August 2014 – The Veltins Arena

You can dress up the fact that West Ham won this game on penalties all you like but in truth it was a terrible exhibition of football. You would have hoped that with a bit of silverware on offer, West Ham would have at least tried to get the ball out of their half. Having seen a picture of the Veltins Cup, I felt it would have looked considerably more impressive in the trophy cabinet than the thumbnail-sized Intertoto Cup that we won back in 1999. It was a good job that penalties were used to decide the issue after 90 minutes rather than extra time, to stop the majority of fans falling asleep. Yes, it was only a pre-season friendly, but surely this should be the time when the manager is being brave, trying out things that could work. So far this season we have seen very little of that in the draws against Stevenage and Ipswich Town and the defeats against Sydney FC and Wellington in New Zealand. With just two weeks to go before the Premier League starts, the club are still desperately trying to bring in some more firepower.

We arrived at the stadium just in time to see Newcastle fall behind to Malaga in the first game. I'd been to the Veltins Arena a few times before yet never seen the home side play. Tickets are incredibly difficult to come by so I had been forced to experience one of the best new-build stadiums in Europe during the Champions League Final in 2004 and then in the 2006 World Cup Finals. However, it seems that the locals weren't particularly interested in the Veltins Cup either. A handful of Malaga fans, a smattering of Schalke fans on the huge terrace and in the far upper corner, around 500 Newcastle fans who were already realising in the same way the West Ham fans had that this Premier League season may be "problematic".

After the third Malaga goal went in just before half-time (the *Daily Mail* summed it up by saying that "even" ex-Man Utd flop Obertan got on the score sheet) a few of us headed out of the stadium to where a few hundred West Ham fans were drinking. Few seemed particularly interested in the game, being here for a weekend away and to experience a more "grown-up" footballing experience (terracing, beer, sausages and no heavy-handed policing or stewards).

West Ham lined up with three up front, although you can hardly ever call Stewart Downing, with four goals to his name in the last four seasons, a striker. Carlton Cole, maligned by many outside of the club (and some inside it), was also in the starting eleven. You know where you stand with Carlton and if we had players with the same work ethic we would have a lot less to worry about. But it mattered very little. The game was tame, with Schalke coming the closest to breaking the deadlock when they hit the post twice. The five hundred or so West Ham fans spread out across SüdTribüne tried to rally the Hammers but it seemed penalties were inevitable.

Fortunately, 39-year-old Jussi Jääskeläinen was still awake and made two excellent saves in the shoot-out, the final one from Borgmann in sudden death to win the game for West Ham, meaning the game 24 hours later against Malaga would determine the first ever winners of the Veltins Cup.

We were one of the last groups to leave the stadium, getting our full money's worth of Veltins beer before heading to the bright lights of Dortmund. It was only a pre-season friendly, but it did give us a taste of how the other half – well, top seven Premier League clubs – live.

One taxi ride later and we were being welcomed into the bosom of Dortmund, Germany's eighth-largest city. The city centre was full of German stag and hen do's, which differed quite considerably from the English version. Back in the UK the focus would range from getting the stag mildly embarrassed at one end of the scale by being taped naked to a lamp-post, to near-death by wandering around naked in Canal Street in Manchester with a Liverpool tattoo on his chest. The hens would all be drunk on Lambrini before 10am before proceeding to a male strip club where the hen would be photographed licking whipped cream off the genitals of a stripper before one of her mates (usually the fattest one) sucked him off for real.

But in Germany, they have a bit more class. The stag is dressed up as a superhero and made to carry out "jolly japes" in the city centre such as dancing on tables of bars, while his mates wheel around a big stereo playing David Hasselhoff's greatest hits. The hens on the other hand all dressed in lingerie and patrolled the bars and clubs, offering us a "dip in their box" for just €5.

Alas, for John, that just meant he paid a fiver to pick out a small thong from the lucky dip box. "Stu . . . what am I supposed to do with this? My missus would kill me if I took it home!" It seemed that a group of Englishmen out on the town were magnets for any money-making scam. An hour after the hen parties had departed, the "Alcohol police" arrived: three not-so-young girls squeezed into policewomen outfits that were far too small, who for just €3 would test the alcohol levels in our blood and tell us whether we were fit to drink. Despite the fact none of us had access to a car, a few of the group lined up to have a blow. They don't get out much.

Sunday morning, for all of its bright sunshine, wasn't a welcome guest in the Fuller hotel bedroom. While the rest of the group were heading back to the Veltins to see if West Ham could actually win a game (they couldn't, by the way), I was heading home with work beckoning. However, it wouldn't be long before I would be back in these parts.

Two weeks later and I was on a plane to Germany once more. Dortmund had tried to break me but it had failed. This time, I was hoping for a more sedate trip with Danny, Stoffers and Kenny, for the annual EFW Board meeting. We had a number of important issues to discuss in person, although football once again threatened to get in the way of official proceedings. A new set of guidelines for our Facebook group, a revision of the EFW rule book, especially the section around asking questions about getting tickets for Bayern Munich games, and a new proposed resolution that would ban the use of the phrase "How do I get to the stadium?"

I have no idea how it happens; no sooner have I agreed to going on one of these trips than the confirmation emails start to appear in my inbox. With my previous jaunt still fresh in the memory (and the liver) I had to stretch to a box of Milk Tray as well as the regular Petrol Station Flowers to appease CMF. She knows the bond I have with the German Cup though, so she did what every good wife does: made me a packed lunch for the train to the airport, told me to give her three rings when I landed, and ordered me not to return with:

a) a tattoo;
b) a communicable disease; or
c) someone else's pants.

She's funny about those things. Women can be strange at times.

We take our duties seriously and that was why Danny and I were on a plane to Hamburg at silly o'clock in the morning. The fact that we would also see games in Lübeck and Kiel over the next 36 hours was a complete coincidence. While the FIFA congress may be happy with dancing girls and Cristal champagne, allegedly, we wanted beer, Regionalliga football and a few bratwurst thrown in for good measure.

Now I don't really have to sell German football to you, dear reader, but it still surprises me how simple it is to arrange a top weekend. There isn't such a thing in Germany as a bad place to go. North, south, east or west there are top destinations that the guidebooks rave about. While most Football Tourists will head for Munich, Berlin, Hamburg or Dortmund, we headed for the bright lights of Wuppertal, Cottbus, Mainz or Rostock. But when it was suggested that we head for Kiel, the comments we found online weren't so complimentary. Kiel doesn't rate highly in many of the guide books about Europe, let alone one for the Danish borders region. Home to the German navy, it can boast a population of around 240,000, a Subway and two breweries. That'll do us.

"A gritty, urban sprawl."

"Lumpen concrete blocks built at speed in the 1950s which are not the place to look for history."

"The city centre is unlovable but unavoidable."

What do they know anyway? Did it have beer? Yes. S sausages? Absolutely! And Football? Well, how about the small matter of a German Cup first-round tie between Holstein Kiel and 1860 Munich? It doesn't take landscaped gardens, thatched cottages, Westfield shopping centres or taking our clothes off to have a good time if you have the three staple ingredients (1980s music gag there, lads, before you start wondering about what exactly we get up to away from home).

Our plan was dependent on us arriving on time in Hamburg. Stoffers had pulled together a minute-by-minute itinerary that ensured we would have fun. As if to underline that fact, he even put on the schedule, between 9.15pm and 9.47pm, in big letters: HAVE FUN. Fortunately, we arrived bang on time and passed through the doors of the airport, and Stoffers' blood pressure returned to normal. There wasn't even time for a group hug before we were marched down to the S-Bahn for the train to the main station.

Hello, who else had joined the party? It was none other than Malta's finest, Ofer Prosner, also now living in Berlin (so that he could use Kenny's free

Wi-Fi apparently), making his EFW debut. Three things you need to know about Ofer before the weekend's tales unfold:

He loves nothing more than 40 winks.
He looks like a young, Maltese Larry David (*Curb Your Enthusiasm*).
He loves nothing more than 40 winks.

As we had landed on time, we qualified for the Stoffers, Option 1 afternoon, which would see us head north to the historic city of Lübeck. *Opens up Wikipedia*: The second-largest city in Schleswig-Holstein and one of the major ports of Germany. Situated on the River Trave, it was for several centuries the "capital" of the Hanseatic League (a medieval SPAR). It is one of the most picturesque cities in Northern Europe thanks to its extensive Brick Gothic architecture, which saw the city listed by UNESCO (a posh version of TripAdvisor that pre-dates the internet) as a World Heritage site. Apart from having a decent Christmas market every year, the city is famed as the birth-place of marzipan, that horribly sickly sweet that your gran used to make you eat for Sunday tea when you were watching *Bullseye*. Oh, and it is also the home of the International Museum of Theatre Puppet. Alas, our plan didn't include a stop at Fritz Frey Junior's museum, which sent Kenny into a right old strop. Stoffers can be a cruel master sometimes.

With Kenny lying on the floor, beating his fists on the pavements at the injustice of the world, we hopped in a taxi and headed for the Stadion an der Lohmühle, or to give it its latest title, the PokerStars.de Stadium, home of Verein für Bewegungsspiele Lübeck. And who said that football clubs have commercially sold out these days? Obvious there are clear synergies between a fourth-tier German side and a poker website. Those marketing guys must have really done their homework to sell the sponsorship to the football club, focusing on shared objectives, demographics of the potential customer base or even the community aspect. Or they just put an offer on the table that the football club, which had been suffering very public financial difficulties, found hard to resist.

Tickets were an outrageous six euros each. SIX EUROS. That's the same price as a hot dog at Stockholm's Arlanda Airport. However, it was spot on in terms of my infamous economic model of Beer v Match Ticket ratio, which, when I am in charge of the beautiful game across the world, will be set at a maximum of 4:1. Yep, we were as happy as Larry, sorry Ofer, with our €1.50 beers, standing in what we thought was the supporters club beer garden. Except it wasn't. We started getting some funny looks when we brazenly wandered in, and now we had made ourselves at home it dawned on us that we had gatecrashed the Ultras bar. German Ultras, in fact Ultras across the world, don't take too kindly to strangers trying to infiltrate them, so with the mood getting a bit frosty we decided to head into the stadium.

VFB LÜBECK 1, SC GOSLAR 0
Saturday 16th August 2014 – Stadion an der Lohmühle

Of course being August we had dressed for the sun. And of course as soon as the game kicked off, the rain started sheeting it down. Six-euro tickets don't give you a roof at football these days so while Stoffers, Danny and Ofer headed for the trees, Kenny and I wandered through an open gate and up into the stand where the Ultras were now doing their thing, waving flags, jumping up and down on the seats and singing songs about Chris Rea (or so it sounded like). But more importantly, we were under cover. The other three followed a few minutes later and were rebuffed, as a steward had appeared from nowhere and pointed out the error of their ways.

"Jog on lads. This is where the big boys play. You will only get hurt if you come in here and then you'll be crying for Mummy to come and wipe away the snot from your nose" is probably what he meant to say to them, instead of simply pointing out their tickets were only good for the terrace.

Beaten, but not defeated the trio skulked in the corner and took a photo or two of us Ultras. Oh, I should point out at this point that Kenny, in order to get into the mind-set of an Ultra, had bought a balaclava on a whim on his walk home from work last week. Girls – form an orderly queue. We were joining in all of the songs, the handclaps and the aggressive pointing at the two away fans at the far end. Two of the main men then headed down the steps, through the gate and went over to Stoffers and Danny. Their photographic activities had made the Ultras concerned. They wanted to know the whys, the whens, the whos and the hows. Surprisingly, none of them had heard of "In Bed with Maradona", so Danny's "research" line didn't wash. Kenny and I felt bad for them for all of five seconds before we had to "jump up and down if you hate BSV Schwarz-Weiß Rehden".

Eventually we felt guilty for them so headed down ourselves, back onto the terrace. Stoffers was like a little puppy, excitedly asking us what it was like and playing down the fact he had been clocked by them. All was well with the world again and another round of beers ensured that the mood was lifted once more.

Of course there had been 45 minutes of football going on in the background. Hardly inspiring stuff, with the home side struggling to break down a dogged Goslar SC 08 defence that had arrived in North Germany rooted to the bottom of Regionalliga Nord with two defeats so far. Not that the home side could say anything, as they were down there too after the opening couple of games. Judging by the standard of play in the opening period you could see why. The second period didn't start much better, with the biggest talking point being the mysterious disappearance of the two away fans, who had failed to reappear for the second half at the far end.

With more rain looming, Danny suggested that we give the last 20 minutes a swerve. Stoffers was of course aghast that he could countenance such a crime and stoically refused to move. Kenny, feeling guilty over Ultragate, decided to stay, which of course meant so did Ofer, as it appeared he was still using Kenny's Wi-Fi. We headed out of the ground just as Lübeck scored the one and only goal of the game. This was Danny's second game of the season and, just like last week at Brighton & Hove Albion v Sheffield Wednesday, he missed the only goal of the game.

We had opted to head north to Kiel for our Saturday night, choosing to forgo the opportunity of tasting marzipan beer. We had also been invited to the house of famous Holstein Kiel fan and chef Matthæus Arminius Kilius, who said he would be honoured to cook for us and then take us to some of his favourite pubs in the city. Who were we to argue? So after a quick change in our luxury apartment overlooking a tug boat pumping out the toilets of a cruise ship, we jumped into a complete stranger's car and headed to the Kiel suburbs.

Matthæus loves his football, you couldn't fail to notice that when you walked into his flat. Football paraphernalia covered every surface. His wife, Frauke, didn't seem to mind sharing her bath with a plastic duck in the colours of every Bundesliga team, nor lying on her Holstein Kiel bedspread. He'd cooked us a local dish with smoked bacon, green beans, potatoes and a big pear right in the middle. A couple of local beers kept us all happily tapping in details to our Untappd app and life couldn't have been better. As we cleared up, Matthæus suggested that €7 each would cover his costs. We all laughed, marvelling at his German sense of humour. Except he didn't seem to be joking.

Our night was still young, and after a trip around a non-league ground in the pitch-dark via a magic door that Matthæus knew about and then driving down a main road on the wrong side of the road, swerving to avoid oncoming buses, we arrived in the centre of Kiel. After persuading Kenny to come out from under the seat we could start our evening. Move along lads, nothing more to see here about our night out. We were all tucked up in bed by midnight, honest.

Sunday morning and we were in the pub again at 11am. Time for a Full German. Like a Full English but with a beer it hit the spot perfectly. The Palenka pub was a stopping-off spot for the Kiel fans on their journey to the stadium so it would be rude not to join them, accompanied by a few German riot police. German football culture has a clear hierarchy and trouble is very predictable based on the teams involved. Clubs often have strong friendships with other clubs, based on a historic event or match, whereas the intense rivalries, such as between Schalke and Borussia Dortmund or FC Köln and Fortuna Düsseldorf, are not always about proximity. There are some exceptions – Dynamo Dresden love nothing more than tearing it up with all comers while everyone outside Munich hates Bayern. Actually, scrub that. Everyone except Bayern fans hate Bayern.

The visitors today, 1860 Munich, had brought a few hundred fans and they were doing what German fans love to do on a Sunday lunchtime – standing on a petrol station forecourt drinking beer. We were immediately singled out as being "foreign" because we were drinking Paderboner beer – the English equivalent of Foster's. Does anyone really choose Foster's when given a choice of beers? Really? Same with Paderboner, which made us look a little bit silly. Then a chap walked past with a pair of home-made trousers made out of old Kiel football shirts and immediately our street credibility rose.

HOLSTEIN KIEL 1, 1860 MUNICH 2
Sunday 16th August 2014 – Holstein Stadion

We took our spot in the away end as the teams emerged. The game had Pokal upset written all over it, with 1860 not enjoying the best of starts to the season so far. Two defeats in their first games had the fans hopping mad, so they hoped that a win against Liga 3 Holstein Kiel would give the squad a welcome boost before they returned to league action at Heidenheim in a week's time. The fans struck up their soundtrack for the afternoon, accompanied by drums and huge flags, all choreographed by a single chap with a megaphone sitting atop the perimeter fence.

For all of the hazards that standing on an open terrace with some hardcore fans brings, during the afternoon we saw the worst of the worst. Someone had left a programme on the floor. Not exactly a small, inconspicuous item, coming in at A4 in size, yet we lost count of the number of people who stepped on it and slipped. One chap took his embarrassment and anger out on it by trying to kick it, which led to him slipping again. Of course we didn't laugh. Much.

After spending most of the last few decades bouncing around the Regional and Oberligas, Kiel were back in the third tier of German football. It's been quite a while since they were a powerhouse in German football. In fact, it's been over a century since that they won their one and only German Championship, back in the amateur days. The locals had come out in force to see whether they could upset the odds in the first round of the German Cup.

With just eight minutes on the clock, a great run to the byline saw the ball pulled back to Kiel's Siedschlag, who smashed the ball home. Instead of groans on the away terrace we all just bounced up and down a bit and sang abusive songs about those bastards in Red (apparently). 1860 simply didn't look like scoring until just after the hour mark when their Austrian forward Rubin Rafael Okotie equalised. Ten minutes later and he put 1860 ahead, converting a penalty after he had been brought down from behind. Game over.

The final whistle brought some good-natured thigh slapping, the sound of flesh on Lederhosen filling the air. A row of blonde female riot police kept the home fans back with minimal effort to let us grab the only taxi in the rank, quite literally, and we headed for the Kieler Brauerei, the one tourist attraction that we all wanted to visit in our 24 hours in Kiel. Sure, there was also The Love Center, but on the drive past, Roxanne hadn't turned on the red light yet so we focused on the dozen or so beers that the micro-brewery served up. Craft beer is the home brew of the twenty-first century but without having to use your best jumper to keep the beer warm in the airing cupboard. The brew house was certainly worth the wait and we had soon sampled our way through most of the menu. Alas, we had a train to catch so we grabbed a takeaway and headed for the station.

Ninety minutes and full renditions of every football song known to man later we arrived in Hamburg. This was where we would be saying goodbye to the Berlin boys but not until we had toasted another successful weekend of EFW business. Stoffers brought our meeting to a close with a toast in Bodega then burst into a chorus of "Fools Gold", dragging a few of the bemused locals up for a quick shuffle around the dance floor. Soon we were all up there and the landlady had declared that in fact not all Englischers were "fucking wankers" and produced some shots from what looked like a carburettor of a 1979 Datsun Sunny, and we all raised our glasses once more.

In the grand scheme of things it had been a pretty good weekend. Although the rain was lashing it down outside, we were happily snuggled up inside. While thrill seekers had headed for the seedy delights on offer on Reeperbahn for centuries, or the lurid window displays of Herbertstrasse where literally anything can be bought, we had chosen to mingle with the locals. Bar Bodega at 10pm on a Sunday night wasn't exactly rocking when we arrived but by the time we left the locals were linking arms, swaying from side to side as Danny led them in a chorus of "No ney never". These were our new best friends.

After an emotional farewell at Altona, we headed to the airport where our beds for the night awaited. By night I obviously mean four hours, which Danny spent sleeping in his shoes, "just in case there was a fire". Of course at 5am on the following Monday morning he couldn't remember any of the events from the night before: the sign of a great night.

Until next season, Germany. Be good, don't go changing.

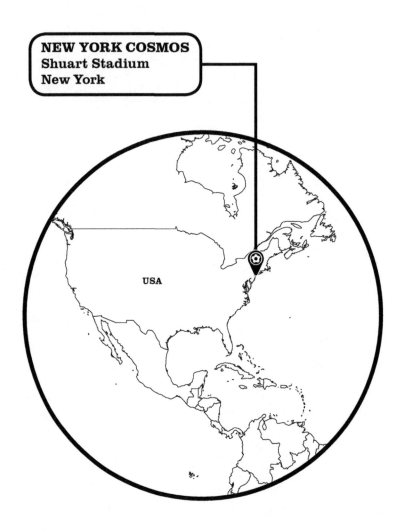

NEW YORK COSMOS
Shuart Stadium
New York

USA

This would be like finding a Bejam's or a Berni Inn,
a chance to revisit something from my childhood.

13. Twice in a Lifetime

As a schoolboy you could hardly ask for a better best friend than someone whose dad was a professional footballer. Obviously, one who has a mum who is a page three model isn't a bad choice either but at the age of 10 when the world was all about "got, got, not got" in the playground, it was all about football. It was luck more than any deliberate ploy on my part that Danny (it's always a Danny, isn't it) and I became best buddies. Paired to sit together at the age of five on the first day of junior school, our only interests apart from football were Dinky toys, Rayleigh Boxer bikes and persuading girls to do handstands. We spent a lot of time in each other's company, building a treehouse (with the help of my dad) in the garden Chez Fuller, plotting and planning our future careers as the world's first inter-galactic Lego architects.

At that age I had no real concept of the nuances of football, despite my dad and brother's Saturday afternoon trips to Upton Park and Dartford's Watling Street ground. We only had three TV channels, the highlight of the week being Brian Moore presenting *The Big Match* on a Sunday where the ONE game featured was a mystery unless you had been at the game in question and seen the single TV camera in the ground. It wasn't until one Sunday when I was watching the game that I saw Danny's dad.

"LOOK! That's Danny's dad," I screamed at the TV, pointing to the man on the TV being kissed by his team-mates after scoring a goal. It appeared that even my mum, who hated football, knew that Danny's dad was a footballer. My brother then gave me the Facts of Life for a West Ham fan, rule number 1 being about hating Millwall and anything to do with Millwall. Danny's dad played for Millwall. And by played I mean he was a club legend and their leading ever goal scorer, an honour he held until the record was recently broken by Neil Harris.

Those of you who can remember the 1970s will now have put two and two together. Danny's dad was Derek Possee, not only a legend for The Lions but also at Crystal Palace and Leyton Orient. Danny had no real interest in his dad's job even if the rest of the class did as the school years passed. Every time I was round his house I would find an opportunity to go out in the garden with a ball and show off my skills. I wore my Coca-Cola Skills

Platinum badge (gained by being able to hoof a ball 50 yards in a straight line) to try and impress him, secretly hoping that Millwall, Palace or Orient would have an injury crisis and would need to bring in a few players.

Back in those days, professional footballers weren't paid the king's ransom that they are today and their needs away from the game were a bit more modest than those of the 18 year old millionaires we see today. The Possees had a normal house, in a normal neighbourhood, drove a normal car and took normal holidays. However, that's not to say he wasn't ambitious, especially with his career winding down towards the end of the decade. Clubs held the power over players back then, with agents unheard of in England. This was in the days before Jean Bosman had even started playing, let alone begun to ruminate about the unjust life of a footballer. Possee had played throughout his whole career without leaving London so when Orient released him in 1977 he looked further afield, signing for Irish side St Patrick's Athletic.

Then in the summer of 1979 Danny came into school one day and told me some devastating news. He was leaving our little village school, heading thousands of miles away where his dad was to be part of the British Invasion of the North American Soccer League.

Possee had become the latest Brit to be tempted by the bright lights of the North American Soccer League, signing for Vancouver Whitecaps. He would be swapping the dank, dark stands and heavily sanded pitch of Brisbane Road for the regularly sold-out, 30,000-seater, plush Empire Stadium with its "Tartan Turf", the first sporting facility in Canada to use an artificial pitch, although a million miles away from the surfaces we have today. He was joined in Vancouver by English goalkeeper Phil Parkes, confusingly not the same goalkeeper who was playing for Queens Park Rangers and West Ham United during the late 1970s. Other notable players who had a stint with the Whitecaps included Bruce Grobbelaar, Alan Taylor, Kevin Hector, Frans Thijssen and of course, Peter Beardsley. To us Brits, American Soccer meant strange names, strange kits and strange rules. Oh, and lots of cheerleaders. Who doesn't like a cheerleader?

Possee wasn't the first Englishman to be lured over to the NASL. He would be following in the footsteps of Geoff Hurst, Bobby Moore, George Best and Gordon Banks. Oh, and Harry Redknapp, but he obviously didn't go for the money. You could see the appeal for these players who were coming to the end of their career. The clubs in general looked after them well with nice houses, first-class travel and almost A-list star status within their communities. Of course the lure of swapping opponents such as Mickey Droy, Billy Bonds and Norman Hunter for Pele, Eusebio, Franz Beckenbauer and Johan Cruyff may have had an appeal as well, as the NASL went into marketing overdrive to try to win the hearts and minds of the attention-deficient Americans. The 1966 World Cup in England had surprisingly fuelled interest in the game in the US, coupled with the strange United Soccer League which had seen European teams such as Stoke City, Hibernian, Sunderland and Cagliari imported into the US to play under the names Cleveland Stokers, Toronto City, Vancouver Royal Canadians and Chicago Mustangs respectively.

The concept of Franchise Football was copied straight from the models adopted by the National Football League, Hockey League and Major League Baseball, with 17 teams ranging from Atlanta to Vancouver taking part in the first season. The franchise from New York, "The Generals", lasted just one season, thus leaving the biggest city in North America without a team. Three seasons later in 1971 the league accepted an application for a new team, which paid the princely sum of $25,000 entrance fee. And so the legend of the Cosmos, and in many ways the NASL, was born.

The NASL still needed to sell football to the North Americans, which was then completely foreign to the majority of them. A number of rule changes were made in those first few years to try to keep the fan's interest. A clock that counted time down to zero, as was typical of other timed American sports, rather than upwards to 90 minutes, was standard at all grounds. In 1972 they implemented the 35-yard line, which meant that players couldn't be offside unless they were in that final zone. But the most famous rule change was the introduction of the Shoot-out in 1974. The US didn't do "tied" games – the concept that you could play for a couple of hours and still not have a winner was just as alien as referring to underwear as pants or not pouring porridge over bacon for breakfast. The concept of the shoot-out was that a player had five seconds to score from running from the 35-yard line. They could take as many touches or rebounds as they wanted as long as it happened within five seconds.

The Cosmos became the NASL to many youngsters like me. They realised that the way to market the team overseas was to bring in the players everyone knew. Cue Pelé, Beckenbauer, Carlos Alberto and England star Terry Garbett (of course, Terry Garbett, ex-Watford and Middlesborough star midfielder) arriving to a great fanfare in the city. For a short time, they became the most talked-about sporting team not only in New York but also in the whole of America. They would dominate the game in the late Seventies and all the talk with Danny before he departed for a new life on the other side of the planet was about when he was going to meet Pelé. The fact that the great man had actually retired two years previously didn't seem to matter. Danny was sure that he would run into him one day at a game and invite him back for a jam sandwich and a bottle of Panda pop.

The Whitecap's, and Possee's, greatest NASL moment came in 1979 when the Canadians made it through to the end-of-season play-off semi-finals, which were played as two-legged affairs. However, they didn't use the concept of aggregate scoring. Instead it was simply the team that won the game, got the point. Two points took you through to the next round. The Whitecaps won the first game in front of a sell-out crowd at the Giants Stadium (today known as the MetLife); the Cosmos levelled the series after one of those shoot-outs. With each team winning one game the tie went to a 30-minute mini-game. That also ended all-square, so another shoot-out took place in which Possee scored the decisive goal to end the dreams of the Cosmos.

In the Soccer Bowl final the Whitecaps beat the Tampa Bay Rowdies, once again in the Giants Stadium, to secure their one and only major honour. The homecoming parade for the team in Vancouver is still to this day the biggest public turnout the city has seen.

Danny and his family occasionally popped back over to the UK and he would shower me with football-related gifts. If we think that Premier League clubs today will stick a logo on almost anything and call it "official merchandise", they would be amazed by the sheer volume of products the NASL clubs sell. I had a Vancouver Whitecaps dog bowl long before the Manchester United marketing machine thought of it, and also a long time before I even owned a dog (that's foresight for you!). Interestingly, according to Danny, the only product they didn't sell was a white cap.

Over time his visits back to the UK got less frequent. Derek Possee retired from the game soon after that Soccer Bowl win, going out on a high, and began coaching, eventually working with the national side. My relationship with Danny, in days before email and Facebook, faded and I didn't hear his name until 10 years later when my mum showed me a story in the *Daily Mail* (of course, the *Daily Mail*) that he had been shot and killed by mistake by the Canadian police in a bungled drugs raid.

In the following years, the popularity of the game started to wane. The league struggled to recruit world-class players and the NASL decided to put the task of selling the game to advertisers in the clubs' hands, which became difficult for some franchises with no national (or international) appeal. At the end of the 1981 season it was announced that the 24 clubs had run up a collective debt of over $30 million. A number of the franchise owners decided enough was enough and pulled the plug on their team. The following season only 14 teams were included in the league.

Many of these new owners were not soccer savvy, and once the perceived popularity started to decline, they got out as quickly as they got in. Over-expansion without sufficient vetting of ownership groups was a huge factor in the death of the league, as was the very small cost to enter.

With the NASL declining rapidly in the early 1980s they needed to think fast how to save the whole sport in North America. An audacious bid was made to host the 1986 FIFA World Cup Finals, although the decision was made in 1983 to give the tournament to Mexico. The league lasted until the 1984 NASL season. On 28th March 1985, the NASL suspended operations for the 1985 season, when only the Minnesota Strikers and Toronto Blizzard were interested in playing. Many teams had decided to join the Major Indoor Soccer League, including the Cosmos, until that went the same way as the NASL in 1992.

As part of the deal that brought the 1994 FIFA World Cup to the United States, a new professional league was announced in 1993. Major League Soccer would start in 1996 featuring 10 franchises, which began to grow as the game became more popular with youngsters, and the US National Team started to perform on an international scale.

In 2009 it was announced that Vancouver had been given a franchise and the Whitecaps were reborn, taking their place for the 2011 season. They joined three other old NASL franchises in the MLS: San Jose Earthquakes, Portland Timbers and Seattle Sounders. Although the New York Cosmos may have hoped to join them back in the top flight of US soccer, their story is a bit more complicated. New York had been given one of the original 10 franchise spots in the MLS, with the catchily titled New York/New Jersey Metrostars kicking off the season in the Giants Stadium at Meadowlands, New Jersey.

As Major League Soccer (MLS) began to expand its borders and bring in players such as David Beckham, Youri Djorkaeff, Lothar Matthäus and Ian Woan to drive its image (and thus overseas TV and marketing rights) during the early parts of this century, chatter began to get louder about the resurrection of the Cosmos. The New York/New Jersey MetroStars made enquiries about who owned the rights to the name before they jumped into bed with Red Bull. In fact, with the Austrian marketing machine agreeing to fund a purpose-built football stadium in Harrison, New Jersey, the city of New York would still be without a team, causing some to hope that there might one day be a resurrection of the Cosmos as a franchise of their own if the MLS expanded. Hopes were raised that the MLS would allow the old Cosmos to be given to a New York side when they accepted the Seattle and Portland applications in 2006 and 2007 respectively.

In August 2010 Pelé put down his Viagra and announced at a press conference that the Cosmos were back. They didn't have a stadium, a team, a league to play in but who needed to worry about the detail. The devil is in the detail, so they lead you to believe, but not if you have the world's best ever footballer wearing one of your football shirts, sitting in front of the world's footballing media.

The detail was left to Paul Kemsley, an ex-director of Tottenham Hotspur, ex-Liverpool CEO Rick Parry and former Chelsea assistant physio Terry Byrne (Byrne would later become David Beckham's manager in Madrid, earning the player's trust after he looked after him in France 1998 when he was sent off playing for England against Argentina in the FIFA World Cup). Eric Cantona was added to the party in January 2011 as their Director of Soccer.

The club had a mission and some of the most qualified people in football to make the dream come true, but at the end of the day they still needed to recruit a team of players. Who wouldn't want to play for a team with the likes of Cantona in charge? Perhaps one who actually wanted to play some games!

Finally, in the summer of 2011 an announcement was released that the New York Cosmos would once again take to the field as the opposition in Paul Scholes's testimonial match at Old Trafford. Speaking at a press conference in Manchester ahead of the game, Cantona announced his squad of guest players such as Sol Campbell, Wayne Bridge, Fabio Cannavaro and Robert Pirès alongside a mixture of the Cosmos youngsters. He tried to explain his motives for getting back involved in football after his sabbatical in the French film industry. The normally enigmatic, confusing and philosophical Frenchman was very forthright in his answer.

"I wanted to come back in a special club, and New York Cosmos is special, the teaching is special and the club is special. The history of the club is great. We have lots of things to do and we can do well . . . we really want to win things, and try to be one of the best teams in the US."

"To be playing the first game at Manchester United is just the biggest thrill in the world," added Kemsley, seemingly filling in the large pauses when Pelé was supposed to produce some appropriate marketing statements.

There was a quiet nod to recently retired Paul Scholes by Terry Byrne, commenting that "we'll hopefully do Paul Scholes justice" in what was to be Scholes's last game for Manchester United, (although he was come out of retirement for a while less than a year later. Cantona, when asked where he ranked Scholes as a football player among all those he has played alongside, described Scholes as a "great player and great personality".

Although the Cosmos were roundly beaten 6-0 in the game, a new generation of football fans now understood a bit about the legacy of the great club. All they needed now was a league to play in.

As luck would have it (funny that) a new league had been created that was perfect for the Cosmos. It was called the NASL. However, this NASL had nothing in common bar the name with the organisation that had disappeared 25 years earlier. This would be the recognised second tier of US soccer, although there would be no promotion to the MLS – the concept of sports meritocracy may take a few decades to explain to US sports fans. The Cosmos' application was accepted and they took their place in the 10-team league for the 2013 season.

Ironically, the newly reformed Cosmos decided to move to Long Island 40 years after they left in 1973. Their home would again be the James M. Shuart Stadium at Hofstra University, some 45 minutes east of Manhattan. The fans hoped the stay in the NASL would be temporary, especially as further expansion plans of the NASL were due to be announced, with one franchise rumoured to be going to New York. Alas, the dream of a return to the top tier of US football was dashed in May 2013 when the MLS announced the new franchise team in the city would be New York City FC, a joint venture between Manchester City and the Yankees, with their marquee players, David Villa and Frank Lampard, announced shortly afterwards.

In their first season at this level the club won the Soccer Bowl. With the season split into two halves, the Cosmos won the "Fall" championship and then beat the "Spring" champions Atlanta Silverbacks to claim the title. Building on the success from that season they claimed second spot in the Spring championship. However, it was in the US Open Cup (the US version of the FA Cup without any need for sponsorship from poor brewers) that the club have once again grabbed the nation's attention. In their first season in the competition they drew the Red Bulls out of the hat and proceeded to smash their richer, more caffeine-boosted rivals out of the park. They then took MLS Philadelphia Union to extra time before they lost 2-1.

Being in New York for business, it was a 100/1 shot that the Cosmos would be at home (honest) but once I saw they were, I had to be there. This would be like finding a Bejam's or a Berni Inn, a chance to revisit something from my childhood.

It is also not often you can tick off two things from your bucket list in one evening without it involving whipped cream, a private room at Spearmint Rhino's, or Holly Willoughby, but the chance to visit the Cosmos out in Long Island delivered just that without me really needing to break into a sweat. It's also not often that many visitors to New York would even think of trying to get to see one of the *50 Teams That Mattered* (an excellent read from the pen of David Hartrick) in the development of the beautiful game. The New York Cosmos' impact on the global game that we see today cannot be underestimated. They were the first global marketing machine, realising the pot of gold that was on offer when selling football in the domestic market and abroad not as a 90-minute game but as a two- to three-hour event.

I didn't need to persuade too much America's greatest sports fan, my friend Andy, to attend the game. I bought the tickets, he bought the beers for the 40-minute train journey to Mineola. The club lays on shuttle buses from the station to the ground. And by shuttle buses what they really meant was those iconic yellow school buses.

Tick one – seeing the Cosmos, tick two – a ride on an American school bus. I felt like I was on the set of *Charlie Brown, Forrest Gump, American Pie* and every other celebrated American film, although the fact we were sitting on a bus drinking bottle of Honker's Ale meant we were probably breaking a thousand laws and would ultimately find ourselves sent to the Principal's office, where of course the attractive secretary would punish us with a cane, wearing . . . stop it Stuart.

Our big yellow bus arrived at the Shuart Stadium at 7.30pm, kick-off time. Of course, being in America meant that the game didn't actually kick off at the official time, but some seven minutes later once the faffing had been completed. While the official attendance was announced later as 4,524, there seemed barely half of that in the stadium. With the sun setting over Manhattan in the distance, the majority of the crowd's applause was reserved for the impressive sunset rather than anything happening early doors on the pitch.

NEW YORK COSMOS 0, FC EDMONTON 0
Wednesday 6th August 2014 – Shuart Stadium

As I entered the stadium I grabbed a copy of the media pack. It was one of the most comprehensive documents I think I have ever seen at a football match. Full details of every game both sides had played, each player's profile and a form guide were standard, but the handy guide produced by the Cosmos Media Team meant we understood not only the background of the visitors from Edmonton, but also how to pronounce their players' names correctly (Tomi Ameobi is: Am-E-O-Be, for your information).

At one end of the stadium the hardcore elements of the Cosmos were actively waving their fans and banging drums. Andy had done some research and told me that there were actually three different groups. The Borough Boys, established in 2007 with the aim of bring soccer back to New York; since the reinception of the Cosmos they have been fully behind the team. Then there are the Cross Island Crew and finally there is the La Banda del Cosmos, whose mission is *"Todas las hinchadas en NYC unidas por la pasion del futbol. Mas alla de las fronteras los trapos, bombos y redoblantes seguiran brillando con LHUNYC."* All three groups combined to keep the tempo up in the first half, bouncing around the stand and giving us all something to sing along to.

The Cosmos' starting eleven included captain Carlos Mendes, who had moved to the Cosmos after six years at the Red Bulls. He has been the talisman for the side so far, scoring twice as many goals (two) in his short career with the Cosmos than he had done in the previous 10 years of his career (one). Norwegian striker, and hero of the win over the Red Bulls in the Open Cup, Mads Stokkelien was only named on the bench.

In the first half the highlights were three yellow cards and then the pint of Samuel Adams beer in the Beer Garden (a roped-off area behind the Main Stand where we still had to prove we were adults by showing ID). The game certainly wasn't a classic, with both teams struggling with the high bounce from the 3G pitch. Both defences played a high line, meaning that the linesmen's right arms were kept busy waving their flags. FC Edmonton had come to grab a point with a defensive 4-5-1 formation which stifled the flow of the game.

We were just finishing our beers when the cheers went up. Not the prolonged cheers of a goal, but the excited chatter that could only indicate a penalty. But to who? The crowd fell silent, then there was a thwack of boot on ball. A groan and a ball sailing over the stand told us everything we needed to know. The Cosmos had blown their big chance. Apparently, Edmonton goalkeeper John Smits fumbled a ball lofted into the box. His attempted recovery brought midfielder Jemal Johnson to the ground. Spanish midfielder Marcos Senna, enjoying his first start for the Cosmos in over two months, took the penalty but sent his shot high over the bar.

The rest of the second half saw the Cosmos try to break down the stubborn Canadians, having fifteen shots to the visitors three. Cosmos coach, Savarese, brought on Stokkelien as a substitute in the 58th minute for the Bulgarian Stefan Dimitrov as they continued to press for a goal. In the 69th minute, Senna came close again when his 20-yard free kick hit the top of the crossbar. With the clock ticking down, Tomi Ameobi, the middle of the three Newcastle Ameobi brothers, put in a two-footed challenge on Szetela which saw him red-carded. A goalless draw did neither team any good, meaning the Cosmos missed an opportunity to leap back to the top of the table. However, it would be no surprise to see them retain their trophy again this year come October time.

Despite the dominance by the Cosmos, the collective group of journalists voted goalkeeper Jimmy Maurer Man of the Match, thanks to a couple of great saves made when he was called upon. Members of the media at the game get to cast their votes to determine the Emirates Cosmos Man of the Match at every Cosmos home game, with the winner receiving an Emirates Boeing 777 model aeroplane with an engraved plaque. At the end of the season all of the votes are added up, with the winning player getting two round-trip tickets on Emirates from New York to Dubai. I'll be sure to tap Mendes up for some duty free if he wins after my vote.

We headed back to our yellow school bus for the five-minute trip to the station. Twenty minutes later we were still driving around side roads, industrial estates and park lots of Mineola. We all got excited at one point when we drove into the car park of the Western Beef Supermarket, which had a special offer on Coors beer –"Buy 12 beers, get a free steak knife" – but it just turned out that the driver was going to get directions. Quite why he didn't think of asking the 40 or so people on the bus, all of whom were scratching their heads, looking at Google Maps, as to where he was taking us, I can't fathom.

Finally, we arrived at the station, where those fans who'd decided to walk had already beaten us there. We had time for a swift beer in O'Carroll's Recovery Room, which lived by the motto of "the hair of the dog is the best medicine", before our train arrived for our journey back into the big city.

It had been an evening of remembering what might have been for the Cosmos. Forty years ago they were riding the crest of the biggest football wave on the planet. Twenty years ago they existed only as a memory and a replica shirt. Today they may still feel bitter about missing out on a spot in the MLS but life looks good for the Cosmos. They are building a supporter base once again and who knows where the next move will take them?

My trip to New York didn't end here. Twenty-four hours later and I was still on the Cosmos Heritage trail, heading by train from Penn Station to Meadowlands, home of the MetLife Stadium. It was here that the dreams of the marketing men came true as the New York Cosmos won the Soccer Bowl with an ageing Pelé in the side. At the time it was known as the Giants Stadium and over 40,000 on average used to come to watch the Cosmos play. It was here back in 2005 that I saw my first (and second) football match in America when England beat Colombia in a friendly, then the Metrostars played an MLS game which even now I cannot remember anything about (sunshine plus beer plus a snooze).

The stadium was demolished in 2009 while the new stadium was being constructed a few hundred yards away. The new stadium opened as a state-of-the-art 82,556-seat stadium, costing a cool $1.7 billion dollars. With the Red Bulls having their own stadium a few miles south in Harrison, the MetLife was a shrine to American Football. The 2013 season had ended with the stadium hosting the 48th Super Bowl during which the fans consumed 11,500 hot dogs, 7,400 lbs of fries, 59,200 chicken tenders (aka goujons), 3,750 meatballs and just 2,340 gallons of fizzy, sugar-filled, soft drinks. Six months later and the stadium was hosting gridiron once more.

Two nights previously, One Direction had rocked New Jersey. Littlest Fuller had set me a mission to track down which hotel the boys were staying at. I'm not quite sure what she wanted me to say to them if I found them but when she Facetimed me, the disappointment in her voice was clear to hear. "You mean you checked EVERY hotel in New York?" Of course I had. Fortunately, and not for the first time, CMF stepped in, pointing out that they had actually headed straight up to Boston from New York, according to Zane's Twitter feed, although I am now concerned that she follows him on social media.

Tonight it was the turn of the New York Jets to provide the entertainment. Well, sort of. This was the first of a couple of pre-season friendlies for the Jets and if we didn't much care for such games in England (of the round-ball variety of course) then there was simple ignorance of them here in America. With upwards of 70 players in their squads, these pre-season games are an important chance to try out their third- and fourth-string players under normal match conditions. They would be facing the Indianapolis Colts, who would also be using the game for the same purpose.

Hardly surprising then that I managed to pick up tickets in the lower tier on StubHub for just $12 each. I only had to mention the word "football" to good a friend, the true Englishman in New York, Luge and he was in. He explained why the crowd for this game would be around a tenth of what it would be if it were a regular-season game.

"Season tickets are like gold dust for both the Giants and the Jets. So the clubs know they have a captive audience. So they make all season ticket holders buy a ticket for pre-season games for every season ticket they have. The fans then try any route they can to recover any cash by selling them on StubHub." That explained why the $127 tickets were so cheap.

As expected, the game was poor, with each side scoring one touchdown. Most fans were concerned with consuming as much food and drink as possible. The strange licensing laws once again kicked in, with alcohol sales stopping at the end of half-time, meaning that everyone who wanted a beer simply queued up, showed their IDs and bought the maximum of four beers, taking them back to their seats. We had a bit more class than that, only taking the three pints of Rebel IPA, but even that couldn't keep us awake as the game entered the final quarter. The Jets Flight Crew did their best to keep our interests up but when they realised they were cheering a losing cause they stopped. So we left. That'll teach them!

Forty-eight hours in New York/Long Island/New Jersey had allowed me to follow in a heritage train of the NASL and the Cosmos, reliving some of my school memories. As Robson and Jerome once sang, "Time passes so slowly, but time can do so much." They also sang "There's always lots of pretty girls, with figures they don't try to hide", so you can't take what they said too seriously.

Oh, and I got to ride on a big yellow school bus.

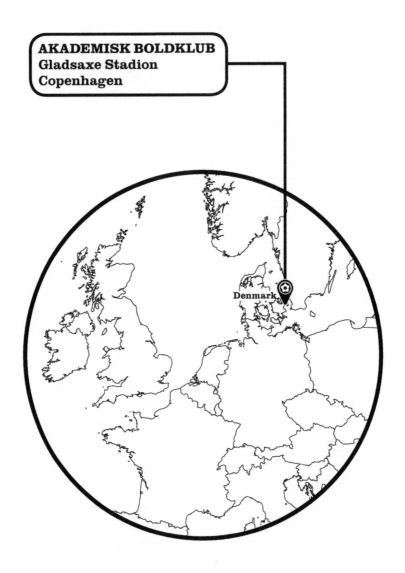

AKADEMISK BOLDKLUB
Gladsaxe Stadion
Copenhagen

Denmark

Their last title was back in the days when
Mrs Robinson was the original MILF.

14. Bloody Students

Like a graceful swan, gliding across the still water, football in Denmark always seems so serene. That is apart from when FCK meet Brøndy four times a year, when anything goes. But on the whole it is a harmonious footballing scene, with clubs, teams and fans getting on famously, which is quite surprising considering the utter chaos that has characterised how the game has grown up in Denmark.

Let me take you back to 1879 when Thomas Edison patented the light bulb, Leon Trotsky was born and Henrik Ibsen's play *A Doll's House* premiered to public outcry in Copenhagen. Perhaps the idea that the conservative values the Danes held in marriage were being challenged by Ibsen was the reason behind a group of young men forming Denmark's first football club on the fields of Fælledparken in Copenhagen. That club, Kjøbenhavns Boldklub, became the first ever organised football team in Continental Europe.

Ten years later clubs had sprung up all over the shop, characterised by initials here, there and everywhere. Kjøbenhavns Boldklub had realised their name was a bit of a mouthful for the majority so they simply became KB. Down the road we had BK Frem, MBK and AB.

Akademisk Boldklub, or AB for those who prefer the modern language of the youth, was formed by a group of academics in the city in 1889, with the only rule being you had to be a student to play for the club. A bit like Team Bath (for those who remember them), but with less of the "jolly japes". Their formation came at a time when sport was becoming more organised in Copenhagen and, at the request of KB, a football tournament was created later the same year.

Seven teams, including KB and AB, applied to take part in the ingeniously named "The Football Tournament", which was played over six rounds, with each tie being decided by extra time if the scores were level at 90 minutes and a replay after that, if necessary. The students won all six games, scoring 32 goals in the process to claim the first ever organised football championship. The impact AB had on football in Denmark cannot be underestimated as they won the tournament seven times in the first ten years, with KB taking the three other titles. Dare I say it, AB actually encouraged academia, with people flocking from all over the country to study in Copenhagen so that they could play for the most successful team in Denmark.

In 1903 the tournament was replaced by the "The Copenhagen Tournament", which aimed to bring in the various footballing groups that had been set up around the city at the turn of the century.

Some of the other clubs, fed up of seeing local players head off across the city to turn out for AB, actively encouraged them to start playing for local clubs. Some even realised that spending their time learning about the History of Fine Art or English Literature wouldn't give them anything more than a chip on their shoulder, so they gave up their studies. AB's domination was broken by the likes of B93, ØB and B1903. The Copenhagen competition ran until 1936 with AB claiming just two titles during this period. KB had risen to be the biggest club in Denmark, capturing 13 titles in the process.

In 1912 the championship was also used as the qualifying tournament for the newly created National Football Tournament, as clubs all over the country sprung up. However, it was still the teams from Copenhagen that dominated football in Denmark. In all its guises, the tournament was won by a team from the capital up until 1955, when AGF Aarhus from North Jutland finally broke the Copenhagen monopoly.

Today, initials still abound in Danish football. Anyone who wants to be taken seriously in these parts needs to complete a university course to learn your AB from your AaB. In the Superliga today we have AaB, AGF, FCK, FCM, FCN and OB. We shouldn't forget that the monsters of Danish football, FC Copenhagen, were formed back in 1992 through a convenient merger of KB and BK1903 and relocated from the west of the city to the brand, new national stadium at Parken. Since then KB have had their guts ripped out and returned back to their roots in the fifth tier of Danish football in the Copenhagen backwaters. Oh, and have I mentioned the likes of GVI, HIK, B93, B1901 and B1909 who litter the lower leagues? If there was ever a need for a glossary of terms, then in Denmark it would be a best-seller.

After my years of wandering the lower leagues of Denmark, my return visits had been few and far between. Alas, sometimes work gets in the way of real life and my skills were required elsewhere in the world. So instead of midweek trips to Køge, Hvidovre and even cross-national borders to Helsingborgs, I had the pleasure of hospitality at Billericay Town, Phoenix Sports and Thamesmead Town. I couldn't be happier. Honestly.

Although I tried to accidentally, coincidentally, as if by chance, arrange meetings and training sessions in Copenhagen when midweek fixtures were scheduled, bad weather seemed to always get in the way.

I had offers of Champions League football at Parken regularly, watching the gravy train roll into town, but at £60 a ticket to watch FCK bravely try to hold on to a draw with the Cypriot/Georgian/Azerbaijani champions it wasn't the best night out. Sometimes we just need an intervention from Miss Fate to bring us happiness, and that is exactly what this tale is all about.

Normally I would be fuming about a technical problem cancelling my flight home, but on a very pleasant summer's evening in August I couldn't have been happier. I was due to leave on the late evening flight back to London, but an issue earlier in the day meant that I wouldn't be going anywhere fast. Fortunately, the airline contacted me in good time and said I could fly back to Stansted on a late flight or have a free hotel room for the night and a guaranteed seat on the first plane out the next morning. And as luck would have it, there was a game being played in Copenhagen. We know what the rules say about that in the European Football Weekend's handbook, and despite the fact it was a Wednesday night, rules are rules. Cinders, you shall go to the game.

I still have good friends in Copenhagen who, in my hour of need, were happy to help me through the pain and would begrudgingly come with me to watch Denmark's first super club, Akademisk Boldklub. Ben offered pre-match beers and Anderson and Ivor agreed to get the sausages in.

Who could refuse such kindness?

"The Academic Football club" is certainly a bold statement in these days when MBAs can be bought online and "Google translate" has negated the need to ever learn a language. One would expect the likes of Wenger to one day arrive here, or that instead of having a boot room they may boast a library containing works by Jean-Paul Sartre, Søren Kierkegaard and Fyodor Dostoyevsky (of course Dostoyevsky). They can claim to have a Nobel Prize Winner among their alumni in nuclear scientist Niels Bohr, who played between the sticks on numerous occasions in 1905, whenever his atom-busting research allowed, alongside his brother Harald, who also turned out for Denmark in the 1908 Summer Olympics where he won a silver medal as the Danes lost to Great Britain in the final at White City. The Danes, playing in what was not only their first major competition, but also their first ever international match, beat France A 17-1 (with Sophus Nielsen scoring just the 10 goals, including a hat-trick by the sixth minute), and France B 9-0, where Bohr scored twice. Good team in those days, France.

Although the club was formed with the intention of giving Danish students a sporting outlet, after the new National Tournament was created on the demise of the Copenhagen version, it once again rose to prominence by winning the Danish National title on no less than 9 (nine!) occasions, only bettered by Brøndby IF and FC Copenhagen in recent times. Oh, and KB, which of course was part of the merger back in 1991 to create FC Copenhagen. So they have a fair footballing pedigree, although their last title was back in the days when Mrs Robinson was the original MILF, Sergeant Pepper decided Match.com wasn't for him and formed a band, and Che Guevara made a fatal mistake by holidaying in Bolivia (that's 1967 for those who can't be bothered to look up those events!). They did of course win the 1999 Danish Super Cup on penalties, beating AaB.

More recently, times have been tough for the Academics. Cash was poured into the club during the late 1990s, both in terms of ground redevelopment and the squad. Two big stands were constructed in 1998 that made the ground one of the best, if not the best, modern stadiums in Denmark. They finished third in the 1999 and 2000 Superliga but four years later they were relegated after being deducted nine points, as one of their players was found to have been registered illegally and the points they had earned while he played for them were removed. In 2007 the AB board announced to a great fanfare another large cash injection that would see the club back in the Superliga by 2010. Alas, despite building it, nobody really came, with crowds falling to below the 1,000 mark, while down the road at Parken, over 30,000 were enjoying the FCK domestic domination and the occasional visit of the likes of Juventus, Manchester United and Barcelona in the Champions League. Five years later and the club still languished in the second tier of Danish football, still counting crowds on two hands. In June 2012 the football club was saved from bankruptcy by the majority vote of the city council, which agreed to put together a financial rescue package. Hard times indeed.

While every year the club start with a clean slate, it seems that the needle is stuck on the record and by the time the winter break kicks in at the end of November it has all gone wrong. Last season they avoided relegation to the third tier of Danish football on goal difference, helped by the mid-season bankruptcy of FC Fyn which resulted in them being withdrawn from the league with each subsequent result awarded 3-0 to their opponents. The 2013/14 season had started as badly for AB as usual, and despite the season being just a few weeks old, it looked like being another long, hard slog against relegation and financial hardship.

So if you cannot win the league, what do you do? Put all your eggs into the cup basket of course! It's all about the magic of the cup, right? Anything can happen in the cup. Except it never does. In the past 10 years, FCK and Brøndy have won the cup six times, while the new kids on the block FC

Nordsjælland have worn the lid of the trophy on their heads in 2010 and 2011. So it seems that even that avenue has been firmly closed to the Academics. But last season we saw hope for all small clubs across Europe, with domestic cup success for the likes of Wigan Athletic, Vitória Guimarães and indeed here in Denmark with Esbjerg fB who beat Randers FC back in May. Perhaps this could be the season that AB once again were being talked about for all the right footballing reasons.

Alas, AB once again had cause to raise their collective fists and wave them skyward when the draw was made for the 2013/14 competition. With teams in the tournament from the regional leagues all over Denmark, AB were drawn at home to Lyngby. Lyngby from just down the road in Copenhagen. Lyngby, who had been in the top division until 2012. Lyngby who were the second-highest ranked team in the competition. The one consolation was that AB would be at home. Not much consolation really when you think about it, with crowds there rarely breaking the 500 barrier.

So AB needed all the support they could get. As if they required any further incentive the winners faced a mouth-watering trip to play Boldklubberne Glostrup Albertslund (remember lesson one about your acronyms) from Brøndby territory in the west of the city in Round Two. Of course, we all have a choice as to how we spend our leisure time and Ben, Ivor and I could have simply headed down to some of our old haunts on Nyhavn and watched the world go by, happy with our lot in life enjoying our £10 Carlsberg sitting in a pavement café. But we are made of sterner stuff and the prospect of an evening watching some desperate football in a crowd of a few hundred won hands down.

It's not hard to find the Gladsaxe Stadion, home of AB, in Copenhagen. Head north from the centre on route 16 and just look for the big TV mast. You can't miss it, it's over 200 metres tall and since 1955 has been transmitting beautiful pictures into the living rooms of Danes. It's thanks to this tower that we are all secretly lusting over Bridget Nyborg Christensen and Katrine Fønsmark, confused by the twists and turns of Sarah Lund, and enjoying the artistic work of Katja Kean today, or is that just me? We've gone all continental in the Fuller household these days with box sets of *Borgen*, *The Killing* and Danish *ColourClimax*. Those long winter nights really do fly by.

I wasn't a stranger to the Gladsaxe Stadion. Back in 2010 while en route to an AB game, Ben and I stumbled on something earth shattering. We'd been at a game just down the road in Brønshoj, ironically in the Danish Cup, and were heading a mile up the road for a second game of the day. Being a native, Ben took us on a "short cut" and as we turned a corner we came across a hill. A bloody hill. In Denmark, one of the flattest countries in the world! Not only was it a hill but there were people all dressed in Lycra, skiing down it. There wasn't a flake of snow in sight but these were land skiers, essentially wearing clown shoes with wheels on. I was surprised that this major geographical feature wasn't mentioned in the guidebooks.

Despite arriving for the game against Lyngby with less than three minutes to kick-off, we didn't have any issues finding a parking space at the ground. It seemed that cup fever hadn't gripped the Copenhagen locals. We were met with such enthusiasm at the gate that it did pass our minds that we were the only paying fans. "I blame Danish TV, deciding to show this game live," the chap on the turnstile told us, trying to explain why so few had come to the game. "But I expect it will be a classic." We had to admire his enthusiasm as we went to find Ivor, who had saved us a few rows of seats each.

AB 0, LYNGBY BK 3
Wednesday 21st August 2013 – Gladsaxe Stadion

The highpoint of the evening was spotting Kim Milton Nielsen, the referee who sent off David Beckham against Argentina in the 1998 World Cup finals. Well, when I say spotted, I mean Ivor spotted him after quite a few beers, standing watching the game with the man who cooked the sausages. It could have been another tall Dane simply having a quiet night out watching the magic of the Danish Cup but I like to believe in the romance of such a key figure in our national footballing history being one of the few hundred watching this game. That single decision split the country. We either hated Nielsen, or Beckham. Golden Balls was either a victim of a cheating Argentinian who tricked the referee into sending off Beckham, or an overpaid prima donna who showed his spiteful petulant side by launching a vicious attack on an innocent opposition player.

Never ones to overreact (and I say this as a life-long fan) West Ham fans hung effigies of Beckham from lamp-posts around Upton Park prior to the first game of the season when Manchester United were the visitors. In turn, every time Nielsen officiated he got a round of applause. Fortunately, football fans have short (ish) memories, and two years later he was a national hero once more. God bless Sir David and all that he has done for football across the world.

Nielsen retired from the game in 2006, after a career that included officiating in over 150 International games and at the 2004 Champions League Final. He seemed to dislike Manchester United though as, apart from the Beckham incident, he also controversially sent off Wayne Rooney in 2005 for sarcastically clapping him after he had been cautioned.

But back to the big match. Four Carlsberg specials, two bread rolls and a rather large sausage accompanied by three Lyngby goals was a decent return for the evening. Two of the goals were top drawer, the first scored by Andreas Granskov with a great lobbed volley and the second by Patrick Mortensen with a sweet side-foot, to which he added the third goal, to wrap things up, a few minutes later. The hundred or so away fans from down the road tried to whip up an atmosphere with a flare or two and some frisky flag waving but in truth everyone was happy to sit back and relax, enjoying the sunshine, including the AB defence who tried as hard as they could to gift Lyngby a goal in the opening 20 minutes.

The talk on the terraces in the first half was about the surreal start to the Super liga season with perennial favourites FCK and last season's champions FCN showing the kind of form that get coaches sacked even this early in the season. In fact this was exactly what had already happened at FCK. Earlier in the day at Parken, the messiah, the special one, the man with the Midas touch, Norwegian Ståle Solbakken, had returned to the hot seat after his achievement of spell in relegating Wolves. Solbakken is the most successful manager in FCK's history and the club hoped he would once again be able to weave his magic and break the recent dominance of FC Nordsjælland. In his five years in charge of the team from 2006 to 2011 he won five Superliga titles, one Danish Cup, two Scandinavian Royal League titles and took them into the promised land of the Champions League Group Stages twice. This was the only news story in the city and there were reporters wandering around the stands asking for people's reaction to the news.

Ben was approached and quoted the examples of Glenn Hoddle at Spurs and Terry Venables at Crystal Palace as to why you should never go back. Ivor, a life-long FCK fan (well since they started winning things in 1995), said it was up there with his wedding day whilst I could only choke on a bit of sausage I had just bitten off. Only time will tell if it's the right move or simply a knee-jerk reaction. Like meeting an old girlfriend years after you split up, you immediately remember all the good times, the night out in Skegness, the family Christmas dinners, and the holiday in Tenerife. But over time, when you start remembering all of those little niggling things that drove you mad, you realise that you can never reclaim those magic moments.

The final whistle was greeted with muted disapproval from the home fans who quickly realised that their season was now over. The few hundred AB supporters knew they were never in the races and that a cup dream would stay just that for another season while they suffered nine months of pain and suffering in the league, dreaming of what might have been if they had not been relegated due to the actions of one player. Lyngby, on the other hand, would prepare for Round 2 of the cup next week against BGA. And for us, hungry, thirsty Brits, Danes and Expats, the night was young, which could only mean a serious headache and a serious dent in the finances in the morning.

Copenhagen – I still bloody love you.

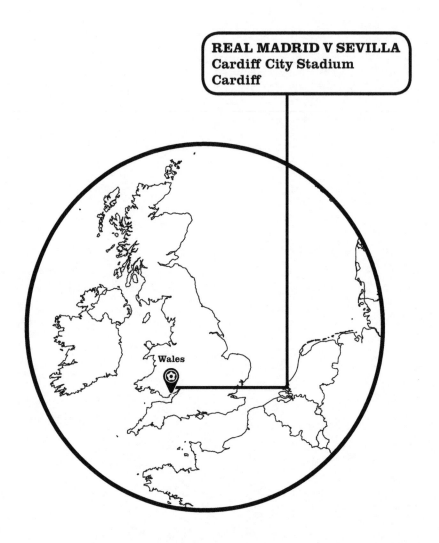

REAL MADRID V SEVILLA
Cardiff City Stadium
Cardiff

Wales

My plan goes swimmingly, right up to the point
where I need to get a train at Swindon.

15. The Half a Billion Team

A few weeks ago I received an email telling me that I had been allocated a media ticket for the 2014 UEFA Super Cup Final. My excitement at going to see Real Madrid play, and potentially get to interview Cristiano Ronaldo, wasn't shared by my work colleagues - in fact few of them could actually remember who was playing, let alone where. The competition, despite featuring a number of English clubs down the years, was a forgotten event of the start of the season.

When I gave them the details, their stock answer was one of surprise, especially when they understood it was being played in Cardiff. "I love the Millennium Stadium," said one, while another colleague assumed it was being held in the Welsh capital because Gareth Bale had chosen it as the venue. Neither could believe when I told them that it was being played at a ground that would be hosting regular Championship football that season. However, there was a lot of logic in the decision to play the game at Cardiff City's recently upgraded stadium. In the last decade the game had been predominantly played at the 18,000-all-seater Stade Louis II in Monaco, in front of average crowds of less than 17,000, with both sides given a small allocation. In 2012, obviously bored with the Monte Carlo nightlife, UEFA announced that the final would be rotated annually, starting with the game between Chelsea and Bayern Munich which was hosted in the Eden Arena, Prague.

The timing of the competition has caused a number of issues in the past. UEFA have moved match to mid-August to try and avoid the issue from previous seasons where the competitors had to cancel domestic league games to travel to play the game. In addition, some clubs also have to play in domestic curtain raisers such as the Community Shield, La Liga's two-legged Super Cup or the German version, which for the third season in a row would be between Bayern Munich and Borussia Dortmund.

The UEFA Super Cup is the Cousin Ruprecht of European competitions. A few years ago there was probably some prestige in playing in the tournament, but now there is so much money in the game that some clubs probably view it as an unnecessary evil associated with winning a major competition, knowing full well of the disruption that a game so early in the season will cause. Clubs take part in the competition purely for pride – the prize money on offer for the winners is less than a Ronaldo, Messi or Rooney gets paid in a few weeks these days. It is the one UEFA competition that has changed very little since its inception more than 40 years ago.

The Super Cup was created in 1971 by a Dutch football writer, Anton Witkamp, who felt that the great Ajax side of the time didn't get enough recognition after winning their first European Cup by beating Panathinaikos in London. At the time the European Cup was only open to the champions of the domestic leagues in the continent, plus the holders. What a bizarre idea? Imagine only the Champions being able to compete for the honour of a Champions Trophy! As if!

Due to its format it also meant that not necessarily the best two sides in the competition would meet in the final. It was also possible, due to different seasons played by some leagues, that not all the strongest sides would be in the competition. Domestic cup competitions were taken very seriously back then by all countries (again, imagine that!) so Witkamp's idea was to create a competition whereby the winners of the two premier European competitions would play each other to decide who were the real kings of Europe.

Witkamp did the hard work himself, setting up a two-legged game between the European Champions, his beloved team Ajax, and the European Cup Winners Cup champions, Rangers. Unfortunately UEFA refused to sanction the game as Rangers were banned from European competition due to the behaviour of their fans during the Cup Winners' Cup Final the previous season in the Camp Nou, Barcelona. As a result, the tie was financially supported by Dutch newspaper *De Telegraaf*, for which Witkamp was the Sports Desk Editor. Ajax defeated Rangers 6–3 on aggregate and thus won the first European Super Cup.

A year later Ajax were once again in the final having retained the European Cup, and this time the competition had the blessing of UEFA. Therefore the first UEFA Super Cup took place in January 1974 with Ajax overcoming a 1-0 defeat in the San Siro against Milan to put six past the Italians in the Olympic Stadium in Amsterdam, sparing the blushes of UEFA from the previous year's controversy.

However, just a year later it appeared the competition was dead and buried as West were due to play East in the form of Bayern Munich versus FC Magdeburg. With political pressure being put on both sides, especially with a FIFA World Cup due to start in Munich a few months later, which both countries would be taking part in, a date for the game couldn't be arranged and the competition was shelved for a year. It was East versus West the following year too as Bayern Munich, retaining their European Cup, played the great Dynamo Kiev side. The crowd of over 110,000 in the second leg in Kiev is still the biggest crowd for a Super Cup final.

The British record in the Super Cup has been very impressive, underlined by the period from 1977 to 1984 when we had a representative in the competition every season. Liverpool, Nottingham Forest (twice) and Aston Villa won the trophy during this period, while the 1985 final between Liverpool and Juventus was the first time the competition was played as a one-off due to the fixture congestion being experienced by both sides, ironically due to both clubs European Cup fixtures that would see them meet again in the infamous Heysel final a few months later.

In 1998 the decision was taken to scrap the two-legged final, played at varying points in the season, and replace it with a one-off game as a curtain-raiser to the new campaign. The UEFA Congress was traditionally held in Monaco every year so they decided to hold the game there. It was unlikely that any of the clubs would complain about a jolly boys outing to Monte Carlo on the UEFA Amex, even if the pitch at the Stade Louis II had come in for criticism over the years as it was built on top of a car park. Chelsea and Real Madrid contested the first "new" Super Cup with the Blues winning 1-0 thanks to a goal from Gus Poyet.

In 2007 I was lucky enough to get an invite to attend, which also included a helicopter transfer from Nice Airport, for the game between AC Milan and Sevilla. In fact, in the last 10 years Sevilla had appeared in more finals than any other side (including tonight's). The tournament in recent years had become a bit of a Spanish affair, with seven out of the last 10 featuring a Spanish team, and only Sevilla's defeat in 2007 to spoil the 100 per cent success record.

The 2013 game in Prague had seen Bayern Munich banish the ghosts of the 2012 Champions League final in Munich as they saw off Chelsea on penalties. Despite both clubs having very sizeable away followings, and Prague being known as a "party town" within easy reach of London and Munich, the crowd was relatively disappointing at the 20,800-capacity Eden Arena. Once again, ticket pricing and timing of the game were brought into question.

UEFA listened (shock, horror – football organisation listening to sense) and a decision was made to play the following season's game a few weeks earlier and in a bigger venue, although few could have predicted it would be in Cardiff. However, as luck would have it, the Gareth Bale connection made everything perfect. It was destiny, the prodigal son was returning home, albeit with a significantly bigger bank balance than when he left.

If Cardiff wasn't a strange enough choice for that year's game then fast-forward 12 months and two of Europe's biggest teams will be heading eastwards (unless of course they are from Azerbaijan or Kazakhstan, in which case it will be westwards) to the former Soviet Republic of Georgia where the fortieth (forty-first if you include the 1972 game) match will be played at the 27,223-seater Mikheil Meskhi Stadium in the capital city, Tbilisi. I'm still trying to work this one out myself. I get the concept of trying to re-energise the one-off game by rotating it around Europe, but who exactly wins from this one?

Tickets for the game in Cardiff went on sale at £40 to £110 each, marginally cheaper than they were in 2013 for Prague, and failed to sell out despite a late push from UEFA. I found it hard to imagine any locals being able to afford to go to the game the following year in Tbilisi. Georgia has a GDP per capita of just over $6,000 (about 150th in the world today) and an average wage of just £195 per month I couldn't see many locals forgoing rent, food and travel costs just to see the game. With difficult transport links into Tbilisi when compared to Prague or Cardiff (there are currently no direct flights to the city), just 61 hotels ranked on TripAdvisor and a stern warning from the Foreign and Commonwealth Office not to go anywhere near certain parts of the country, it looked like a trip for only the bravest and most loyal fans.

But back to 2014 and the question that most of the footballing world was asking. How do you solve a problem like Real Madrid? After a few years of "near misses" in Europe, the previous season they had turned on the style when it was needed and captured their tenth European Cup/Champions League when they beat Atlético Madrid in Lisbon, although their city rivals pipped them to the La Liga title. But Real Madrid aren't a real football club any more. The club is the world's richest in terms of revenue, with an annual turnover of €513 million, and the most valuable sports team, worth €2.4 billion according to *Forbes Magazine*. The team that took the field in Cardiff in the Super Cup Final could well be the first half a billion pound starting eleven in world football.

Not content with having one of the world's best players in Ronaldo, the most expensive in Gareth Bale and a World-Cup winner in the form of Toni Kroos, they'd dipped into the transfer market that summer to sign the star of the 2014 World Cup, James Rodriguez, for a mere £63 million from AS Monaco. Some may have considered this a good problem to have, but how would Carlo Ancelotti keep all of those four happy with game time? Last season Bale and Ronaldo managed 46 La Liga goals between them with the lone striker at the club, Karim Benzema, adding 17 of his own. Scoring goals has never been an issue for Los Merengues – it has been the erratic defending, summarised by players like Pepe and Sergio Ramos, both of whom failed to cover themselves in glory in Brazil. It is surprising, given their love of defenders who enjoy wandering about the pitch, that the club didn't put an offer in for David Luiz, especially as Ancelotti signed him for Chelsea back in 2011.

Talking of players who had a nightmare in the FIFA World Cup, you will undoubtedly remember the torrid time that goalkeeper Iker Casillas had. Despite his iconic status within the club, with him having made over 500 appearances for them, there were widespread concerns that he had entered a terminal decline. After initially being dropped by former boss Jose Mourinho three years earlier, he had been replaced in La Liga the previous season by Diego Lopez, only appearing in cup games.

And although Casillas ended up winning the Champions League, his personal performances were less than convincing: he was at fault for Atletico's goal in the final in Lisbon and rated his performance in Spain's opening game of the FIFA World Cup where they lost 5-1 to the Netherlands as his "worst ever". During the summer he also looked unsure in the Guinness International Champions Cup, especially in the defeat to Manchester United. It wasn't as if many people were watching either – the crowd for the game in Michigan was only 109,000. Ancelotti could not afford to have his players make mistakes. While the retention of the Champions League would be a prime objective, the preceding season's third-place finish in La Liga could not afford to be repeated. So it was unsurprising that he had already brought in a new goalkeeper, Costa Rica's star stopper, Keylor Navas.

But was everyone forgetting that there were two teams playing in the game? Sevilla are no mugs and the fact that this would be their third appearance in the Super Cup Final in the last decade underlined one major fact: they had won more European trophies in the past 10 years than Real Madrid. They had won the Europa League/UEFA Cup on three occasions, including the final last season in Turin where they beat Benfica. They weren't coming to make up the numbers. Last season they had finished fifth in La Liga, beating Real Madrid at home (although they would not want to be reminded about the 7-3 defeat in the Bernabéu I am sure) and Unai Emery's side would surely be hoping that to break into the top four that season.

So match day in Cardiff. My plan went swimmingly, right up to the point where I needed to get a train, at Swindon. The golden rule in Great Britain is 'never trust a train' but instead of driving the whole way down to Cardiff, and because I really object to having to pay a toll one way on the Severn

Bridge but not the other, I chose to drive part-way then train the rest. After all, according to the Tourism Wales website, plenty of buses would take fans arriving by train to the stadium from 6pm.

My original plan was to arrive around 5pm in Cardiff, then head down Westgate Street for a couple of beers, then catch the bus to the stadium. Alas, Great Western Trains put a spanner in that. You wouldn't have guessed there was a problem when I arrived at Swindon, with my train only two minutes late. Two minutes after it should have arrived, it became another two minutes late. And so on for the next 35 minutes. According to my good friend Twitter, this is because they use some super-duper technology on the tracks that senses when a train passes and relays the info to the information boards. So if it passes point 1 and then not point 2 it assumes it is delayed, and delayed by a default 2 minutes. Pointless.

The train was full of Spaniards heading for the game, dressed in full kit (the ladies) and shorts and vests for the men. Oh how they laughed as we passed under the River Severn and out into a monsoon. Our train pulled into Newport and their faces simply said "Where have we come?" I pointed out that Cardiff was much better – after all, it did have a Waitrose.

A few of them were in a heated debate as to where the stadium was. It seemed that it wasn't just my work colleagues who had assumed it was being played at the Millennium Stadium. They were struggling to find the Cardiff City stadium on their phones. "Don't worry" I said, "they are laying on buses to take you to the stadium."

I waved my new Sevilla-supporting friends goodbye as they turned right and I turned left out of the station. I had time for a swift half or three in the City Arms where I had spent many a happy hour before the normal English Rugby Union humiliation by the Welsh. In fact the only time I had seen any team apart from the Welsh win in any sport in Cardiff had been on my first visit to the Cardiff City stadium where Valencia had beaten the Bluebirds, as they still were back then, in a pre-season friendly on my wedding anniversary. Romantic, you may say. Absolutely. I'd even bought her a pair of Cardiff City slippers as a present. She wasn't with me, mind. She had surprisingly chosen to stay in Barry Island with Littlest Fuller on a Gavin & Stacey Heritage Walking Tour.

I've been a regular visitor to Wales in the past. The Gower Peninsula is still one of my favourite places to head for a long weekend, with the remote clean beaches, great nightlife in Swansea (you cannot fail to pull/get into a fight/get food poisoning after a night out in Wind Street) and of course the fantastic Welsh people. Charlotte Church (voice of an angel, liver of a wino according to Catherine Tate), Imogen Thomas and of course Catherine Zeta-Jones. I wanted to call my first daughter Catherine but CMF stopped me as she felt my motivation was not in the right place. Many a time we've driven up and down the roads of Swansea hoping to catch a glimpse of the lesser-sighted CZJ, but after a few days even the kids started to question my three-hour route to the beach, which was visible from our holiday home.

Back in a previous life (which is code at home for when I am about to tell a story featuring a romantic interest prior to the arrival of CMF) I went out with a Welsh girl whose parents had a house in Swansea, so I was forever taking her up the Mumbles (insert Finbar Saunders giggle at this point). Despite living in Jack Town, she was a true Bluebird and on a number of occasions we went to Ninian Park, back when Cardiff really were crap. None of this protesting about whether the kit should be red or blue. Back then it was whether anyone on the Grange End would get showered with bits of the roof every time that Nathan Blake took a shot on goal (and thus ended up hitting the roof of the stand). After the football we had walked along Ninian Park Road and into the city centre for a few Brains, a bag of Teisennau Tatws and a quick fumble on the train back to Swansea.

Cardiff today is a very different beast. The construction of the Millennium Stadium transformed the Riverside area, and huge developments on Cardiff Bay brought in overseas investment, making the city almost unrecognisable when I visited for the first time in years back in 2002. The redevelopment of Sophia Gardens from a tired old county ground to an international venue left Ninian Park standing like a sore thumb on the outskirts of the city centre. But that all changed in 2007 when work started across the road from Ninian Park on a brand-spanking-new stadium that would be home not only to Cardiff City but also the Cardiff Blues Rugby Union team.

The new stadium, aptly named the Stadiwm Dinas Caerdydd, or Cardiff City Stadium, opened in July 2009 as a 26,000all-seater arena, which was more than ample for the club, who were playing at the top end of the Championship. However, the arrival of new owner Vincent Tan not only saw the club promoted to the Premier League for the first time, but also saw the sacking of popular manager (and Lewes FC owner) Malky Mackay, and the changing of the club colours, and the club badge, from blue to red. It was fair to say that the fans weren't totally happy with what was going on on Soper Road. Tan's plans of grandeur didn't stop at rebranding. He agreed to increase the capacity of the stadium to 33,000 with an additional tier added to the east side of the stadium, which would be ready in time for the Super Cup final.

An hour in the pub was enough so I headed back down to the station, only to see the same Sevilla fans, now very wet and very mad as no buses had turned up at all. I slipped on my baseball cap and set off down Tudor Street, deciding that the evening stroll would do me a world of good. Hardly the most romantic of routes for the travelling Spanish fans heading to the ground, although a lot quicker than those who were still waiting for the buses to arrive. The city had tried to make an effort by adding banners to the lamp-posts but with rain falling, everyone had their heads down and missed the inspirational messages such as "O Gaerdydd mae Gareth Bale", which of course we all know from our O-Level Welsh means: "In Cardiff there will be Gareth Bale."

The Cardiff City Stadium certainly looked smart, the recent redevelopment work now complete though the new red seats looking a little out of place within a mostly blue stadium bowl. We all knew it would be only a matter of time before the whole of the stadium was decked out in Tan Red, as the colour would be called in Dulux paint terms. Talking of paint, this was to be a historic event, as English referee Mark Clattenburg was handed the "golden spray can", the first official in a European game to be able to use the vanishing spray.

The opening ceremony was bizarre, as they usually are. Without some kind of audio commentary it is difficult to know what is actually going on, and where you should be looking. What was very clever though was the way the word CARDIFF, spelt out in big white letters, suddenly disappeared, merging into the names of Real Madrid FC and Sevilla FC. Not content with the usual plinth with the match ball on, tonight we had three. One for the ball and then as the teams emerged, the two captains placed the respective European trophies on the other two. Quite what happened to them both is a mystery as the opening ceremony reached a climax and our attention was diverted away. Clever ruse and one that will no doubt feature in *Ocean's Seventee*n.

Ancelotti had managed to shoehorn in all of the £500 million-plus talent into the line-up, which a tactical aficionado like Michael Cox or Jonathan Wilson, would describe as 4-1-1-2-1-1 (or the "Crucifix", as I am christening it). But the rest of us would call simply goal hanging city. The Sevilla fans got the party going with a fine scarf-twirling routine along with what sounded like a much better version of Lady GaGa's "Fine Romance". The fans at the other end waved bits of white toilet paper.

The game ebbed and flowed nicely without either side really creating a great chance. Both keepers were called into making bread-and-butter saves, although in Casillas's case that was probably more important than for Beto. Twenty-five minutes in and Ronaldo created the best chance of the game, spinning in the box with the ball miraculously tied to his feet before shooting straight at Beto.

Slap-bang on the 30 minute mark the old partnership worked its magic. Bale was given far too much room down the left-hand side and whipped in a cross to the far post where Ronaldo – who else? – slid the ball home. Sevilla were almost level within a couple of minutes as Caricco took advantage of a slip by Rodriguez, found some space in the area and fired across the goal, but Casillas was wise to the danger and saved smartly.

The midfield battle was shaping up nicely, with Bale and Modric pulling the strings. New signing James Rodriguez looked off the pace in the first period, unsure where he should be playing as Bale, Benzema and Ronaldo all interchanged positions. A couple of the Sevilla players welcomed him to Spanish football with little taps on the ankles. All part of the game.

Sevilla underlined their tag of rank underdogs coming into the game and rarely suggested they had the resources to upset the odds during the first period. Real had slowly taken a grip on the game, and even with some defensive failings they showed enough of their relentless attacking drive in the first half to make every team in Europe sit up and take note. Claims that they are aiming to win six trophies that season may have been exaggerated, but they had started in the right way, exhibiting the steel and determination that would be needed to achieve such a feat.

Half-time and I ventured back down to the Media room. The beer fridge was firmly locked. "Heineken would love to share a beer with you post-match." As if lazy journalists even considered staying down here, drinking the free beer and just filing their report from what they were watching on the TVs. I grabbed a free cup of water and headed back up to my seat to watch the first-half highlights on the TV screen in front of me. The chap to my left was engrossed in Holby City on his, obviously taking his duties very seriously.

We had hardly switched our laptops on when Ronaldo doubled the lead, finishing with style from the left after Benzema had put him through. Even with 40 minutes to go it was game over. Ronaldo, put through by Bale, went down far too easily under a challenge and waved his hand to Clattenburg suggesting it was a bookable offence. A girl behind me, wearing her Welsh shirt with pride, stood up and shouted, "Get up you tart. You go down easier than xxxx after a Breezer on Wind Street" (I have removed the name of said lass just in case it isn't true and I am sued. However, I am willing to do some research if you want to provide the Bacardi Breezers). Sevilla tried their best to force Madrid onto the back foot where their Achilles heel has been for a number of seasons, but they lacked the patient approach play. Manager, Emery, sporting some very natty elbow patches on his suit that I expect took his mum all night to sew on, tried to change things around so that their one danger man, Suarez, saw more of the ball. But in the end it finished 2-0 and no surprises to see Ronaldo awarded Man of the Match, receiving his award from his former boss, Sir Alex Ferguson, who when asked later confirmed that, unlike Ian Wright and Glenn Hoddle, he was still referred to as "gaffer" by the striker.

The pitch became a mass of white and blue confetti as the fans waved even more white toilet paper. One down, five to go. I headed down to try and get into the press conference or even grab a word with Ronaldo or Bale. Of course I could claim that the following quotes were given to me exclusively, but you would never believe that. After all, I struggle to get a word out of Jack Walder, the Lewes captain these days.

Real Madrid manager Carlo Ancelotti was relatively humble in his post-match words, although he must have said them with a very big smile on the inside, mentally counting his end of season bonus already:

"The team played very well, especially bearing in mind we didn't have much time to prepare. The game worked out pretty well. I think we might be starting a very important cycle. We have a squad of extraordinary quality – I am fortunate to be able to coach an outstanding group of players. It's hard to improve this team. We have an outstanding set of players, and it is important to use the squad to its full capacity. To be competitive in all competitions we need to rotate players."

I had a train to catch so headed off out into the bright lights of Leckwith. The last service out of Cardiff to Swindon took us on a long detour of what seemed every town in Gloucestershire and Wiltshire, picking up Bristol City and Oxford United fans along the way who had decided that the Capital One Cup was a better way to spend their evening. We all know that alcohol, football fans and trains can be a volatile relationship and it seemed that getting off at Swindon was a wise move before the combined forces of Oxfordshire and Avon tried to take on a carriage full of Spanish fans.

Getting home at 3.30am was a small price to pay for a slice of the action. Real Madrid are once again the side that everyone wants to see, apart from Barca and Atletico fans, and they didn't disappoint. Of course we had no idea whether they would win all six trophies that year, but got the feeling that it would be sure to be entertaining regardless. And as for Cardiff? Well apart from the issues of getting to the ground it had proved to be a perfect host. I fear that we won't be saying the same things after the 2-15 final.

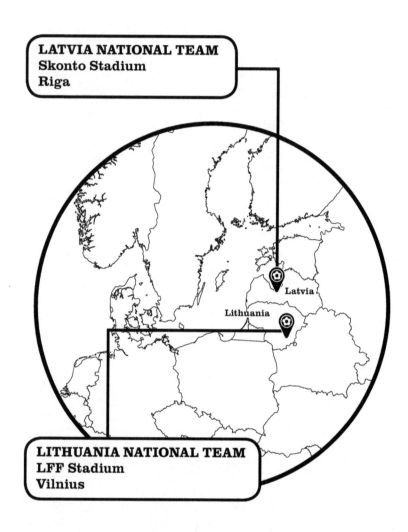

LATVIA NATIONAL TEAM
Skonto Stadium
Riga

Latvia

Lithuania

LITHUANIA NATIONAL TEAM
LFF Stadium
Vilnius

The FA's Marketing and Spin Department
would have to go into overdrive to make
these games attractive.

16. A Former Soviet State of Affairs

After years of distinctly average performances in major tournaments, and the continued blinkered approach taken by our own Football Association, love for our national side had fallen to an all-time low. Need any proof of this? Well how about the lowest attendance for an international at Wembley since it reopened for the game in September 2014 against Norway, the fact that *The Great British Bake Off* got more viewers than ITV's live coverage or that Wayne Rooney actually pays a lookalike to play in these meaningless games so he can stay at home in Manchester – well two out of those three are correct and the third is open to debate.

The Premier League season hadn't even started before it was time for an international break. Premier League managers were up in arms about losing players for days on end each month as they jetted off to the four corners of the world to go through the motions of caring about representing their countries. The format of UEFA's European Championship now meant that each country basically had a one in two chance of qualifying for the 2016 tournament in France. England's win in early September away at group second seeds Switzerland all but secured their place in France with nine games still to play. With matches at Wembley against San Marino, Estonia and Lithuania subsequently to try and fill, the FA's Marketing and Spin Department would have to go into overdrive to make these games attractive, while ITV would be preparing to lose audience share to re-runs of *The Vicar of Dibley* on UK Gold.

The question of the use of Wembley for all England games once again raised its head after the debacle of the Norway game. The FA are allowed to count the thousands of Club Wembley seats within the official attendance, whether the holders choose to attend or not, so actual ticket sales had probably been on a par with a mid-table Championship side (which ironically sums up the performance against Norway pretty well). The FA's stance was unwavering: Wembley was a £200 million millstone around the national team's neck and even if attendance figures fell to three figures, England will be running out at Wembley for decades to come. Who needs fans when you have corporate patronage and a new light system powered by a mobile phone company, even though said company can't actually provide a signal to four people in the Fuller household, let alone 80,000 in the stadium?

But then there appeared to be a change in thinking. The money men at the FA saw the tills ringing when American Football came to town in late September, and instead of worrying how to entice people to watch the national team they asked themselves: how about bringing more of the US's best loved sport to London? If that happened then it would be a case of "run along England, back to the provinces". After all, FA is an anagram of AF, standing for American Football. Tenuous enough? I'm sure it would do.

While there were dozens of reasons to hate these international games, there was also one fact that was simply too good to miss. Obviously someone in UEFA liked a road trip or two and decreed that the international break would actually be six days of games across football. Should you be so inclined, you could go to a game a day for nearly a week. That would obviously be very silly, wouldn't it . . . and expensive.

"That's just silly and a waste of money," The Current Mrs Fuller told me as I floated an idea of a Baltic road trip for the October internationals. "And aren't you forgetting the small matter of my birthday during that break?" She was right. I had forgotten that her birthday would be slap-bang in the middle of the trip. But what girl wouldn't want to spend her special day in an Irish Bar in Tallinn prior to the game between Estonia and England with hundreds of pissed-up England fans? "Fair point," I said. After all, I'd want to save such a special treat for her fortieth birthday next year.

Marriage is all about compromise, so we agreed that in exchange for a day at a posh spa as a birthday present, I could head off to the Thursday and Friday games. Two new countries presented themselves to me: Lithuania and Latvia. Sharing a border, the two former Soviet States were two of the newer members of the European Union, and had adapted to life without the apron strings better than some other countries, notably neighbouring Belarus.

It all looked so easy on paper. Fly from Luton to Vilnius, capital of Lithuania, watch them take on Estonia, then head up to Riga for Latvia v Iceland before a dawn flight back to Blighty, all for under £150. I opened a bottle of Chateau Neuf De Pape before she could change her mind. It would undoubtedly be the best trip ever.

Trip. Now there's a relevant word. For a number of reasons, not least to prove to myself I had the willpower to achieve it and the fact I was due to have an operation on my knee, September was deemed a no-alcohol month. Despite the pressures of a new job, an office move and a disastrous start to the season by Lewes, I managed a full 32 days from the 30th August to 2nd October.

And then I fell off the wagon in spectacular fashion. Perhaps it wasn't wise to spend a day in Lille for "research" purposes as my first day back on the beer. By the time I arrived home at 7pm I was tired and emotional. I agreed to all sorts of requests from the little Fullers, each exploiting the weakness that a dozen strong French beers had caused in my armour.

Around 9pm I decided to bring a full cup of tea, a laptop and a large book down the stairs. A simple job when sober, but when under the influence it was like a task from the Krypton Factor (kids: ask your dad). And of course I slipped. I still claim one of the cats ran past me, causing my fall, although I did deserve a round of applause for not dropping the book or laptop and hardly spilling a drop of my tea. The subsequent damage to my ribs, arm and thigh, however, initially brought out the family's sympathy. I think I pushed that too far when I suggested that CMF slip on her saucy nurse's outfit. Apparently our teenage daughters didn't need to know that, or the fact I liked her to dress up as an air stewardess, Snow White or the left back from Bristol Academy Ladies team. Can't do right for doing wrong sometimes.

A week later and I passed a late fitness test on my ribs and was allowed to travel. First up I had to negotiate the delights of Luton Airport. It doesn't seem to matter how much money is spent on our airports (or how many TV programmes are made about them), they aren't designed with passengers in mind. Luton is exceptionally bad, with huge queues for everything and the airport trying to milk every penny out of passengers, such as charging a premium to get to the front of the security queues, which they seem to deliberately make so long by only opening a small section, or having the cheek to charge a pound for one of those plastic bags for your liquids. Unfortunately it was a necessary evil for this trip.

Two and a half hours after take-off from gloomy Luton we landed at gloomy Vilnius to a round of applause. I still fail to understand this custom, which seems common among Eastern and Central European citizens. It's like tipping your binmen or postman at Christmas. We don't tip our doctors or dentists who have our welfare in their hands, so why show gratitude to a pilot (or his auto friend) for doing their job?

What can I tell you about Vilnius that you don't know about already? Well how about these five facts just for starters.

1) The city has some of the fastest internet speeds in the world, with average download speeds of 36 MB/s.
2) Vilnius has some of the cleanest tap water in the world due to the

number of freshwater lakes it has.

3) CNN voted the Christmas tree in Cathedral Square as the best in the world in December 2013. Woof.

4) The city is the birthplace of Hannibal Lecter. . Well, that's what author and creator Thomas Harris said anyway.

5) The Easter bunny is old hat in these parts, replaced by the Easter Granny or Velyku Senele, if you are in the know.

It also has an UNESCO World Heritage Site Old Town, dozens of stunning buildings and a thriving economy. Alas, I wasn't going to see much of Vilnius at all, which was one downside of the packed agenda. It's supposed to be a beautiful city but from touchdown to departure on my executive bus it would be 11 hours of darkness. My taxi driver from the airport offered to show me the sights of the city on the way to the hotel.

"There is Ikea. Now we go to McDonald's and then a brothel." I managed to convince him that McDonald's, being opposite my hotel, was actually a better alighting point. "But no titty-titty?" He looked crestfallen that I preferred a McFlurry to a "naked help-yourself buffet" but soon cheered up when I gave him a 10-litu note as a tip (which incidentally had a picture of the Kemp twins on it).

I'd struck lucky in picking the hotel, not only because it was opposite a 24-hour fast-food outlet but because it was a five-minute walk to the LFF Stadium. Oh, and it had a bar offering 50-pence beers open until everyone had gone to bed, which. as I learnt later, was about 6am.

There would be some domestic interest in my first destination, with England due to visit Vilnius in exactly a year for the final game in Group E. Both teams had won their opening match, so it was possible for a brief moment that one of them could top the group come full time. With some bookies offering odds of 5/1 on San Marino getting a corner, let alone a goal, at Wembley against England, the Three Lions would be top at the end of the evening on goal difference, if not points.

Press pass collected, I was ushered into the inner sanctum of the stadium and given a mini tour by my own personal escort. CMF had already given me strict instructions about asking nice ladies about extras so I bit my lip and just asked for a coffee when she asked if she could do anything more to make my visit to Lithuania more pleasurable.

Estonia had travelled in decent numbers, with a few hundred fans having made the short trip south. Despite some of the worst attendances in domestic game (I once watched league leaders Ajax Tallinn play in the national stadium with just 43 other fans), the national team is well supported, and despite the warnings of sleep-inducing performances, the game on Sunday against England was a complete sell-out in the Le Coq Arena in Tallinn.

Despite their love of basketball, the locals had also come out in numbers. Luke Winn, a writer for *Sports Illustrated*, said in an August 2011 story about the passion for the sport in the country that "Basketball is the only sport Lithuanians truly care about – it is their second religion, after Catholicism, and their success is proportionately stunning." This is borne out when you look at the average attendance of the A-Lyge, the top division here in Lithuania, which is just 744, making it one of the 10 worst-supported leagues in Europe. The top club in terms of crowds are the current champions FD Žalgiris Vilnius, which gets 1,256 in the LFF Stadium.

It was a balmy evening in Vilnius, which in Lithuanian terms means it wasn't raining or snowing – a good job really as, bar a few rows of hospitality seats, the LFF Stadium is completely open to the elements. It is still a work in progress and has only a fraction of the capacity that the country's biggest ground has, the 15,000-capacity Žalgiris Stadium down the road. The hardcore fans in the corner of the stand behind the goal (there is only one, as the other end appears to have been stolen) stood, bounced, chanted and waved scarves, while the fans around the rest of the ground politely clapped when the Lithuanians broke.

The 3G pitch proved to be a challenge for both sides. The first chance of the game fell to Lithuania's Deivydas Matulevičius in the sixth minute, but the ball ran away from him on the fast surface as he broke free of the Estonian defence and the Finnish keeper smothered the ball.

Arvydas Novikovas of Bundesliga club FC Erzgebirge Aue was the stand-out player in the first period for the home side, causing the Estonian defence no end of problems, mainly because he had mastered the bounce of the artificial surface, and his shot from distance in the 36th minute was the first real chance to break the deadlock.

Chances were few and far between as both five-man midfields cancelled each other out, leading to long periods of play when the most exciting thing to watch was the stunning full moon. Lithuania showed more purpose and finally got their reward with 15 minutes to play when a shot bobbled up off the artificial surface which the Estonian keeper Sergei Pareiko could only push into the path of Matulevičius and he squared for substitute Saulius Mikoliunas to head home. Almost matching the cheers for the goal was the applause for a second yellow for Estonia's right midfielder Ken Kallaste, tormented all night by Novikovas.

With the game kicking off at 9.45pm local time, it was past midnight once I left the stadium. With another home game to follow on Sunday against Slovenia, Lithuania could have a 100 per cent start to their qualifying campaign and a real shot at the play-offs in the group. Back at the hotel the locals had taken over the bar and I was welcomed to their bosom. They were keen to talk about London and some of the things they should see and do when they came in March for the game at Wembley.

They seemed pleased we too had Ikea and McDonald's although I'm not sure they will be too impressed when they arrive and ask a cabbie to take them to the home of "hot and spicy birds, Nandos". Well, what do I know about that sort of thing?

At 3am I had to call it a night. Some strange, sweet, brown liquid was being poured into shot glasses and this wasn't going to end well if I stayed, what with a 5.30am alarm call.

My method of transit between the two capital cities was a "luxury, executive coach". Apparently for €25 I would be transported between Lithuania and Latvia in unbridled comfort with a reclining leather seat, free Wi-Fi, free breakfast and movies on demand in my own screen. Yeah, right.

OK, sometimes I'm wrong. The description was spot on. This was possibly the best coach in the world, even complete with warnings about not using the Wi-Fi to watch "movies that may offend other passengers". Four hours after leaving Vilnius and cruising across the incredibly flat plains of Lithuania and Latvia we rolled into a murky, grey Riga.

I've done a bit of travelling in Eastern Europe and the former Soviet States and all the hallmarks were clear to see as the coached pulled up at the bus station. The huge, ornate palace-type building, the onion-domed churches and the criss-cross of wires above the road for the trolley-bus network. Everything looked grey. Even the girls in their high boots looked moody. This wasn't how I imagined Riga.

After checking into my hotel I headed out to explore. Riga, it seemed, was like pass the parcel. Remove the outer wrapping of the crumbling Soviet buildings, the potholes and cheap-looking shops around the edge of the city and you are rewarded by a magnificent old town with a beautiful park alongside the Pilsêtas canal and some jaw-dropping architecture such as the Melangalvju Nams (rough translation: "the blackheads house") which according to the guidebook was a stopping point for unmarried merchants – so a brothel then? One bit of Latvian I learnt quickly was that they love adding an 's' to words even though they aren't plurals. Bars means a singular bar, for instance, although I'm not sure how you would describe a street that had a few of them.

Cultured out, it was time for a local brew or two. I was aware that a number of England fans were in the city, fresh from the glorious slaughter last night of the footballing superpower of San Marino, so I gave the Irish Bars a swerve where out of tune – badly sung verses of Wonderwall were already polluting the air – and went to Ala Pageabs in the Old Town, tempted by SIXTEEN local beers on draft and a decent pepper steak all for less than €20 (not covering all 16 beers I hasten to add!).

The catchily named SMSCredit.lv Virslīga is the top division in Latvia and was dominated by Skonto Riga after independence from Russia in 1991 with 13 consecutive championships. These days it's FK Ventspils who get the pulses racing, although the average attendance in the league is still only on a par with Lewes FC's Ryman Premier League average of just over 500. Like Lithuania, football takes second place in national sporting interest. Ice Hockey is the real passion in these parts. Skonto these days struggle to break the 400 fans mark on match day at the 10,000-capacity national stadium. In contrast, Dinamo Riga average over 8,000 fans for their ice hockey games at Arena Riga.

Latvia has had relative success in international terms compared to some of the countries that it would consider to be its rivals (i.e Lithuania, Belarus and Estonia). Back in 2004 they qualified for the UEFA European Championships in Portugal, beating Turkey in the play-offs to reach a major tournament for the first time. Despite being the lowest-ranked team in the tournament and drawn in a very tough group, the Latvians held their own and made a whole nation proud. They took the lead in their first game against the Czech Republic with just 20 minutes left but fell to two late goals in the scorching sun of Aveiro. Then they held the mighty Germans to a goalless draw in Porto before losing their final game against the Netherlands.

That squad of players including such familiar names to us English football fans as Marians Pahars, Igors Stepanovs and Aleksandrs Kolinko should have gone on in the next few years to bigger and better things. However, 2004 remains their peak, although the current qualification tournament for an expanded championship in France does offer some hope that the good times may return. Pahars is now national team coach and Latvia can lay claim to being the best team in the region after back-to-back Baltic Cup Championships, the last of which was in May when they beat Lithuania. They started their qualification campaign with a 0-0 draw in Kazakhstan last month and welcomed Iceland to Riga as one of the "must win" games in order to finish in the top two in Group A.

Goalkeeper Kolinko had survived from that team back in 2004 and 10 years later the former Crystal Palace keeper, now plying his trade in the Russian enclave of Kaliningrad for Baltika, lined up in the three-quarters-full Skonto Stadium. Ah yes, the stadium. I've been in plenty of three-sided affairs before, such as the LFF Stadium in Vilnius just 24 hours previously, but how about a two and two-thirds one? At one end of the stadium the presence of a large sports hall meant that the stand only ran to where the goal was, giving the whole ground an unfinished feel – a bit like Dean Court or Bloomfield Road before they filled the ends in.

At least there was a bit of an atmosphere as the hardcore Latvian fans had given ice hockey a swerve for the night and come out in numbers to support the team. Heck, they even had a few Scottish fans in there as well, as you do. The Iceland fans had also come in numbers and were making themselves heard with their repertoire of English 1980s pop classics. "Just Can't Get Enough", "Tom Hark", "Da Da Da", "Come On Eileen" and "Save Your Love" were chanted in the first half to take our collective minds off the game. One had even brought a vuvuzela – what fun that was!

Despite having home advantage, Latvia played with a strange 3-1-4-1-1 formation, christened 'the jumbo jet' based on how it looked on paper which, placing my scouting hat on, meant that Valērijs Šabala in the "false-nine" position should have been able to drift across the Iceland back four causing them confusion as to who would pick him up. Alas, it didn't. The Iceland defenders looked very comfortable with the ball, playing it in triangles around the Latvia midfield in the first half although with no penetration.

Any real hope of getting the home win they needed disappeared in the 55th minute when midfielder Vladislavs Gabovs saw a straight red for an ugly challenge. Pahars, looking very Roberto Martinez-esque on the touchline with his long black coat on, pondered a different plan. As he looked on, trying to think up a new formation, Iceland took the lead when Swansea City's Gylfi Sigurdsson's shot from distance was deflected past a helpless Kolinko.

Now here was an unusual sight. With 20 minutes to go, Austrian referee Robert Schörgenhofer decided to take himself off after suffering cramp. Fortunately these days the officials team consists of assistants and additional assistants (those chaps with the Harry Potter wands behind the goal) so there was no need to put out an announcement for any qualified refs in the crowd to step up to the plate. Modern football is rubbish sometimes. We all want to see incidents like that, or outfield players having to go in goal after the goalkeeper is sent off.

Two minutes after the restart and it really was game over for Latvia. A needless free-kick was conceded in the corner, Emil Hallfredsson whipped the ball over, and skipper and Cardiff City midfielder Aron Gunnarsson leapt like a killer whale to head home. Swansea 1, Cardiff 1.

The final act came in the last minute when substitute Rúrik Gislason broke free of his marker and drilled the ball into the corner of the net. Latvia had been well and truly beaten, paying the price for playing in such a defensive formation that had hardly led to a single threat on Hannes Halldórsson's goal.

As I walked back to the hotel, the whole city centre had transformed. It was Friday night – "Stag and Hen night" in other words – and the pavement cafés had given way to heaving pubs and clubs, all trying to outdo each other with louder music, garish lighting and scantily clad girls trying to entice in male customers. Nobody wants to see that surely. . oh, they do. OK, but for me, with a 4am alarm call, it would have been a disastrous move. Honest.

So while the stay-at-home fans and Premier League managers might hate these international breaks, they had given me the opportunity to experience new adventures in virgin Football Tourist areas. It had been a great little trip, one I'd recommend to anyone. The football hadn't been great but that's not that important really. Although Great Aunt Helga and Cousin Jãnis may disagree but, both games and all four teams had been poor. But that's what we've come to expect these days. Far too much rides on these games for anything other than a cautious approach. The same couldn't be said for the cities of Vilnius and Riga. Sign me up again please! Oh look, there's another international break in four weeks. Should I? Could I? It would be rude not to.

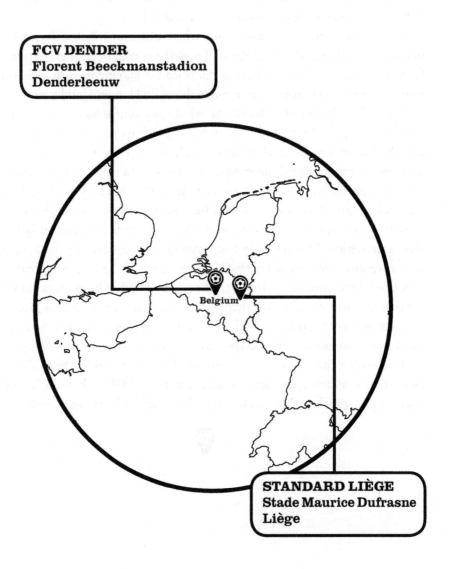

FCV DENDER
Florent Beeckmanstadion
Denderleeuw

Belgium

STANDARD LIÈGE
Stade Maurice Dufrasne
Liège

Within minutes we were munted millionaires,
ready to treat all our new friends with our
pile of plastic coins.

17. Brussels – the New Nirvana

A few years ago we were all raving about Germany being THE place to get your European footballing kicks. Their hosting of the 2006 World Cup showed the hundreds of thousands who visited the country that you could dress like an extra from Spinal Tap and still look cool. Today the stadiums up and down the leagues are awash with visiting Brits each weekend, lured by the cheap (proper) beer, great value and relatively easily obtainable tickets, as many sausages as you could possibly imagine, and a bevy of beauties that will . . . well, let's leave it there. The budget airlines also wised up and every week carry hundreds of Brits to Cologne, Hamburg, Stuttgart, Munich and all points in between.

Life couldn't get any better, could it?

Fast-forward to June 2012 and Poland was raising its collective shot glasses and wishes us *Na zdrowie* and *Sto lat*, filling our senses with even cheaper beer (even if it was called Plop), even meatier sausages and a bevy of beauties who for 50 per cent less would . . . well, would give us 50 per cent more.

Everyone was flying back from the likes of Łodz, Krakow, Gdansk and Szczecin (of course Szczecin) on a Sunday night with a big smile on their faces. Life couldn't get any better for the travelling football fan than a trip to Poland where your zloty went a long long way.

With a gap that we needed to fill in the European Football Weekends calendar, the team discussed options over a virtual beer on WhatsApp. Germany had two votes (unsurprisingly from our German-based contingent ,even though Stoffers wasn't even coming) and Poland was the venue of choice from Danny and myself. Having four directors is a problem when the "next EFW" item comes up on the monthly board meeting agenda. We rarely agree on such matters, so we drew up a simple "Pros and Cons" list and 10 minutes later agreed on Belgium. Of course, Belgium.

I made the fatal mistake of asking the Littlest Fuller what she would do. I told her all about the bratwurst and bitburger in Germany, and the warka and wolowina pieczona in Poland. I regaled her with stories of flares and fanatical support, the derbies of Munich, Krakow and Warsaw. And she said: "If I was allowed to go I would go to that place that had the chocolate . . . and the chips."

I assumed she was referring to Belgium (although for one minute I did think of Bournville). She is a bit logical for her 10 years so she explained why we should go to the land of Tintin.

"They have fruit-flavoured, chocolate-favoured, even chip-flavoured silky smooth beer. And sausages? Well they have waffles, smothered in chocolate with a dollop on top. And football . . . good old-fashioned football . . . with flares and fences.

"Well, you can look at flying, and flight times are short, but flying there is a bit pointless and expensive due to the real lack of competition in the budget airline space. You see, budget airlines work on a strict revenue yield model which means they cannot discount for flight times of less than an hour. I suggest you look at the train."

She was right. I bitch and moan about having to get up at 4.30am on a regular basis to get the Eurostar to Paris but such trips had perks. Eurostar miles. Hundreds . . . nay, thousands of them. They were my currency to a weekend of the best beer, the best chips and of course the best football in Europe. So you see, it wasn't my, or for once, Danny Last's fault. It was my daughter's. My lovely, logical daughter, who made us get up at 7am on a Saturday morning in mid-October to travel to St Pancras International, dragging Big Deaksy along for company, and boarding the first train to Brussels. CMF could hardly complain – I was simply trying to please my daughter. Her fee? A bag full of chocolate-shaped Louis Tomlinson figures.

Of course the weekend wasn't only going to be about football, beer, chocolate and twice-cooked chips. Oh no. We had a cultural agenda as long as your arm. Well, that was what Kenny Legg told us, who was arriving from his secret location somewhere in NordRhein Westfalen where he was still "doing stuff for Her Majesty". He had prepared the itinerary for our weekend. Museums, art galleries and a classical music concert, he told us the night before we arrived. Only he left the plan in the Legg Arms in Düsseldorf on Friday night while he sang Trio's "Da Da Da" on the Karaoke. Bad form Kenny, bad form. What to do? We mused on the train as it swished under the Channel. Deaksy bravely suggested we revert to plan A of football, beer, chocolate and twice-cooked chips and the motion was carried 3-0.

Saturday. Midday. Brussels Midi Station.

Like Marmite, you either love Brussels or hate it. I am a lover, while The Current Mrs Fuller is a hater. "A dull, grey concrete jungle filled with Eurocrats gorging themselves on tax-payers money" was her summary a few years ago. She had been to the city once, back in the day, and was still bitter that Anderlecht had changed their game at the last minute for TV and thus denied her an opportunity to take in a game. On the other hand I had always enthused about visiting the Belgian capital and had many a good night in the city. Euro 2000 was a good tournament in many ways.

Sure, the Dutch and the Belgians didn't really get on despite their love of chips with mayonnaise, but for the travelling fan it was the best four weeks ever. Six of the eight stadiums used were within a two-hour train ride, so Brussels provided a perfect base for excursions.

The semi-final between France and Portugal held at the Konig Baudouin Stadium (aka Heysel) was as dramatic as the tournament got, with the French eventually prevailing in the dying seconds of extra-time with a Golden Goal (remember that stupid idea from FIFA) from a penalty by Zidane after Xavier's handball, and the red card for Nuno Gomes, but ironically not for Xavier who committed the professional foul. Somehow after the game, a friend and I got caught up in a private party making their way back into town and ended up in a night club, with hostesses on hand to provide "anything sir desired". "When in Rome," my friend Pete said as he ordered a bottle of Johnny Walker Blue Label and we dug in for the night, watching the girls work the room. At one point one came over, kicked off her dangerous -looking heels and sat with us, enjoying a drink. Somehow, talk turned to bathroom redecoration (don't ask, it was just one of those conversation flows) and despite our different languages, different backgrounds and differing job objectives, we both went home eventually at the end of the night with some new grouting tips.

Since then the city had been more of a transit location for our forays into more exotic Belgian locations. Brugge, Oostende, Antwerp and Ghent. But now we were here to put over 10 years of hurt behind us.

Saturday. 3pm. Rue De L'amigo.

Plan A was going down well, very well indeed. Danny had researched a few decent pubs that would take us from our hotel to Brussels Zuid station, via one or two mystery destinations. We didn't get off to the best start. Pub number one, Le Corbeau, offered us a rather dull choice of expensive beers and had us in a fluster as to what to choose. For one brief moment we considered a Stella, using the same logic about drinking Guinness in Dublin "because it tastes different here, don't it?" but we quickly came to our senses and ordered four Krieks. The last thing we wanted to do was draw attention to ourselves so we went with a safe bet. And by inconspicuous we of course meant drinking bright red, cherry-flavoured beers out of test-tubes on steroids. We had made a rule that we would only have one beer in each bar and so after a rocky start in Le Corbeau the afternoon got better and better.

One such pub summed up our afternoon perfectly. Saturday shoppers and tourists alike simply walked on by a tiny doorway in between a Hush Puppy shop and a make-up shop. A bit like one of those secret alleyways in the Harry Potter films which only the wizards could see. Wander down into the darkness and on the left was the smallest of bars called Au Bon Vieux Temps, or as we came to know it, the good old days. None of your pints of Foster's, *Only Fools and Horses* on the TV and pictures of dogs playing snooker. Au Bon Vieux Temps offered us a selection of 12 (Twelve!) Belgian beers ranging from a strong Orval (who is your best friend?) at 6.2 per cent to a hallucinogenic Rochefort 1-10 coming in at 11.3 per cent, all topped off by a bowl of plastic cheese cubes with a mustard and pepper dip. Naturally. We scoffed at the thought of the tourists in the English Bar down the road, tucking into a pint of cooking lager and fish and chips. Mustard-coated cheese, that's the real Belgium.

"Lads, I have a real treat for you," Danny told us as we polished off our mind-bending Delirium Tremens and headed onto the 82 tram, destination Chataîgnes Kastanjes (The Chestnut Forest).

He'd been in touch with manager of the supporters bar at Royale Union Saint-Gilloise no less, and we had an invite to sink a few beers in his fine establishment in the ground. "And get your cameras ready because the magic door is going to be well and truly open."

Twenty minutes later and we were banging on the door of the most shut-the looking bar you will ever see in your life. It seemed that the invite had somehow got lost in translation. So we were forced to head across the road to the unofficial supporters bar and join the locals for a Saturday afternoon of Jupilers and watching Belgian Teletext for the football scores across Europe. Twitter is the great mediator and it appeared the confusion had been caused by the good old-fashioned time zone issue.

Exactly an hour after we thought the bar would be opened, the lights came on and the door swung outwards. "Welcome Gentlemen of London, England" our genial host announced. Within seconds we had a beer in our hands and were sitting in the home dug-out. Stade Joseph Marien is the best ground in Europe: fact. Set within the trees of Parc Duden with a big sweeping terrace down one side and a large main stand on the other side, the smell of days of glory was floating around the stadium, memories of their 11 Belgium

Championships. Back in the day they were one of the most feared teams in Europe. Alas, those days are long gone and instead of welcoming the likes of Anderlecht and Standard Liège, match-days are filled with games against RJS Heppignies-Lambusart Flerus and URS du Centre. After soaking up the history of Les Unionistes, it was time to move on. We'd exhausted trying to find things in Brussels that were "Bigger than Deaksy" and made a big dent in the list of the 10 strongest Belgian beers. Now it was showtime. Our treat for the evening was a trip to the metropolis of Denderleeuw, just 20 minutes from Brussels, or as Kenny put it, "THE place to be on a Saturday night in Belgium." Did we believe him? Of course we did. The fact we'd had a bellyful of Orval and Chimay had nothing to do with our senses being slightly clouded.

Saturday. 7pm. Denderleeuw.

"Denderleeuw is a municipality located in the Belgian province of East Flanders in the Denderstreek.

The municipality comprises the towns of Denderleeuw proper, Iddergem and Welle. On January 1, 2012 Denderleeuw had a total population of 19,069. The total area is 13.77 square kilometres which gives a population density of 1384 inhabitants per square kilometre. The current mayor of Denderleeuw is Jan De Dier, from the N-VA."

Wikipedia is rarely lost for words, but the above is the full description of the town of Denderleeuw.

No cultural highlights, no famous people, and not even an interesting insight into a local church. As the train pulled away from the platform we stood alone. The wind blew the tumbleweeds across the track and we slowly made our way out into the heart of the town. A single light, coming from a restaurant opposite the station, drew us in. "Table for four please?" Kenny asked, putting on his best governmental accent. "Have you booked?" asked the waiter, turning around to reveal an empty restaurant. "Erm, no. Is that OK?" "Of course. Come in my friends." Cue the biggest pizzas known to man, washed down with a never-ending stream of cold beers. The staff were all dressed up in bow ties, hovering by the door. We weren't sure if they were simply hoping for more custom, or trying to intimidate us to stay longer. But we weren't having any of it. We had a game to get to, and football waits for no man.

The walk from the restaurant to the Florent Beeckmanstadion took us through the heart of Denderleeuw. It seemed that everyone had shut up shop early to get to the game. Shutters had been pulled down over shops and houses alike, as if the locals were expecting the likes of 1970s Millwall rather than Belgian third-tier side Racing Mechelen.

FCV DENDER 1, RACING MECHELEN 1
Saturday 19th October 2013 – Florent Beeckmanstadion

During the week via a conversation on Twitter, the club had promised us beer, belly-laughs and a bloody good night out, and they delivered on all three. Even though this was "just" a Belgian Third Division A game watched by just a few hundred we were welcomed like long-lost friends as we walked into the club bar. The club house was of the breeze-block variety, and still had the remnants of a wild night of celebration from a few days previously when the national team had qualified for the World Cup Finals. OK, a few red, black and yellow balloons stuck to the wall hadn't quite deflated yet. We had to fight our way to the bar, where we rejected the ubiquitous Jupiler for something from "under the counter". Well, technically in the cupboard behind the bar, but when the barman opened those doors it was like that feeling when you went into the video shop when you were 14 and managed to rent a copy of *Porky's*. Four bottles of Yea Oldie Ale (seriously) were soon being consumed, the right sort of pre-match warm-up for the 90 minutes ahead. The Florent Beeckmanstadion is a great little stadium for football at this level. We could have bought tickets in the "Old Trafford Business Seats", or even a place in the "Stamford Bridge Business Lounge" that they market on the website, but the €10 place in the stand behind the goal was more than enough for our viewing pleasure. Three covered stands were more than sufficient for the Dender fans, all of which seemed relatively new, representing a club with grand ambitions.

I'm sure you have all read the match reports in the papers by now so you don't need me to go into great detail about the entertaining score draw. The undoubted highlight of the first half was the appearance of Fergie-lad, our jovial Tranmere fan who has a habit of popping up to see us in random places across Europe. He'd decided to give Prenton Park a miss and hopped on a Ryanair special to Brussels (well, Charleroi) for a couple of games. Faced with a choice of Brugge or Denderleeuw – he had also read Wikipedia – after which a trip to Denders was a no-brainer.

The visitors, Racing Mechelen, not to be confused with big brothers KV Mechelen although they had once finished runners-up in the Belgian First Division, had brought a noisy bunch of a couple of hundred fans who knew more English than any of us five put together. Every song was sung with gusto and, dare I say it, a slight Norfolk accent, while the hard core home fans responded in their natural tongue informing their visitors that they would be going home in a Flemish ambulance.

On the field, Arne Naudts put the away side one up after 20 minutes but you already knew that.

The second half saw Dender fight back, with Brian Moding levelling the scores with just 10 minutes to go, which of course you also already knew. The goal was greeted with pure joy in our stand, with one chap so excited he ran to the front and tore off his jacket, jumper and woolly vest before leading a chant of "There's only one Brian Moding", until his mum came along and gave him a clip behind the ear for being so silly.

Full time and honours were even. Football, beer and a decent little atmosphere had been the winners. There was just time for us to act like the proverbial (Wal)loons and get ourselves photographed by the *Denderleeuw Echo* under the headline of "Loyal fans show their love for Moding". Despite the tempting offer of a night in Denderleeuw, the plan was to head back to the sleepy backwater of Brussels. Although the train trip was only 30 minutes we needed some food so we bought what Kenny told us was "a big bag of chips". So big was the portion that it was served in a carrier bag. Now that is what I call a takeaway.

The remainder of the evening was spent in the small bars around St Katherine's, where we met a man with six fingers, a woman who used to be a lion tamer in the circus, and a couple who said they once won Belgium's equivalent of *Blockbusters*. We didn't believe them after they failed to see the funny side of the "Can I have a P please Bob" joke for the twelfth time.

At 2am the cry went up from Big Deaksy, now bored with the game of "replace words in song titles with Big Deaksy": "Gentlemen. To bed. For tomorrow we rise at 9am for Liège."

Sunday. 9.14am. Brussels.

"Are you getting up or what?" Danny wasn't happy on the other end of the phone. It seemed that Kenny had forgotten to change the time on his mobile from German to Belgium time, or so he told me, and we were late. And if there is something that Danny hates more than Crystal Palace, its people being late. Oh, and flying, but that's not really relevant here.

Ten minutes later we were downstairs, raring to go. It was 9.25am. Although *we* were awake, Brussels certainly wasn't. Keen tourists gave us a wide berth as we marched across the old town wielding our croissants with menace. Street cleaners were clearing away the detritus from the remnants of a lively Saturday night and the noise of their work echoed through our collective hangovers. Was it too early for a beer? Despite all the rules in the EFW charter about being awake on foreign soil for more than 30 minutes and passing open drinking establishments, we stoically continued on our journey with only an espresso for refreshment. We had a train to catch at 10am. We were heading in a south-easterly direction from the capital to Liège, the economic capital of Wallonia.

Today was the day of the 'Hate Derby'. League-leaders Standard Liège versus Sporting Charleroi. The rivalry between the two biggest teams in the French-speaking province of Wallonia wasn't quite at the level of a Partizan v Red Star, or a Lazio v Roma. In fact it was in the same league perhaps as a Lewes v Worthing. In Belgium everyone hates Anderlecht and one other. In the case of these two, the secondary hate was reserved for each other. A few years previously there had been some trouble in this fixture, so the Belgium police still classed this as a 'Bubble' game, with a few hundred Zebras fans being bussed direct from South Brussels to the ground.

Despite my eldest child being born just eight days prior to the start of Euro 2000, I spent a couple of weeks hopping around Benelux during the tournament (minus the Lux apart from one day when I headed the wrong way down the A13) taking in games virtually every day. I was present for the birth, and every couple of days I would turn up at home, to be met with a frosty reception from my mother in-law who had decided that I wasn't capable of looking after my new family and had moved in our small two-bedroom house. So I went to stay in a hotel. Granted the hotel was slap-bang in the middle of Belgium and that this was while the second-biggest football tournament in the world was taking place, but it was pure coincidence. But Liège was the only venue I hadn't visited during the fantastic summer of football and in the proceeding 13 years it had somehow eluded my attentions.

As the train eased into Liège-Guillemins railway station we all let out a collective "ooooh". For those with a bit of an interest in architecture and the work of Santiago Calatrava will know that the €300 million new railway station is up there with his best work alongside the terminal at Bilbao Airport, the Cuitat de las Arts i les Ciences in Valencia and Turning Torso in Malmö. This man can do wonders with a bit of steel painted white and some glass, I will have you know.

"Snap out of it Stuart." Kenny brought me back to the present by wafting an open bottle of Orval under my nose, enticing me onto the waiting bus that would take us along the banks of the Meuse River to the Stade Maurice Dufranse. Despite the short hand on my digital watch only just reaching 11, and the game some three hours away, the area around the ground was a hub of activity. Supporters bars were opening up ready for the marauding hordes, cranking out the tunes and turning on the big TVs. It seemed that the biggest show on Belgium TV on a Sunday morning was a programme called *"September Revisited"*, which was essentially a round-up of all the best goals in Europe from the past month. Relatively interesting at 11am but by 1.30pm, when it was still on, it got a tad boring. The inclusion of the solitary West Ham effort from the month was a low point and one that sent us in search of the heart of the Standard Liège hard-core fans. We had found a home in the Bois d'Avroy, one of the bars opposite the stadium. While the rest of the Standard fans were tucking into the Jupiler, we had asked for the "special stuff" from the barman, who gave us a wink and plonked four bottles of Chimay on the bar. Yes, it was three hours until kick-off but we could handle the 8.5 per cent of Belgium's finest? Well, three of us could, while one nameless member of our party (called Kenny) was struggling to hold down a Maes.

Despite hundreds of fans flooding into the bar, service had been nailed down to a tee. A group of young female waitresses roamed the room, looking for vulnerable beer-free fans, and pounced on them to take their orders. We all had our favourites and were willing to wait that extra time until our chosen one could serve us. It was just as efficient outside the bar, where fans had taken over the road and the waitresses out there had their wares on brazen full display. The football-shirt-clad girls worked the crowds with their trays full of €2 beers. What more could a football fan want?

We were joined at the table by Mark, a Standard die-hard who gave us the low-down on the finer points of watching the game (and the fans) in Liège. It seemed that the performance of the national side in recent years had given the domestic game a long-overdue boost and crowds were once again returning to clubs. The game today was deemed a sell-out by Standard, but it appeared that Charleroi had only been allowed a few hundred of the seats in the away end for their own protection.

Fully up to date on the state of the nation, we headed into the stadium. The Stade Maurice Dufrasne was a cash-free zone, with the munt being the only currency recognised in these parts.

Within minutes we were munted millionaires, ready to treat all our new friends with our pile of plastic coins. Alas, bizarre stadium regulations meant that you cannot take any of Belgium's finest treats into the seating area. I can understand the problems a beer may cause, but does a hot chip really constitute a weapon these days?

Ten minutes before kick-off and the stadium was rocking. The small band of away fans, safely housed in the middle tier of the North Stand, made a fair din but it was the home fans who stole the pre-match show with their display of a huge St George's Cross made up of individual banners at the far end to welcome us English fans. Pleasantries over, it was time for battle to commence.

STANDARD LIÈGE 2, SPORTING CHARLEROI 2
Sunday 20th October 2013 – Stade Maurice Dufrasne

Standard came into the game top of the league with nine wins from their opening 10 games and a 100 per cent record at home. A few commentators were suggesting this was the best Standard team for decades. The visitors were mid-table and had struggled for points on the road. Nobody really expected any other result than a home win, apart from the few hundred Sporting Charleroi fans.

The first half was a cagey affair, with Standard appearing to be biding their time before they struck.

However, current form often counts for nothing and it was the visitors who took the lead in the 37th minute. The scorer was former Lens striker David "the chicken" Pollet, who disappointingly didn't do a Kevin Nolan-style flying chicken impression. What would Ray Winstone do in this situation? Apart from growing a 10-foot-tall head and spinning round like someone possessed he would have backed the draw. And that is exactly what I would have done, apart from the fact I had a little snooze. A combination of a late late night, a few Chimays and the warm sun on my face provided ideal conditions for 40 winks during the first half. But if I'd been awake I would have almost certainly backed the draw. At half-time we went on a munt spending spree. We had learnt from bitter experiences in Arnhem and Tilburg that you don't want to be stuck with munts at the end of the game. The value of the munt to the euro falls dramatically as the game progresses so we spent unwisely on beer, burgers and waffles.

Fully refreshed from the first-half snooze and the half-time treats we went into the second half with hopes of a Standard bombardment. Although they certainly started on the front foot, it took 20 minutes before Jelle Van Damme (the more timid of the Van Damme brothers) equalised on 65 minutes. From this point onwards Standard would surely easily go to win the game and cement their lead at the top of the table. That was until the 80th minute, when Dewaest put Charleroi in front again.

That wasn't in the script. Standard threw everything they had at Charleroi until finally they broke them down in the 91st minute when Ezekiel salvaged a draw for Standard. A draw wasn't in the plan for the league leaders and the fans trooped out into the Sunday afternoon sunshine ruing the wasteful nature of their first-half display.

We headed to the fans bar in the stadium, where Deaksy invented a new game involving three one-euro coins which, rest assured, will be the biggest-selling children's game this Christmas. Who needs an X-Box, Game Boy or even a MegaDrive when you could have a game for all the family such as DeaksyBall. A trip next door to the shop produced a big fat zero on the football socks scale, but a 10 for the football club ruler. Who said football clubs weren't original in their design of merchandise?

We wanted to experience the real Liège so we headed into the old town, sampling some of the local beers and a dish of oversized meatballs in a pear and apple sticky sauce (Boulettes Liègeoises), which was basically a plate of oversized meatballs in a thick sauce. The road of bars that Danny remembered from his time here in Euro 2000 had been replaced with strip joints, which at 4pm on a Sunday afternoon wasn't appealing. We finally found some life in a Turkish Tapas bar which appeared to be hosting an over-60s singles party. Amusing to stand back and watch for a while, until the ladies wore out their potential male partners and turned their attentions to us youthful bucks.

We managed to resist their advances long enough to make a swift exit. The night could have gone seriously downhill from this point so we took the easy option of a carrier bag full of plantain crisps (despite living on his own, Kenny still hasn't got the hang of shopping) and a pocket full of Belgian beer for the train ride back to Brussels.

We could have simply had an early night, ready for our return to the UK on Monday morning, but that would be what the sensible Danny, Deaks, Kenny and Stuart would have done. Instead we headed back into the backstreet bars of Brussels and found the same characters in the same bars as we had 24 hours previously.

Another cracking European Football Weekend drew to a close in an all too familiar way – lively debate over a small beer or five about the best ever player to wear a headband, whether the Stuart Surridge red and white ball was the best ever, and what the purpose is of flags on the half-way line. Belgium had delivered on almost every level for us, underlining our judgement in choosing the lowlands of Europe over Germany and Poland. Would we be back? Could we be back? Should we be back? A resounding YES from the quartet of Englishmen.

Acknowledgements

In the Football Tourist I waxed lyrical about all of those people who helped bring the project to life and into the hands of the millions of people around the world who (ahem) I'm sure bought the book. Many of those individuals played a big part in this book ever reaching this stage and once again, they are thanked from the bottom of my heart.

To tell you the truth I never thought the Football Tourist would travel again after the journey to the end of the first book. Work started getting in the way of fun and for a period of time I had no trips in the diary. Well, when I say a period of time I meant January 2013. Come February I was back in the arms of my main partners in crime, Danny Last, Stoffers and Kenny Legg. Once again those three names are always behind the concept, planning and execution of a great European Football Weekend. At 3am in a strange bar in an even stranger city centre, these are the sort of chaps that you want by your side.

Work has opened up some new horizons for me, as well as some new cities and continents to explore. Singapore, Hong Kong and Australia are now stamps in the passport, with football tickets to match, and I'd like to thank my new travelling companions there, even if they know absolutely nothing about the game – Ed, I am talking about you here! A doff of the cap also to my American cousins, Luge and Andy Mac for always keeping me entertained with random, pointless facts on our travels around New York "soccer" stadiums.

Once again Dave Hartrick has been the perfect publisher. By perfect I of course mean one that is located in the dark and distant North, where they are still getting used to telephones and his main method of communication is carrier pigeon.

Finally, I have to raise my bat to the pavilion to salute the unwavering support of my three girls, the Fuller family, who have ensured that my underwear was ironed, I was fully stocked with Mars Bars and demands for presents from foreign lands were kept to a minimum. Everyone needs an inspiration and these are mine. Viva the Current Mrs. Fuller!